IDENTITY AND DIFFERENCE

Identity and Difference

Studies in Hegel's Logic, Philosophy of Spirit, and Politics

EDITED BY
PHILIP T. GRIER

STATE UNIVERSITY OF NEW YORK PRESS

Published by
State University of New York Press

Printed in the United States of America

For information, contact State University of New York Press, Albany, NY
www.sunypress.edu

Production by Diane Ganeles
Marketing by Fran Keneston

Library of Congress Cataloging-in-Publication Data

Identity and difference : studies in Hegel's logic, philosophy of spirit, and politics / edited by Philip T. Grier.
p. cm.
Includes bibliographical references and index.
ISBN-13: 978-0-7914-7167-8 (hardcover : alk. paper)
ISBN-13: 978-0-7914-7168-5 (pbk. : alk. paper)
1. Hegel, Georg Wilhelm Friedrich, 1770–1831. I. Grier, Philip T., 1942–

B2948.I35 2007
193—dc22

2006028018

10 9 8 7 6 5 4 3 2 1

CONTENTS

ACKNOWLEDGMENTS

The original versions of the chapters collected in this book were all presented at the Eighteenth Biennial Meeting of the Hegel Society of America, held at UCLA on October 22–24, 2004. I wish to thank conference hosts Professor John McCumber and the Department of Germanic Languages and Literature for their generous support. I also wish to thank Benay Furtivo for the excellent arrangements for the conference.

Introduction

Philip T. Grier

Framing the Issues

All too frequently in the contemporary world we find groups obsessed with asserting the "identity" or "sameness" of their members in order to affirm the contrast with what they perceive to threaten them as "different" or "other." The perceived differences may belong to any number of familiar typologies, including race, religion, ethnicity, gender, class, sexual preference, or other status taken to be "fundamental" in some supposedly alarming sense. And of course some of the most violent boundary-drawing exercises occur where multiple attributes of perceived "difference" are thought to be simultaneously present, such as, for example, when a different religion, race, and ethnicity are all thought to characterize a specific "other" at once. Such particular manifestations of the politics of "group identity" are the frequently appalling stuff of daily news.

But not all construals of identity are motivated simply by the "political" desire to exclude some specific other. Prior to such potentially pathological forms of the construction of group identities there are a number of more fundamental and essential forms of identity to be achieved, in the absence of which we would be unable to construe ourselves as moral or political agents at all, indeed, in the absence of which we would be unable to construe ourselves as *selves*. These more fundamental forms include the constitution of self-conscious individual identity in relation to other individuals, the constitution of self-conscious individual identity in relation to some larger, all-embracing communal identity, such as that represented by the state, and the constitution of national identity in relation to other nations. (Each of these aspects of identity constitution is treated by contributors to the present volume.)

Central to the challenge of constitituting these various types of identities is the issue of how we negotiate the fact of *difference*. Obviously we cannot speak of identity without simultaneously speaking of difference, yet there exists a variety of ways to theorize the relation of identity to difference. Failure to grasp the implications of each of these distinct theories of identity and difference may ultimately lead to a failure of practice, or to an inadequate comprehension of practice. (1) Identity may be conceived as a practical matter of achieving *separation* from the different; (2) identity may be conceived in a purely formal way as a matter of identity of the object with itself (without logical connection to the other); (3) or, identity may be conceived as developing from, and essentially constituted through, the mutual recognition of samenesses and differences through relation to the other. In other words, difference may be thought to be logically involved in the constitution of identity. (This particular formulation is taken from Nuzzo's contribution.)

For example, the first of these theories of the nature of identity—that it is achieved through the mechanism of *separation* of the group from its other—may lead to the political demand for the simplest and crudest of solutions: driving the "other" away through violence. However, such a strategy of group (or national) autism, the construction of enclaves, will almost inevitably lead to the impoverishment of the very identity the protection of which is being sought (Nuzzo and Buchwalter). Still more pointedly, as one of the contributors here argues, the very act of drawing such a boundary is often a tacit confession that the asserted "identity" does not in fact exist; drawing the boundary and enforcing it is intended to bring the asserted identity into being (Nuzzo). Such an understanding of the constitution of identity is thus highly problematic.

A different sort of problem arises from the second theory of identity, as merely formal. The widespread assumption that this theory "must" be the only correct one at some fundamental level has long inhibited serious examination of the theoretical alternatives. This book is devoted, among other things, to encouraging just such an examination of alternative accounts of identity in relation to the abstract formal one (Yeomans, De Nys, and others).

The third theory of identity figures quite prominently in this book. It construes genuine identity as something constituted only through a process of mutual self-conscious recognition of one another as essential to the construction of the identities that make us "the same," where that sameness also necessarily involves difference. It is asserted that only such a mutually constituted identity could be something actual or concrete. Indeed, the theme of mutual recognition by one another of self-conscious selves is almost as central a focus of this book as the theme of identity and difference (Williams, Nuzzo, Buchwalter, and others).

These and other aspects of the problem of identity and difference are explored from multiple perspectives by the contributors here. It is a thesis implicit in several of the chapters that behind many of the manifestations of practical, political conflict over such issues of identity and difference, as well as failed attempts to theorize the nature of identity, lie some deeper philosophical confusions over the very concepts of identity and difference that tend to inhibit our ability to think through these challenges successfully.

A number of the contributors here find something crucial, potentially decisive, in Hegel's account of identity and difference, and they attempt in various ways to show the fundamental importance of his approach for the resolution of certain of these difficulties. However, in much contemporary philosophical discussion there are two distinct barriers to the successful appropriation of Hegel's contribution. The first of these is, in effect, a refusal to take Hegel's approach seriously, to reject it out of hand as resting on a series of "obvious" mistakes, a view usually rooted in the assumption that only some version of the second theory of identity, mentioned earlier, the abstract, formal one, could be correct. This response has been characteristic of much analytic philosophy, at least until fairly recently. The second barrier has most often arisen in the context of continental philosophy, where one still finds widespread the conviction that Hegel's own thinking of identity and difference privileges identity over difference to the ultimate exclusion of the reality of the other.

These two continuing barriers to the appropriation of Hegel's thought on identity and difference are explicitly taken up in part 1 of this book in the hope that they can be set aside and will no longer stand in the way of an appreciation of the details of Hegel's contribution, and hence of a more wide-ranging examination of alternative theories of identity and difference. The first two contributors (Maker and Williams) offer compelling arguments on behalf of the conclusion that Hegel's theory privileges neither identity nor difference, and that claims to the contrary rest on misinterpretation. All four contributors in part 1 (Maker, Williams, Yeomans, and De Nys), plus Nuzzo in part 3, take up the challenge of articulating the details of Hegel's treatment of identity and difference by engagement with alternative conceptions. Each in his or her own way attempts to show that the problems to which Hegel offered his theory as a solution cannot be set aside, and that none of the alternative theories clearly deals with that set of problems as successfully.

With these impediments to a more wide-ranging examination of possible theories of identity and difference hopefully diminished, if not removed, a number of more specific problems can then be explored. In the first of these Hegel's distinctive but neglected account of the development of the unity of mind out of the differences of psyche, consciousness, and intelligence in the third part of the *Encyclopedia* is illuminated by an important new reading that sketches an alternative program for contemporary philosophy of mind (Winfield).

Listing some of the other problems dealt with in the book, one might begin with what is arguably the most fundamental problem, that of self-identity. How is the identity of the self-conscious individual constituted? Our understanding of Hegel's famous argument, that such a process is to be understood as possible only via the mutual recognition of one another by a plurality of self-conscious selves, is here deepened by a radically innovative interpretation of dialectical mediation in Hegel's speculative thought as necessarily involving a *double transition* (Williams). That deepened understanding of dialectical mediation has implications for the theory of identity and difference itself as well as for the theory of recognition. The claim that recognition itself is essentially involved in the constitution of genuine, concrete identity is explored in this book not only by Williams but also by Nuzzo, Buchwalter, Howard, and Kowalski.

Another fundamental problem examined here from multiple perspectives is how the identity of the autonomous, freely willing individual can be thought to involve essential connection, even unity in some sense, with the universal ethical substance of the rational state even while that individual retains his or her individual autonomy. This is of course a classic problem of modern political theory, here cast in Hegelian terms. That problem is confronted explicitly by three authors (in a skeptical spirit by Flynn, and in a more affirmative manner by Howard and Kowalski).

Even if a generally convincing account of the moral and political agency of the autonomous individual in relation to the modern state could in principle be supplied, there remain other potential obstacles to the acceptance of such a view. Traditional political theories have typically construed the forms of political agency made available to the individual in conspicuously patriarchal terms. Hegel's theory is a notorious offender in this respect: He treats feminine identity as a bar to full participation in the public activities of citizenship in the nation-state. Another contributor here teases out the ultimate conceptual sources of Hegel's apparently prejudicial treatment of the feminine in terms of his conception of the particular and its relation to the universal (Simpson).

Yet another problem arises in connection with the identity of the nation via other nations. If we take seriously Hegel's usual claim, that concrete identity can be achieved through a process of mutual recognition, then what sort of international order would be required such that the identity of one nation could be constituted through the recognition of others? Is not any such actual international order rejected by Hegel's political theory? But if so, how is genuine national identity possible? (Buchwalter)

Finally, a distinctive problem of racial identity affecting the proper interpretation of Hegel's account of the development of Greek culture from its Egyptian roots is examined, and a widespread but mistaken assumption concerning this aspect of Hegel's philosophy of history is corrected (Bernasconi).

Taken together, the chapters in this book illuminate the fundamental logic of identity and difference in a variety of practical contexts, invite consideration of the details of Hegel's contribution to the debate, attempt to remove some of the most enduring impediments to taking his views on identity and difference seriously, and in some cases offer path-breaking innovations in the interpretation of Hegel's texts. A brief synopsis of each of these essays, in sequence, is supplied in the following overview.

The Structure of this Book

Part 1. Identity and Difference in the *Science of Logic*

Part 1 of this book contains four chapters, each of which undertakes to explore some aspect of Hegel's treatment of identity and difference in the *Science of Logic*. In his contribution, William Maker issues a vigorous challenge to the familiar accusation that Hegel is the consummate *Identitätsphilosoph,* privileging identity and sameness over difference and otherness. On the contrary, he argues that "Hegel may fairly lay claim to being the philosopher of difference, otherness, and non-identity." Still more strikingly, Maker turns the tables and argues that the very demand for systematic completeness of thought evinced in the *Logic*, commonly held to be the ultimate source of an all-devouring identity of thought with itself that finally tolerates nothing that is not thought, leads on the contrary to the requirement of an ineradicable *difference* which is other than thought, in the absence of which thought could not achieve systematic completeness. The difference ultimately required for the completion of the system of thought is the other of thought: *nature*. Maker argues that this outcome can be seen as inevitable once we properly think through the implications of the demand that thought, in the context of the system, be both autonomous and self-grounding. This demand can be satisfied only if thought can be exhibited as self-determining, and the latter can be achieved only through a dialectic in which neither identity nor difference is privileged as an originary determining ground.

Just how the dialectic must be interpreted if neither identity nor difference is to be privileged is the problem taken up next by Robert R. Williams. In his contribution, Williams introduces the crucial topic of *double transition* in Hegel's explication of speculative reasoning. This topic has been largely overlooked in previous Hegel commentary, but without a grasp of the role of double transition in Hegel's argument, according to Williams, some of the most deeply contested issues of Hegel interpretation cannot be properly framed. The first of these issues to be addressed is the much-tortured question of identity and difference in the system. The conclusion that Hegel's system ultimately eliminates genuine otherness, or difference, is among the most commonly offered grounds for a dismissal of his thought, or, justifications of the need to "move beyond" Hegel. Williams here calls that conclusion into question by drawing attention to a series of passages—especially to changes that Hegel himself introduced into subsequent editions of the *Logic* and the *Encyclopedia*—in which the idea of a *double transition* is advanced as crucial to the comprehension of dialectical mediation throughout the system. Williams's thesis—that the standard reading of Hegel's dialectic throughout the system must involve double transition—represents a major innovation and promises to have a significant impact on Hegel studies. He further illustrates the importance of such a reading by extending it to the theme of recognition, a topic on which he has written extensively elsewhere.

Christopher Yeomans next undertakes a particularly subtle analysis of the problem of identity and its intrinsic connection to difference as Hegel presents it in the *Science of Logic*. The framework of his analysis is a logic of question and answer, an erotetic logic, modeled on Bas Van Fraassen's work, in which to put a question is to imply certain presuppositions in the context of which alone it can be determined what counts as a meaningful answer. Within such a framework Yeomans analyzes Hegel's treatment of identity as formulating the problem context within which the inquiry into identity makes sense, and he is then able to show how difference comes in as part of a meaningful answer within such a problem context. Yeomans develops his analysis by way of contrasts with a number of other treatments of identity in the current literature, including those by Colin McGinn and David Wiggins.

Martin J. De Nys also takes up the problem of Hegel's treatment of identity and difference in the *Logic*, though the scope of his discussion is broader—it eventually focuses on the general problem of the relation of thought and being in Hegel's philosophy, as well as on the significance of Hegel's treatment of identity and difference in the history of philosophy. De Nys situates his own account in relation to the accounts of Heidegger, Taminiaux, Desmond, Di Giovanni, and Burbidge. His view supplies an additional standpoint from which to resist the conclusions of philosophers such as Desmond and Taminiaux to the effect that difference does not receive its due in the Hegelian system. In this respect, his analysis converges with Maker's and Williams's.

Part 2. Identity and Difference in the *Philosophy of Mind*

In part 2 Hegel's doctrine of identity and difference is employed as a guide for interpreting a crucial section of the third part of Hegel's *Encyclopedia*, the *Philosophy of Mind.* In a path-breaking study of Hegel's account of how mind achieves unity in difference by integrating psyche, consciousness, and intelligence, Richard Dien Winfield lays out a new program for the philosophy of mind that constitutes a radical alternative to a widely familiar program in contemporary analytic philosophy, sketching out possible solutions to a series of impasses encountered by that theory.

The familiar standard program for the philosophy of mind in contemporary philosophy traces its origins to Descartes, then recapitulates Kant's distinctive contributions, along with the impasses to which it leads. These difficulties inherent in the Kantian perspective are widely supposed to have been overcome by a further development of the philosophy of mind emerging especially from the work of Wittgenstein, Sellars, and Davidson in the twentieth century. Proceeding from Wittgenstein's denial of the possibility of a private language, the dominant contemporary conception holds that "the acquisition of the concepts making knowledge possible is bound up with the intersubjective process of learning and using a language."

However, Winfield argues that this familiar holistic, relativist account is also beset by several deep difficulties, which he succinctly enumerates, and that it offers no prospect of ultimate success as a program for philosophy of mind. In Winfield's view, Hegel's much-neglected account of the unity of mind conceived through the differences of psyche, consciousness, and intelligence, as presented in the "Philosophy of Subjective Spirit" in the third part of the *Encyclopedia*, provides a thoroughgoing alternative program for the philosophy of mind, one that promises to avoid numerous impasses and lacunae afflicting the familiar conceptions from Descartes forward. He supplies a careful and clear exposition of the Hegelian account, tracing the emergence of mind through each of the three subordinate moments, indicating the outlines of a research program appropriate to the further development of this alternative concept of mind.

Part 3. Identities and Differences: Peoples, Genders, and Nations

The next series of chapters in part 3 of this book, turns more overtly toward the realm of the political, dealing with several of the issues described earlier.

Angelica Nuzzo proposes that we must first broaden our conception of the treatment of identity and difference in Hegel's *Logic*, focusing not simply upon the moment of "identity" as a determination of reflection within the sphere of Essence but equally upon the Logic of Being, the Logic of Essence, and the Logic of Concept. In a sensitive rereading of the text as a whole, she argues that Hegel's logical solution to the problem of identity and difference must be comprehended as a dialectical progression involving all three parts of the *Science of Logic*. In the successive moments of this dialectic she sees an explication of two fundamentally distinct conceptions of *political identity* in the contemporary world, one of which depends upon *separation* from the other, sometimes literally enforced by the construction of walls, and the other of which can be exemplified in the formation of a *cultural identity*, which depends upon a free interplay and interaction with *others* where differences as well as identities are constituted through mutual recognition.

This theme of *cultural identity* is taken up by the next contributor, Andrew Buchwalter, in an innovative analysis of Hegel's conceptions of national identity and the nation-state within the international order.

He points out that much commentary on Hegel's conception of the international order has failed to notice that in his account *Äusserstaatsrecht*, often mistranslated as "international law" rather than as the more accurate "external law of states," contains two components: *Staatenrecht*, or interstate law, and *Völkerrecht*, the law of peoples or international law, properly speaking. *Staatenrecht* concerns the formal and external treaty relations among states and is appropriately conceived in terms of a realist view of international relations. On the other hand, *Völkerrecht* concerns nation-states in their *cultural* dimension, embracing relations of mutual cooperation and interdependency, presupposing reciprocal relations of mutual recognition, and developing toward a notion of common or "universal" human identity. On the basis of this starting point, Buchwalter is able to advance a very different analysis of Hegel's conception of the international order as a substantial corrective to those usually encountered in the Hegel literature.

In the following contribution Patricia Anne Simpson approaches the theme of identity and difference through an examination of Hegel's categories of the universal and the particular, more precisely, of the power of the universal over the particular, with respect to two important topics in the *Phenomenology of Spirit* and the *Philosophy of Right*: gender and nation. Hegel's treatment of the universal and the particular, as it intersects the themes of freedom and autonomy, has become the subject of a growing literature in the feminist and cultural studies approaches that inform her contribution. Exploring arguments offered by a variety of contemporary commentators, Simpson interrogates the category of particularity as it represents the feminine and the national in the context of Hegel's theory of the modern nation-state.

In the final contribution in this section Robert Bernasconi directs new light on a particular issue in Hegel's philosophy of history: the racial identity of the Egyptians. He points out that most discussions of Hegel's writings on the ancient Egyptians have proceeded, since the middle of the nineteenth century, on what is almost certainly a mistaken premise—that Hegel and the majority of his contemporaries would have believed the ancient Egyptians to be Caucasian. Instead, Bernasconi argues convincingly, on the basis of a painstaking reconstruction of the history of assumptions concerning Egyptian racial identity in late eighteenth- and early nineteenth-century European sources, that Hegel and most of his contemporaries would have believed the ancient Egyptians to be predominantly *black*. Since the achievements of ancient Greek civilization were in many instances said, by the Greeks themselves, to be inspired by Egyptian models, the "hierarchy" of cultural achievements would contradict the parallel "hierarchy" of races increasingly promoted by white supremacists in the period following Hegel's death—which eventually led to the "conversion" of ancient Egyptian racial identity from black to white in European texts. Correcting the anachronistic assumption of the "white" identity of the ancient Egyptians poses the necessity of rereading all of Hegel's texts concerning the *cultural* identity of the Egyptians, their racial and cultural relation to the rest of Africa, Hegel's notorious treatment of sub-Saharan Africa, and the role of the Egyptians in the dialectic of history. Bernasconi here makes a significant contribution toward this necessary, systematic rereading of the relevant texts.

Part 4. Identity and Difference in the *Philosophy of Right*

In part 4, the final section of this book, three contributors explore interrelated aspects of the theme of identity and difference, all focused on Hegel's *Philosophy of Right.* Erin E. Flynn raises the question of the extent to which the relation of the individual to the ethical substance (*Sittlichkeit*) can be successfully characterized as a unity of identity and difference. Recognizing that Hegel makes very strong claims of this sort, and also recognizing that an impressive array of recent scholarship testifies to the defensibility of Hegel's claims that the "right of subjectivity" can nevertheless be sustained in this unity of the individual with ethical substance, Flynn chooses to test the plausibility of these claims from *within* the structure articulated in the *Philosophy of Right.* As a test case he takes up the problem of legal punishment, first in the context of civil society, and subsequently in the context of the political state. Flynn undertakes to show that an individual subjected to punishment as the outcome of a trial could not regard the enforcement of these legal norms as the actualization of his or her own freedom in any meaningful sense but must instead regard them as the intrusion of a "meaningless" external contingency thwarting the affected individual's plan of life.

In the following contribution, Jason J. Howard accepts the challenge posed by this residual contingency and indeterminacy conditioning us as particular individuated subjects. He argues that the experience of this very contingency is essential to the individual's development beyond the immediacy and potential alienation inherent in our individual self-certainties. Mediating this alienation inherent in being a particular, finite individual is necessary if freedom is to be realized as concrete or actual within the modern state. Howard approaches the problem of the mediation of the individual as the emergence of "true conscience" out of "formal conscience," focusing especially upon Hegel's notion of *patriotism* as the highest and final form of true conscience (superseding *piety* within the family and *rectitude* in civil society). The development of patriotism enables individuals to recognize their own *accountability* within that larger community that is the politically governed state, mediating personal self-insistence with the universality of common purposes and goals. Such accountability demands that individuals submit their own private projects, interests, and visions of the good to the test of political participation and dialogue, obtaining recognition and confirmation from the wider community of the objective validity of what survives this process of dialogue and confrontation.

In the final contribution, Maria G. Kowalski explores this same theme of the requirements for the realization of substantial freedom in Hegel's doctrine of the ethical state from a less familiar perspective: the identity of rights and duties. She explicates the process of the mediation of the individual will through inclusion in the political state as involving not merely the right but the *duty* of the free will to will the free will. That is, the duty to which she directs attention is not in the first instance a duty to the state but a *duty to self* that each individual has to actualize in order to achieve concrete freedom. Duties to the state arise only as a consequence of the prior duties the individual has to the self to realize freedom for the self. That duty then grounds a series of duties to produce and maintain the means to realizing one's freedom, and these may ultimately constitute duties to the state. Kowalski develops this analysis of the identity of right and duty from its grounding in abstract right, through morality, to its realization in the ethical state. In particular, she argues that duties to oneself on Hegel's account are not grounded either in the right to freedom or the well-being of other persons. Since the duties an individual has to belong to an ethical community and to fulfill the obligations of citizenship can be shown to be based on a prior duty to the self, she argues, a commonly encountered interpretation of Hegel's political philosophy as anti-individualistic can be set aside.

Part 1

Identity and Difference in the *Science of Logic*

Chapter 1

Identity, Difference, and the Logic of Otherness

William Maker

> It is in this dialectic as it is here understood, that is, in the grasping of opposites in their unity or of the positive in the negative, that speculative thought consists. It is the most important aspect of dialectic, but for thinking which is as yet unpracticed and unfree it is the most difficult.
>
> The advance of culture generally, and of the sciences in particular, gradually brings into use higher relationships of thought. . . . It is a matter of infinite importance that in this way an advance has been made beyond the form of *abstraction*, of identity, by which a specific concept . . . acquires an independent self-subsistence, and that prominence and currency have been given to the *determinate* form, the difference, which is at the same time an inseparable element in the identity.[1]

More often than not, Hegel is understood and criticized as the consummate *Identitätsphilosoph*, disparaged for propounding an onto-theological, authoritarian metaphysics that has swallowed everything into the Absolute Idea.[2] Of late, as postmodernists have railed ceaselessly against grand metanarratives and taken pen in hand to defend difference and otherness against the depredations of Western logocentrism, Hegel has faced increased obloquy as the systematic philosopher who brings the reductionistic, devouring quicksand of rational thought to the abyssal depths of its nadir of completion.[3] While this view of Hegel's system as an intolerant omnivore has a pedigree going back at least to Kierkegaard, it suffers from one defect. It is altogether wrong.

In what follows I will contend that Hegel is not guilty of the charge of reductionistic absolutism with which he is so frequently smeared.

Hand in hand with this, and on a positive note, I will indicate how he in fact crafts a philosophy that may successfully comprehend difference (the nonidentical or otherness) in a radically nonreductionistic manner. In short, my thesis is that Hegel may fairly lay claim to being *the* philosopher of difference, otherness, and nonidentity.

The usual basis for charging Hegel with reductionism has been his very idea of philosophy as a rational system that promises to be unconditional, comprehensive, and complete. Conventional wisdom holds that such a system must manifest a totalizing logocentrism that betrays the inescapable finitude and incompleteness of our knowledge and denies the genuine independence of a reality given apart from thought, even as it offers an unavoidably distorted account of it. The crux of the criticism seems to be that the systematic demand for comprehensive completeness must privilege an idealistic notion of identity that cannot abide the truly different and nonidentical, that which is radically other than thought itself. Hegel's critics hold that thought that purports to be unconditionally true and complete must be totalizing, allowing only for the truth, reality, and value of that which it can grasp in terms of its own primal and definitive identifying features; according to them, whatever else systematic thought may even attempt to conceive must be construed in terms of the identical, or ignored altogether. The lust for finality and inclusivity mandates a homogeneity of thought that denies, devalues, and denegrates the heterogenous. The view I will present is diametrically opposed in holding that the key to appreciating Hegel as the philosopher of difference lies precisely in his notion of philosophy as a comprehensive systematic science. So just what his critics see as the source of Hegel's monological, totalizing, and authoritarian abrogation of difference I will present as the basis for his multifaceted, differentiated, and liberating celebration of it.

As Hegel frequently insists, the logic first establishes and articulates the scientific character of the whole system. Throughout the system, Hegel refers us back to the logic as the resource for understanding and justifying what he presents elsewhere only, as he says, "in outline" form.[4] Thus the logic and its notion of science are definitive for understanding any further treatment of identity and difference in Hegel. What we will see generally is that the fundamental nature of Hegel's conception of science necessarily and unequivocally precludes reductionism. Hegelian philosophical science will be shown to necessitate a mode of logical conceptualization and development that engenders a conceptual framework where difference, the nonidentical, is given full and undistorted acknowledgment, insofar as this is attainable in thought. So what are the distinctive features of Hegel's conception of philosophical science? First I will discuss Hegel's concept of science in a general way, focusing on how and why it shapes the system as a philosophy of difference. Next I will show how difference is crucial to the very opening of logical development and will sketch its role in the logic of essence and the logic of the concept. In conclusion I will consider how logic's completeness requires a further differentiating in the conceiving of nature as a radical other to thought.

As is well known, Hegel asserts that science must begin without any presuppositions regarding either its form or its content.[5] Instead, it must commence in and with what he refers to as the indeterminate immediate, that which is devoid of determinacy both within itself and in reference to anything else.[6] It is easy to see why Hegel insists on just such a beginning for philosophical science. For one thing, if science opens with some determinate content given from outside, then the completeness of what comes to be systematically articulated as its subject matter could never be vouchsafed. (It could always be asked whether that given content has been adequately conceived and whether other unincorporated contents may have been omitted altogether.) Furthermore, were science to start with any determinate notions either about its method or its subject matter, these predeterminations would stand in need of further demonstration, since philosophy is precisely that discourse which aims, unlike all others, to provide a complete justification for what it asserts.[7] If philosophy begins with anything determinate as the given, determining ground for what follows, then the requisite attempt to justify these predeterminations must lead either to bad circularity or an infinite regress, and philosophy would have to jettison its definitive claim to be self-grounding and to offer unconditional truth. And if these ideals must be abandoned, then any and all truth claims would only be true relative to the ungrounded assumption(s) on which they rest.[8] So truth and the necessary philosophical account of it require that philosophical discourse be radically autonomous and self-grounding.[9] Only thought that is independent of all given external determination may be complete and final both in terms of its subject matter and its justification.

For Hegel's critics, it is just such completeness and finality that require a discourse which is self-grounding in the totalizing sense that everything addressed in it is ultimately reducible to and incorporated in the all-determining ground from which it begins. But in fact, with Hegel, just the opposite is the case. The inescapable demand for self-grounding inherent in a coherent notion of truth, the demand that thought be autonomous and self-determining, requires philosophical science to systematically conceptualize nonidentity and articulate difference. In a nutshell, autonomy and self-grounding necessitate conceptual self-determination[10] and such self-determination may only transpire through a conceptual dynamic—dialectic—where identity and difference are mutually implicated and neither is a privileged, originary determining ground.[11] Why is this? Why must such discourse entail the genuine acknowledgment of the other rather than a reductionistic incorporation where the determinacy of the other is parasitical upon an original determinacy?

If the system is scientific in virtue of its autonomy, the absence of any presuppositions in terms of which the determinacies of the system are determined, then this means that there can be no foundational determinacies of form or content given from outside.[12] Thus the only way in which determinacy could emerge from indeterminacy must be through a process of strict, autochthonous self-determination. But insofar as there is nothing already present as determinate in reference to which determinacy could be determined, how indeed may any determination arise? What I shall explicate generally is this: Hegelian self-determination takes place as a *forward*-moving process whereby what is determinate comes to be determined in and through a mutually constitutive determining relation to its other. Broadly speaking, for Hegel, there can be no thought of what is without thinking its opposite or negation; there can be no thought without difference. In addition, the primal demand that thought be autonomous and self-determining, and that form and content be one also means that self-determination denotes both the methodological procedure and the subject matter. The system is about the many modes of autonomy. What we will see as a consequence is that thought's completion of *its* autonomous self-determination, its comprehension of itself as a self-determining totality, requires that it conceptualize its difference from what is other than itself by the acknowledgment of an autonomous, radically different other—nature as that which is different from and autonomous of thought, and which is autonomous in its own fashion, different from the manner of thought's autonomy. Having self-determination as its method and content means that Hegelian science comprehends autonomy—what it means for something to be determined in its own right—and such comprehension can only take place as thought progressively differentiates itself, both within itself, and, finally, from itself altogether; not the elimination but the proliferation of difference is the heart of Hegel's system. The autonomy of self-sufficient self-identity is impossible without the articulation and sustaining of irreducible, nonderivative difference.[13]

What this signifies generally is that Hegelian thought turns the traditional notion of identity inside out. Unlike traditional metaphysicians, he does not fetishize identity, and unlike postmoderns, he does not fetishize difference.[14] Thus he may avoid altogether the heteronomous, hierarchical, and hegemonic logic of reductionism that is found throughout the history of thought in the manifold attempts to find some primal, privileged determining ground from which all else is derived. Rather than reverting to a foundational determining ground, the minimal requirement of scientific systematicity for presuppositionless self-determination requires a process of thought that cannot appeal to the antecedently given and thus *must* come to think the other just in order to first determine itself. Thus *ab initio* the demands of scientific philosophy for self-grounding self-determination preclude just that mode of thinking whereby difference, nonidentity, and otherness come to be thought as secondary, as derivative of some primal, originary determinacy whose legitimacy and authority are neither established nor questioned. In stark contrast, in Hegelian discourse, nonidentity and difference are not secondary and derived, mere variations upon an originary determinacy. Since there is literally no originary determinacy here, identity and difference will be seen to emerge together inescapably at the very start and to remain inextricably involved with one another in the further development of the process and its march toward completeness. The general Hegelian view is this: To be is to be determinate, and being may come to be fully and finally determinate only insofar as a manifold variety of differentiating relations to others is both realized and brought to thought. Self-sufficiency and autonomy are not attainable in isolation, by excluding or incorporating difference, but rather only by establishing and sustaining it.

In broad terms, how can we find the logic revealing and developing the notion that identity without difference is unthinkable, as the process of logic's conceptual self-determination unfolds in each of the three logics of the logic and culminates in logic's attaining completeness through the transition from thought to nature? In considering the general nature of the logic of being, the logic of essence, and the logic of the concept, I will focus on highlighting how each of these illustrates my central claim that self-determining discourse is a differentiating process, requiring an other-emergent, forward moving from the indeterminate to the determinate, rather than an other-subsuming, backward moving return to an already determinate ground. The beginning is crucial here, for if the process of self-grounding self-determination is compromised by the involvement of an originary determinacy as determining ground, then no conceiving of difference in its genuine autonomy would be possible.[15]

According to Hegel, the logic proper begins when we make "the resolve" to think purely and take up the indeterminate immediate.[16] Such resolve means that we will not invest any determinacy in the indeterminate simply in virtue of its being an object of thought; to proceed in that fashion would be to introduce determination from without and thus to void the scientific character of this discourse. We need to think it just as it is in its nature as the indeterminate immediate, as being. Hegel explicates this thinking as follows: "In its indeterminate immediacy it is equal only to itself. It is also not unequal relatively to another; it has no diversity within itself nor any with a reference outward. It would not be held fast in its purity if it contained any determination or content which could be distinguished in it or by which it could be distinguished from another."[17] So, according to Hegel, thinking the indeterminate immediate just as what it is as thoroughly and purely indeterminate is the thinking of that which lacks any determinate characteristics either within or in reference to an other, and, thought just as utterly devoid of determinacy, being is (or has become) indistinguishable from and is the thinking of nothing: "It is pure indeterminateness and emptiness. There is *nothing* to be intuited in it. . . . Just as little is anything to be thought in it, or it is equally only this empty thinking. Being, the indeterminate immediate, is in fact *nothing*, and neither more nor less than *nothing*."[18]

Before considering the next forward movement, a few observations are in order to bring Hegel's nonreductive approach into relief. The determinacy of being's other, nothing, is not grounded in or derived from being as its determining source, since being cannot even be distinguished successfully from nothing, nor vice versa. Since neither being nor nothing is thinkable either in isolation or in a stabile determinate relation to its other, neither can stand authoritatively as "that in terms of which" the other is determined.[19] Difference and otherness cannot be swallowed up into being here, or even be said to be derived from it, simply because there is no stable determinate being present for them to be swallowed up in or derived from. On a more positive note, being can only be initially thought as inextricably and dynamically conjoined with its radical other, the (seemingly) absolutely different nothing. At the crucial beginning of Hegel's science, difference is not denied, diminished, or derived but is equally originary with identity, as the two can be thought neither as at one nor as separate.

Note also that the movement of thought is inexorably forward, since there can be no retreat to an already determined self-identical ground that could sustain the contrasting difference as an identifiable contrasted pole. Pure being simply cannot be thought without this thinking being the thinking of nothing. And nothing is initially no more determinately distinguishable from being than being initially is from nothing. Thus what emerges is thinking as a forward moving into a *vanishing contrast* between being and nothing; what is initially fundamental in this project is difference, or a certain mode of differentiating (insofar as talk of difference presupposes a stabile relation between determinate differentia). "But it is equally true that they are not undistinguished from each other, that, on the contrary, that they are not the same, that they are absolutely distinct, and yet that they are unseparated and inseparable and each immediately *vanishes in its opposite*."[20]

Hegel's last words are telling: The thinking of pure being, that which in its limitless, totalizing generality is all encompassing and all-inclusive, cannot take place without conceiving the negation, the radical other of being, as that into which being vanishes or disappears, and so too, the nothing into which being disappears cannot be thought without disappearing into being. Also, since this is a vanishing contrast, neither self-sameness, identity, or being, on the one hand, nor difference, non-identity, nothing, on the other, is privileged; identity and difference are equiprimordial. The radical inextricability of identity and difference could not be more fundamentally asserted: We neither start with identity and move to difference, nor vice versa. Neither is thinkable, except for the dynamic oscillation between identifying and differentiating, and this very oscillation is something inseparable from the thinking of being and nothing while yet now emerging as a new and different determinacy that is *other than both*: becoming.

"But the third in which being and nothing subsist must also present itself here, and it has done so; it is *becoming*. In this, being and nothing are distinct moments; becoming only *is*, in so far as they are distinguished. This third is an other than they; they subsist only in an other, which is equivalent to saying that they are not self-subsistent."[21]

Rather than being *derived from* a given determinacy that proceeds it, the emergence of becoming out of the dynamic instability of being and nothing first bestows a minimal and newly attained stability on being and nothing as distinct moments. Yet becoming does not incorporate, swallow up, the being and nothing with which we began, for being and nothing, as distinct moments, are now different from what they were.[22] But what is the relation of becoming to what has come before? Becoming here does and does not depend upon what precedes it. Logically, it does depend on what comes before in that it has come after and as a logical consequence of what precedes it; importantly, however, becoming does not depend substantively on what comes before, in the sense that its determinacy is not derived from and as a variation of an already established determinacy. In logic generally the development of determinacy is more prospective than retrospective: Something comes to be and is yet transformed in its other and its other in it, and the modes of transformation are themselves transformed—differentiated—as we move through the three logics.[23] We find this forward-moving, prospective development in which determinate negation—difference and otherness—is driving, because, in accordance with the minimal requirements for scientific philosophy, we began without a given determinacy as a point of reference. So for Hegel it is the system's fundamental scientific character as presuppositionless and self-determining that demands and which makes it a logic of difference, otherness, and determinate negation, rather than identity, sameness, and simple affirmation.[24]

The centrality of moving forward into a relation with an other comes to an initial completion, and is itself transformed, in moving from the logic of being to the logic of essence. The truth of the logic of being that emerges as the transition to the logic of essence is this: Being only is what it is in terms of its relation to an other, but this other only is what it is in terms of its relation to *its* other, which can only be being, so what is, is as a self-diffentiating relation to a posited other. In the logic of essence being no longer *dis*appears in its other but *appears* in and through it, and is determined in virtue of the self-contrasting, as a result. The logic of essence then unfolds as an effort to think the determining side of the self-differentiating contrast; if no given determinacy is postulated, if the process of strict self-determination is held to, then the nature of the contrastive differentiating that established determinacy must emerge as reciprocal in character. Neither side can be held fast as primal determining ground upon which the determinacy of its other depends and from which it is derived. Each is equally what it is as the other of its other, but *this* other only is what it is as the other of *its* other—to be itself, to be self-identical, is to be the other of the other, thus (now explicitly, or posited) to be in a mutually differentiating relation with the other is just to be oneself.

Since each is otherwise indeterminate except as the other of the other, each *is* the "other of the other" and is self-identical just in and as this sustained differentiating; to be other is to be oneself and just thereby still to be differentiated from this other. Since being or selfhood only is as the other of the other, otherness and difference constituted both poles of identity, thus differentiating is now explicit as the truth of identity.

> The *unity* of substance . . . in positing itself through the moment of absolute negativity . . . becomes a *manifested* or *posited identity*, and thereby the *freedom* which is the identity of the Notion. The Notion, the totality resulting from the reciprocal relation, is the unity of the *two substances* standing in that relation; but in this unity they are now free, for they no longer possess their identity as something blind . . . on the contrary the substances now have essentially the status of an *illusory being*, of being moments of reflection, whereby each is no less immediately united with its other or its positedness and each contains its positedness *within itself*, and consequently in its other is posited as simply and solely identical with itself. With the Notion, therefore, we have entered the realm of *freedom*.[25]

The truth of pure, self-determining thought attained and then articulated in the logic of the concept is this: Differentiating is self-determining, self-identification; logical identity is neither a reduction of the other to self nor a return out of the other to self but a mutually established differentiation of reflection between self and other where the self's identity is found in the other only through and as their dual differentiation. Pure identity is a doubly negative process of mutual differentiating where identity emerges in the differentiating. Previously being disappeared, then appeared in the other. Now being develops in the other as what Hegel calls posited or manifested identity. Since it is now explicit that identity is differentiation, differentiating must take place and does so as the logic of the concept unfolds.

How does the logic as a whole reach its completeness as a self-determined totality? The view that Hegel propounds an absolute metaphysics as a totalizing logocentrism holds that the reality conceived in his *Realphilosophie* is a mere extension of logic, a development of the absolute idea predicated on the notion of a fundamental underlying identity of thought and the real.[26] On this view, if the real is just the idea in otherness, then systematic thought can claim to comprehend it *a priori* and in a complete, all-inclusive fashion. Of course, if this interpretation is correct, then Hegel is guilty of a totalizing reduction of difference and otherness to thought; thought is everywhere and is everything, in some more or less literal sense. But this is not how the transition from logic to *Realphilosophie* takes place as the completion of logical self-determination at the end of the logic. Both a consideration of the logic as the completion of thought's autonomous self-determination and of the actual transition to the philosophy of nature indicate that, for Hegel, autonomous identity necessitates the establishment of difference through the acknowledgment of the other as autonomous in its own right.

Realphilosophie cannot be an extension or a development of logic, simply because attaining the complete *self*-determination and certified autonomy of the logical necessitates the thinking of that which is *not* logical at all, through the conceptualizing of an ontologically distinct domain of that which is not thought or thoughtlike. For logical thought to be complete, a new, *nonlogical* method of conceptualizing must emerge (albeit, from out of logic's methodological recapitulation) as well as a new, *non-logical* domain of determinacy. If such a radical differentiation does not take place, then the logical cannot be complete, nor can it certify the autonomy required for science. If the logical extends into the other as the determining ground from which the determinacies of reality are derived merely as variations on the idea, then logic has no self-sufficient finality. Completeness requires closure, and save for the self-limitation arising from the acknowledgment of nature as an autonomous other, logic cannot be complete. Nor could the logical be autonomous if it extends in some determinative fashion as logic into its other, for then its own determinate nature would depend upon this quasi-other, and thorough self-determination would be lost. So logic's completeness and autonomy can only be demonstrated insofar as something radically different is conceptualized; only in coming to think something distinctly nonlogical can thought unequivocally claim to have completed the thinking of the logical as self-sufficient.

That the move from logic to *Realphilosophie* is properly characterized as a further differentiating demarcation where a new autonomous domain of determinacy is acknowledged, rather than as a reductive inclusion where thought usurps the autonomy of the real by claiming to be its source, can be seen if we look at some of the features of the actual move from logic to nature. In the final chapter of the *Science of Logic*, Hegel discusses "the Absolute Idea" that "does not have the shape of a content, but exists wholly as *form*," whose "universal aspect" is "the *method*." [27] "The method is the pure Notion that relates itself only to itself. . . . But now it is also . . . the *Notion that comprehends itself*. . . . in it the *science of logic* has grasped its own Notion."[28] Hegel makes clear, however, that logic's consummating self-comprehension is at once the beginning of something distinctly new and nonlogical, that it is a radical differentiation, for "this Idea is still logical, it is enclosed within pure thought, and is the science only of the divine Notion. . . . Because the pure Idea of cognition is so far confined within subjectivity, it is the urge to sublate this, and pure truth as the last result becomes the *beginning of another sphere and science.*" This emergent differentiation between logic and nature is such that both are free, and free of one another, for logic's self-sublation takes place as an "absolute *liberation*," the idea "freely releases itself," and the "form of its determinateness is also utterly free—the externality of space and time existing absolutely on its own account without the moment of subjectivity," that is, no longer as logic at all.[29]

So the relation of logic and nature is not of determining ground to subordinate other but of mutual, utter, and absolute independence. Of course, the thinking of this absolute independence (of what is thought about in logic, on the one hand, and in *Realphilosophie*, on the other) is required by the completion of logic, so it too is a mediated independence. (As we have seen, what Hegel criticizes and rejects throughout is "abstract" or atomistic identity where self-identity and independence are held as existing prior to and apart from difference and mediation.) But, while philosophical thinking continues, what is thought *about* in *Realphilosophie* (what it says about the real) is not thought of as having the character of the logical; for Hegel, natural things are not thoughts or thoughtlike. In addition, the method of this thinking is also different from logic's in that now empirically given observations are required rather than banned, as they were in logic.[30]

The character of this autonomous domain as distinctly and irreducibly nonlogical is also evident when we consider the first determinacy of nature: externality or space as self-subsistent otherness.[31] Here we find a domain whose determinacy consists in being "other than," as being "apart from" or "outside of," a new notion of otherness that is nowhere to be found in the logic itself. Yet the logic's discovery, that (logically speaking) self-subsistent self-identity must involve irreducible difference, persists but it is markedly different from what it was as a purely logical relation: Space is just that which may be thought as self-identical and self-subsistent, because each space of space is identical through its capacity of sustaining difference as sheer outsideness. Every space of space is outside of—different from—every other, and just as such, all space is this sheer outsideness and is everywhere the same. As such, space is a domain that can sustain determinacies as given independently of one another. Thus with the move to the philosophy of nature, *given* determinacy as the antithesis of the logical (as the arena of pure, self-determining determinacy) is introduced, and we come thereby to think nature, as the domain of the given, as nothing like the logical. Of course this is a *thinking* of nature, but one predicated not on any purported sameness or similarity between thought and nature but rather just on the notion of their absolute difference. We can do this—think nature such that our thinking does not taint this other than thought by assuming that its determinate character is in some fashion like thought (just a quasi-other)—simply because we have now first fully conceptualized the domain of self-determining thought. Pure thought as logic has thereby been captured and closed in its completeness, so to speak, and we may come to conceive of something as utterly free of thought's determination, for we know just what the latter is and also what autonomy consists in. We have fully comprehended what the autonomy *of* thought means, and with that, we have come to know why and how we now need to think what is autonomous *from* thought itself.

Still, as a thinking about nature, is it not guilty of refusing to recognize an otherness that simply cannot be thought at all, and is not this an important complaint of Hegel's critics? In fact, Hegel does not refuse to recognize nonthinkable otherness and allows that there are aspects of the real that cannot be brought to thought, things that, like Herr Krug's pen, cannot be deduced.[32] Furthermore, philosophical attacks on Hegel that argue, and not merely assert, such otherness must of course do what they claim cannot be done, conceptualize what it is about this other that ostensibly escapes the grasp of thought. Take, for example, Kierkegaard's discussion of existence.[33] In so doing the purportedly unthinkable X has been brought to thought. In principle, Hegel has no problem with this, as he does it himself (e.g., in the discussion of the necessity of contingency), and he also recognizes nonsystematic modes of thought as capable of grasping what philosophy cannot, as being valid in their own right, and as in some important respects essential for systematic thought.[34] All of these are also ways in which Hegel specifically acknowledges the limits of systematic philosophy. What is wrong from the perspective of Hegel's system is the tendency to absolutize the other as a purportedly given, all-determining unmediated immediacy that thought must surrender to as its master. This fails to overcome absolute metaphysics, for it simply inverts it. The larger problem for Hegel's critics is that they ignore Hegel's method for the autonomous acknowledgment of difference and otherness, and thus their attempts to articulate, describe, and glorify radical otherness or difference must be tacitly, if inadvertently, idealistic and unwittingly guilty of the charge of authoritarian reductionism that they erroneously lay at his feet.

Notes

1. G. W. F. Hegel, *Hegel's Science of Logic*, trans. A.V. Miller (London: George Allen and Unwin, 1969), 56, 32–33, emphasis in original. Hereafter, *Science of Logic*.

2. See, for example, Michael Rosen, *Hegel's Dialectic and Its Criticism* (Cambridge: Cambridge University Press, 1975), 174. In *Metaphysical Aporia and Philosophical Heresy* (Albany: State University of New York Press, 1989), Stephen David Ross asserts, "He [Hegel] insists that the Absolute not only organize the whole of determinate and complete knowledge—all contingent and finite events—but that it *be* the whole" (274), emphasis in original.

3. See, for example, Martin Heidegger, *Hegel's Concept of Experience* (New York: Harper and Row, 1970); Jacques Derrida, *Positions* (Chicago: University of Chicago Press, 1981); Emmanuel Levinas, *Totality and Infinity: An Essay on Exteriority* (Pittsburgh, PA: Duquesne University Press, 1969); Paul S. Miklowitz, *Metaphysics to Metafictions: Hegel, Nietzsche, and the End of Philosophy* (Albany: State University of New York Press, 1998.) A more nuanced and subtler view of the matter may be found in Stuart Barnett's introduction to *Hegel after Derrida* (New York: Routledge, 1998).

4. For example, *Hegel's The Philosophy of Right*, preface, 2, trans. Alan White (Newburyport, MA: Focus Philosophical Library, 2002).

5. "Thus the beginning must be an *absolute*, or what is synonymous here, an *abstract* beginning; and so it *may not presuppose anything*, must not be mediated by anything nor have a ground; rather it is to be itself the ground of the entire science" (*Science of Logic*, 70, emphasis in original). "In no science is the need to begin with the subject matter itself, without preliminary reflections, felt more strongly than in the science of logic. . . . These other sciences are . . . permitted to speak of their ground and its content and also of their method, only as premises taken for granted. . . . Logic, on the contrary, cannot presuppose any of these forms of reflection and laws of thinking" (*Science of Logic*, 43). "Philosophy, if it would be a science, cannot, as I have remarked elsewhere, borrow its method from a subordinate science like mathematics, any more than it can remain satisfied with categorical assurances of inner intuition, or employ arguments based on grounds adduced by external reflection. On the contrary, it can only be the

nature of the content itself which spontaneously develops itself in a scientific method of knowing, since it is at the same time the reflection of the content itself which first posits and *generates* its determinate character" (*Science of Logic*, 27, emphasis in original). "This [that the method of the logic is "the only true method"] is self-evident simply from the fact that it is not something distinct from its object and content; for it is the inwardness of the content, the dialectic which it possesses within itself, which is the mainspring of its advance" (*Science of Logic*, 54).

6. *Science of Logic*, 70, 82.

7. *Science of Logic*, 43; *Hegel's Logic, Being, Part One of the Encyclopedia of the Philosophical Sciences* (1830) trans. William Wallace (Oxford: Clarendon Press, 1975), §9. Hereafter *Encyclopedia Logic*.

8. ". . . filling the abstract basis of Logic acquired by study with the substantial content of absolute truth and giving it the value of a universal which no longer stands as a particular alongside other particulars but includes them all within its grasp and is their essence, the absolutely True" (*Science of Logic*, 59). Of course, for Hegel, according to whom anything and everything is both mediated and immediate (*Science of Logic*, 67), even absolute truth is 'relative': the beginning of the science in logic is relative to the prior mediation of the *Phenomenology of Spirit* of 1807, which consists precisely in the self-disclosed failure of attempts to demonstrate that all truth must be relative to or mediated by some predetermined determination.

9. "Henceforth the principle of the independence of Reason, or of its absolute self-subsistence, is made a general principle of philosophy, as well as a foregone conclusion of the time" (*Encyclopedia Logic*, §60, Remark).

10. "It is by the free act of thought that it [philosophy] occupies a point of view, in which it is for its own self, and thus gives itself an object of its own production" (*Encyclopedia Logic*, §17). "I maintain that it is this self-construing method alone which enables philosophy to be an objective, demonstrated science" (*Science of Logic*, 28). "What we are dealing with in logic is not a thinking about something which exists independently as a base for our thinking and apart from it, nor forms which are supposed to provide mere signs or distinguishing marks of truth; on the contrary, the necessary forms and self-determinations of thought are the content and the ultimate truth itself" (*Science of Logic*, 50).

11. "All that is necessary to achieve scientific progress . . . is the recognition of the logical principle that the negative is just as much positive, or that what is self-contradictory does not resolve itself into a nullity. . . . Because the result, the negation, is a *specific* negation it has a *content*. It is a fresh Notion, but higher and richer than its predecessor; for it is richer by the negation or opposite of the latter, therefore contains it, but also something more, and is the unity of itself and its opposite" (*Science of Logic*, 54, emphasis in original). "That which enables the Notion to advance itself is the already mentioned *negative* which it possesses

within itself; it is this which constitutes the genuine dialectical element" (*Science of Logic*, 55, emphasis in original).

12. *Science of Logic*, 43. In "With What Must the Science Begin," *Science of Logic*, 67–78, Hegel makes clear that the science must be devoid of any presuppositions and that this means beginning with the indeterminate immediate.

13. In this chapter I will use the terms *identity* and *difference* in their usual philosophical senses. While Hegel specifically discusses identity and difference in the logic of essence, I am not addressing his use of the terms there.

As will be indicated later, what I mean here by nonderivative difference is not that difference and otherness somehow appear mysteriously out of nowhere. As the logic unfolds they are logically derived from what comes before, just in the course of the preceding's coming to be determined, but, save for the logic of essence, their determinate nature is not derived from what comes before in the sense of being a variation of a prior determinate ground. Just that mode of derivative determination—the reductive logic of heteronomous determination—is considered and superseded in the logic of essence. Unfortunately more often than not Hegel's system as a whole is erroneously seen to instantiate and to function in terms of that superseded logic.

14. A case can be made that postmodernist attempts to overcome metaphysics fail to critique the root source of metaphysics—seeking a given, determinate ground for thought and reality—and only substitute a new candidate for what is fundamental and all-determining. Of course, when difference is fetishized, it just becomes a metaphysical, authoritarian determining ground in its own right.

15. See "Anfang und Methode der Logik" in Dieter Henrich, *Hegel im Kontext* (Frankfurt: Suhrkamp Verlag, 1971).

16. *Science of Logic*, 70.

17. Ibid., 82.

18. Ibid., 82, emphasis in original.

19. "It is therefore inadmissable to employ more developed forms of mediation here and to hold being and nothing in any kind of relationship—the transition in question is not yet a relation. Thus it is impermissible to say: nothing is the ground of being, or being is the ground of nothing or nothing is the cause of being, and so forth" (*Science of Logic*, 103).

20. Ibid., 83, emphasis in original.

21. Ibid., 92, emphasis in original.

22. "Becoming is as much the subsistence of being as it is on non-being; or their subsistence is only their being in a one" (Ibid., 92).

23. This is, of course, a simplification in two respects. First, there is a retrospective or backward- looking moment in logical development in that, for example, the truth of being and nothing is revealed in becoming. The truth of the whole previous logical development is attained at the end of the logic. See *Science of Logic*, 71–72. In addition, "transformation" does not do justice to the

different ways in which being and other are dynamically related in each of the three logics. More accurately, transformation takes place in the logic of being (e.g., being vanishes into nothing), appearing takes place in the logic of essence, and development takes place in the logic of the concept.

24. "That which enables the Notion to advance itself is the already mentioned *negative* which it possesses within itself; it is this which constitutes the genuine dialectical element" (*Science of Logic*, 55, emphasis in original).

25. Ibid., 581–82, emphasis in original.

26. See Edward C. Halper, "The Idealism of Hegel's System," *The Owl of Minerva* 34:1 (Fall–Winter 2002–2003): 19–58.

27. *Science of Logic*, 825, emphasis in original.

28. Ibid., 842, emphasis in original.

29. Ibid., 843, emphasis in original.

30. *Encyclopedia Logic*, §9, Remark. See also *Hegel's Philosophy of Nature, Being, Part Two of the Encyclopedia of the Philosophical Sciences* (1830) trans. A.V. Miller (Oxford: Clarendon Press, 1970), §250, Remark. Hereafter *Philosophy of Nature*.

31. *Philosophy of Nature*, §254.

32. Ibid., §250, Remark.

33. *Concluding Unscientific Postscript*, trans. D. F. Swenson and Walter Lowrie (Princeton, NJ: Princeton University Press, 1941).

34. *Philosophy of Nature*, §246, Remark.

Chapter 2

Double Transition, Dialectic, and Recognition

Robert R. Williams

In what sort of discourse is Hegel's thought to be discussed, evaluated, and criticized? This is not simply a question of how to translate Hegel's obscure and complex German into English. Rather, it is a question about the discourse in which Hegel's thought is formulated and expressed by scholars and interpreters, both critics and defenders. The question concerning the language in which speculative thought should be expressed is an issue that Hegel himself repeatedly addressed and struggled with. How should a speculative dialectical philosophy be articulated? Can it be expressed in ordinary propositional discourse without distorting it? This issue is not merely of concern to scholarly "drudges," it is also of concern to Hegel himself; he frequently observes that the propositional form of judgment is inadequate to express speculative truth. The formulation of speculative truth in judgments leads to its distortion and misrepresentation. The truth of reason is mishandled by the understanding (*Verstand*).

On the other hand, some believe dialectic itself is a reductive distortion of otherness and difference. Hegel's critics believe that Hegel fails at his ambitious project of reconciling and transcending the oppositions he seeks to mediate, and that speculative dialectic is just a more subtle form of domination by a privileged, one-sided unity. These charges play out especially on the themes of other, otherness, identity, and difference. Hegel's French students, who subsequently turned against him, charge that Hegel privileges identity over difference and reduces difference and otherness to negation, and thus to a subordinate, negative moment of identity. They point to an early Hegelian phrase, "the identity of identity and difference." Here difference is expressed as the negative moment of dialectic (opposition to identity), which is in turn itself negated in the second affirmative moment of negation of negation. The negation of negation (difference) allegedly reinstates the original identity, thus difference is eliminated. Further, the critics observe that here difference is thought dialectically by means of identity and thus is a difference that has been tamed. The critics seek a difference that is not subordinate methodologically to dialectical opposition in which it is mastered by, reducible to, or eliminated by identity. For example, Deleuze writes concerning Hegel that "difference is crucified . . . only that which is identical . . . or opposed can be considered different: difference becomes an object of representation always in relation to a conceived identity."[1] In contrast, Deleuze wants a difference that is not a negation or derived from a dialectical opposition that reinstates identity but an unrecognized and unrecognizable difference, a difference affirmative in itself.[2]

Such criticisms of Hegel's speculative dialectic are found not only in his critics but also among Hegel scholars. Some note that in Hegel's phrase, "identity of identity and non-identity," the term *identity* appears twice; consequently, identity, they maintain, is the controlling term. Difference is thus subordinate to identity.[3] This subordination leads, they allege, to Hegel's apparent privileging of community (state) over individuals (difference) in his social and political philosophy.

Perhaps the most sustained analysis and critique of Hegel's thought on this issue by a Hegelian scholar belongs to William Desmond who charges that Hegel's thought is at best ambiguous and at worst reductionist. According to Desmond, Hegel's dialectical treatment of the mediation of difference (otherness) by identity threatens to reduce mediation by other to self-mediation. In Desmond's words, "The logic of dialectical self-mediation includes a reference to what is other, but also always ends by including that other as a subordinate moment within a more encompassing self-mediating whole."[4] According to Desmond, Hegel fails to safeguard or to do justice to the other and to the inherently plural, doubled character of intermediation: "The doubleness of the self and the other is not fully recognized as the basis of a togethemess that is irreducibly plural; it becomes dialectically converted into a dualism that is to be mediated and included in a higher and more embracing process of self-mediation."[5]

In what follows I want to examine and respond to Desmond's critique, because he formulates succinctly views of Hegel that are widespread. His probing, brilliant traversal of Hegel's thought from a sympathetic, yet divergent perspective both throws light on the problems in Hegel, which he and others have identified, and at the same time engages the problems in formulating Hegel's speculative philosophy noted earlier.[6] Desmond's corrective to Hegel's dialectic is what he calls the "metaxological view," which is hostile to any reduction of otherness to identity, "and to the reduction of a pluralized intermediation to a singular self-mediation."[7]

I shall show first that Desmond's critique of the logic depends on a reductive reading of speculative dialectic from the perspective of *Verstand.* It is ironic that Desmond, who charges Hegel with reductive mediation, bases this very charge on a reductive and distorted reading of Hegel's logic. Second, I shall show that Hegel is not only aware of the distortion of speculative dialectic when it is formulated and interpreted at the level of judgments and propositions, but he also seeks to correct this distortion by insisting on what he calls "double transition." Double transition is for Hegel a transcategorical principle, applicable throughout the whole scientific logical method. Double transition prevents any reduction of mediation by other to singular self-mediation; it safeguards difference against subordination to identity, and it clarifies the nature of the speculative holism that Hegel intends. In short, Desmond's critique of Hegel is part of Hegel's own self-critique. Hegel is not a "Hegelian" in the sense rightly deplored by Desmond and others, namely, one whose method intends or requires the reduction of the other to the same or a reduction of plural intermediation to self-mediation. This will become clear both from an examination of the logic and from the concept of recognition as a "syllogism" developed both in the *Phenomemology* and in the mature system (*Encyclopedia*). I shall not develop a global interpretation of the logic but instead examine some categories and relevant texts that clarify Hegel's position.

Hegel's Critics: Dialectic as Reductive of Otherness and Difference

In spite of his reservations, Desmond concedes that speculative dialectic is an important third alternative to the univocal sense of being as sameness, and the equivocal sense of being as irreducibly plural. The former favors abstract identity and universals, while the latter regards the irreducible plurality of being as precluding any mediation. The rejection of mediation leaves a plurality of beings indistinguishable from dispersal and fragmentation, an option toward which deconstruction is inclined. However, the possibility of mediating differences is opened up by dialectic.[8] Desmond agrees with Hegel against deconstruction and pluralism that mediation is necessary.

What is at issue is the nature of this mediation, this togetherness that defines the community of self and other in their identity and difference. Desmond acknowledges the need for mediation but criticizes what he believes is Hegel's "tendency to interpret all mediation primarily in terms of self-mediation. The togetherness of self and the other and their intermediation is, in the end, seen in the light of a certain privileging of self-mediation. . . . The doubleness of self and other is not fully recognized as the basis of a togetherness that is irreducibly plural; it becomes dialectically converted into a dualism that is to be mediated and included in a higher and more embracing process of self-mediation. The dialectic converts the mediation of self and other into two sides of a more embracing and singular process of total self-mediation."[9]

Desmond is not hostile to universals and to mediation as are many of Hegel's critics. But he protests what he believes happens in Hegel's dialectic, namely, "the reduction of a pluralized intermediation to a *singular* self-mediation."[10] Desmond believes that, in dialectic, "mediation by other turns out, in the end, to be a mediation of the self [by itself] in the form of its own otherness, and hence not a mediation of an irreducible other at all."[11] If in Hegel's thought all mediation by other turns out to be self-mediation, then such thinking seems to privilege its own internal self-coherence and may renege on "potentially dissident forms of otherness that resist complete conceptualization."[12] Hence the French critics of Hegel are right. Granted the apparent failure of Hegel's dialectic, Desmond argues for a fourth alternative that "articulates the space of a middle that is open to a *double mediation,* a double that is no dualistic opposition. The middle is plurally mediated; it can be mediated from the side of the dialectical self, but also it can be mediated from the side of an otherness that is not to be reduced to a moment of self-mediation."[13]

> Can Hegel really count to two, or count to a real two? This seems a ridiculous question since Hegel is notorious for his stress on the number three, and all its trinitarian implications. I ask the question in all seriousness. I also ask for a mindfulness larger than univocal literalness. If what I said about the double mediation of the metaxological in contrast to the singular process of dialectical self-mediation has been understood, then we can say this: Hegel counts to three, but in dialectically

> counting to three, he is finally counting to one; the third turns out to be the first; for the second, in dialectically turning into the third, also turns out to be the first; three turns out to be one, two turns out to be one, hence Hegel does not finally count beyond one at all.[14]

Thus Desmond's Hegel is a dialectical monist who regards otherness and difference "as a self-division, hence a halving of the original unity."[15] Hegel treats otherness simply as a self-diremption or negation of a primordial unity or identity, and, by a second negation of negation, he reinstates the original unity or identity. This reinstatement of unity means that Hegel does not count beyond one at all.

Desmond seeks to correct what he considers the monistic tendencies of speculative dialectic. He maintains that reality is irreducibly plural and pleads for a genuinely plural, two-sided "between" and the continuation of the double as "ineradicable."[16] Only if the "between" is preserved by double mediation can there be an adequate account of relation and nonreductive togetherness. The problem he finds with Hegel, the "essential core of the Hegelian position," is that "the double mediation collapses into this total and single self-mediation."[17] "Hegel's absolute is erotic, and in the end every other is the other in which the self-constitution of Hegel's absolute, its self-recognition and self-appropriation, is effected. That is, there is no absolute other in the end."[18] Desmond, like many others, dissents from such monism: "I think this is wrong. The double mediation is irreducible."[19] It is difficult not to agree with Desmond, chiefly because Hegel makes the same point concerning the necessity of double mediation in his *Logic* as I shall now show.

Preliminary Reflections: Plurality and Measure

I first discuss Desmond's quasimathematical test to decide whether Hegel is adequately pluralistic. Double mediation implies and presupposes irreducible plurality. But what is plurality and how are we to conceive it? Desmond tackles this question with a quasimathematical test, namely, counting. He asks, can Hegel count to two? Although the question has an obvious clarity about it, it is misleading. It is worth reminding ourselves of Hegel's views on counting and quantification. Quantity is a logical category that must be accorded its due. But Hegel observes that it is easy to overestimate its importance, exaggerate the scope of its validity, and perhaps even take it as the absolute category.[20] This is what happens when "only those sciences whose object can be submitted to a mathematical calculus are recognized as *exact* sciences. . . . There would indeed be something badly amiss . . . if we had to renounce the possibility of exact cognition of objects such as freedom, law, ethical life, and even God himself, because they cannot be measured and computed or expressed in a mathematical formula."[21] When this view is pushed to the metaphysical level, it becomes atomism, which, as Hegel notes, surfaces not only in materialistic views of nature but also in politics, for example, the social contract theory of the state.[22]

Hegel insists that speculative truth cannot be properly expressed in quantitative, numerical language. Such language implies that irreducible plurality means a numerical aggregate. Number is an abstract unit that is externally related to and equal to other abstract units. In the *Logic* Hegel inveighs against mathematization and formal views of syllogism; he complains that "numbers are a conceptless material and operations of arithmetic are an external combining or separating of them."[23] He contends that with regard to spirit and ethical life, "It is futile to seek to fix [these] by spatial figures or algebraic signs."[24] According to Hegel, the formal syllogism collapses into tautology because of the formal equality and interchangeability of its terms, that is, its three terms all reduce to one.[25] Thus Hegel anticipates Desmond's critique but criticizes its formalist implications and presuppositions. Desmond's counting test for plurality brings with it presuppositions concerning abstract identity and sheer external relations. Abstract identity implies that all relations are external, even so-called "internal" relations. Hence, relations have no implications for their terms, which remain indifferent and formally equivalent, that is, interchangeable. However, as far as Hegel is concerned, such formal, merely external relations are not genuine relations at all.

Further, a purely formal system of thought could not generate contradictions in Hegel's sense, because as he points out in his critique of Kant's formalism, "A contradiction must be a contradiction with something."[26] Desmond's charge—that Hegel cannot count to two or three—assumes that Hegel's logic and dialectic are formal. This is doubtful in view of the fact that Hegel brings the emptiness charge against formal logic and propounds dialectical logic as a nonformal alternative.[27] Moreover, Hegel counters Desmond's counting test to determine whether plurality is real and/or genuine. He observes, "If one insists on counting . . . instead of a triplicity the abstract form may be taken as a quadruplicity; in this way the negative or difference is counted as a duality."[28] Here, *pace* Desmond, Hegel is insisting that difference is not eliminated in singular self-mediation; rather, difference counts as duality and as a presupposition and requirement of double mediation.

Whatever the plurality of spirit may be, it cannot be conceived adequately in the abstract and external form of counting, for here the categories of abstract identity, abstract difference, and external relation hold sway. The counting test is not sufficient to determine the unity, the plurality, or the vitality of spirit. But Desmond's advocacy of the counting test suggests that the perspective, the categories, and the language he uses to formulate his critique of Hegel reflect the standpoint of the understanding, *Verstand.* To be sure, this is not false per se but nevertheless part of the problem, the restriction, that Hegel is concerned to overcome.[29] The counting test implies a metaphysical atomism and abstract individualism that underlie the social contract theory of the state. Hegel rejects these presuppositions.

Second, Hegel's analysis of the category of being-for-self (*Fürsichsein*) is relevant to the issue of plurality. Hegel can claim to be a pluralist. The starting point is that being-for-self is conceived as a negative unity that excludes all otherness from itself. However, as Hegel observes, this negative and exclusive being-for-self subverts itself: "Self-subsistence pushed to the point of the one as a being-for-self is abstract, formal, and destroys itself."[30] The purely negative being-for-self undergoes a dialectical reversal. The negative One reverts into positive plural ones: by excluding everything from itself, the One shows that it stands in relation to what it excludes, that is, the many. The consideration that establishes the exclusive unity of the monad also establishes the positive plurality of the many, that is, it is dialectical. The reverse is equally true: The plural many also are one. Does this reversal mean that Desmond is correct when he charges that Hegel reduces plurality to unity? Yes and no. Hegel elaborates:

> It is an ancient proposition that the one is many and especially that the many are one. We may repeat here the observation that the truth of the one and the many expressed in propositions appears in an inappropriate form, that this truth is to be grasped and expressed only as a becoming, as a process, a repulsion and attraction, not as being, which in a proposition has the character of a stable unity . . . each is one, each is one of the many, is by excluding the others—so that they are absolutely the same . . . This is the fact and all that has to be done is to grasp this

> simple fact. The only reason why the understanding stubbornly refuses to do so is that it has also in mind, and indeed rightly so, the difference; but the existence of this difference is just as little excluded because of the said fact [of identity] as the said fact [of identity] is excluded by the difference. One could, as it were, comfort the understanding for the naive manner in which it grasps the difference, by assuring it that the difference will also come in again."[31]

Hegel notes the limitations of the propositional form, namely, that it portrays being as something static and fails to capture becoming and process. The understanding's basic categories are abstract identity (unity) and an equally abstract difference, or plurality. The understanding *(Verstand)* thinks plurality and difference naively as something exclusive of and apart from abstract unity. But dialectical reason breaks down and overcomes such abstractions by showing that the opposed terms are related. Separation implies and presupposes relation. Opposition and contradiction do not annul relation but rather are forms of relation as Hegel explains: "In accordance with its concept the One forms the presupposition of the many and it lies in the thought of the One to posit itself as what is many. *In other words, the One which is for-itself is . . . not something that lacks relation—instead it is relation.*"[32] But it is equally true that relation implies and presupposes separation, otherwise the difference of the *relata* would collapse. Relation and separation are reciprocal, thus relation is constituted by the double transition of each term into its opposite. The double transition breaks down the assumption that the one excludes the many, and vice versa, and rather transforms them into a process of mutual-reciprocal relation, that is, repulsion and attraction. The double transition shows that *being-for-self (Fürsichsein)* and plurality cease to be mutually exclusive and thus cease to be opposed. Instead, they become mutually coconstitutive of relation.

Hegel's Corrective: The Double Transition

The preceding discussion has brought to light an important feature and principle of Hegel's method that, once appreciated, can be discerned throughout his logic on all levels of the logical categories.[33] This principle Hegel calls "double transition," *der gedöpptelte Übergang.* It is a principle that Hegel enunciated in the latest editions of both his *Logic* and *Encyclopedia,* which suggests that he had gradually become aware of a potential misunderstanding that may arise when the logic is read and discussed at the level of the understanding (*Verstand*), ordinary language, and propositional judgments. Double transition is explicitly formulated in the second 1830 edition of the *Science of Logic*, buried in a not widely read discussion of quantity and quality.[34] The passage is as follows:

> The positing of the totality requires the *double transition,* not only of one determinateness into its other, but equally the transition of this other, its return, into the first. The first transition yields the identity of both, but at first only in itself or in principle; quality is contained in quantity, but this is still a one-sided determinateness. That the converse is equally true, namely, that quantity is contained in quality and is equally only a sublated determinateness, this results from the second transition—the return into the first determinateness. *This observation on the necessity of the double transition is of great importance throughout the whole compass of scientific method.*[35]

The first transition of one term into its other is not yet their full identity but only the implicit, *an sich,* identity of the two. This identity is not yet the full concrete, mutually mediated, and jointly constituted identity; rather, it is abstract, one-sided, and reductive. It results from the disappearance of one term into the other, or the subordination of one term to the other. In contrast, the concrete, actual identity is the accomplishment of the full double transition. Both terms transition into their opposite. Hence, instead of a simple subordination of one term to another, double transition means a mutual, joint, and reciprocal mediation in which both terms are sublated and together constitute a new whole. Anything short of full double transition short-circuits the process of mediation and reduces it from double to single mediation. Single mediation is an incomplete, partial, one-sided mediation and results in a forcible, reductive identity whereby one term is reduced to or subordinate to the other.

It is remarkable that Hegel would bury this important observation on double transition in the middle of his discussion of quantitative ratio. However, this does not mean that the passage is an empty rhetorical flourish tacked on to a monist system. On the contrary, it clarifies what is at stake by subverting the monist reading of mediation as singular self-mediation. It seems that Hegel reflected on the importance of double transition—which was already an element in his method in quantitative ratio—and wanted to make it explicit and generalize it in order to forestall precisely that misreading of his thought presented by Desmond and others.

Any suspicion that the double transition passage cited earlier is merely a rhetorical excess, unimportant, and at best marginal to Hegel's thought can be laid to rest by the fact that Hegel makes the same point about double transition at the conclusion of the logic in the final 1830 edition of the *Encyclopedia.* He says:

> *The development of this sphere becomes a return into the first, just as the development of the first is a passage to the second.* It is only through this doubled movement [*gedoppelte Bewegung*] that the difference gets its due, since each of the two differences, considered in itself, consummates itself in the totality and in this totality works out its unity with the other. Only this self-suspension of the one-sidedness of both [sides] in themselves prevents the unity (totality) from being one-sided.[36]

The double transition is Hegel's response to the limitations and distortions introduced into speculative thought when the latter is expressed in judgments and propositions at the level of the understanding (*Verstand*). Such judgments tend to assert identity and suppress difference. The first transition, he says, yields the implicit but one-sided identity of both *relata,* both terms. The second transition corrects this one-sidedness by articulating and preserving their difference. This reciprocal double transition or *Aufhebung* prevents the resulting totality from being one-sided and reductive. This is Hegel's response to the half-truth distortion that the speculative dialectic reduces mediation by other to singular self-mediation, or reduces the other to the same. Double transition has profound implications for difference, otherness, plurality, relation, and the space of the "between." It is only through the double transition that the difference gets its due. Instead of being subordinate to identity, difference is preserved as coequal and equiprimordial to identity.

Double transition is Hegel's antireductive, antimonist corrective of the abstract identity favored by the understanding. When employed by the understanding, abstract identity results in metaphysical atomism, and in a mechanical mode of thinking, "Its nature is an act completely external and devoid of thought, so that it can be performed even by a machine. Here there is not the slightest trace of a transition to an other."[37]

This remark implies that a transition from one term to another implies and presupposes the difference of the two terms. Collapse the difference as formalism does and there could be no transition. The difference cannot be collapsed into abstract identity or unity without undermining and denying not only transition but the very possibility of transition. Transition, like contradiction, presupposes real, nonformal difference.

There can be a double transition only if there is another, second term that is irreducible to the first. If there were no other, then there could be no double transition. Indeed, if there were no otherness in any sense, then there could be no transition at all, not even a tautological reiteration of the one and the same. If there is to be a genuine transition, then it must be a transition to an other, and this other must be irreducible to the first. Transition requires an other, a double, but this is a prenumerical plurality, a prenumerical difference. The same is true for the second transition: it too presupposes a double, an other. Both transitions together constitute the double transition. Double transition constitutes a relation between terms that can neither be identified nor separated. This "between," the space of the middle, has to be jointly and reciprocally constituted from and by both sides. To return to the so-called "counting test," we can say that doubling implies at least two; but if there are two then there must be a third, namely, the transition and relation (of some sort) between them. This relation must be two-sided and reciprocal, because "a one-sided relation is no relation at all."[38]

Double transition clarifies the nature of the totality that Hegel intends. The whole cannot be simply identified with one of its terms, nor can it be produced by eliminating one term or reducing one term to the other. The unity that resulted from such suppression of the other would itself be a reductive unity, a closed and an exclusive unity. But if there is to be a whole at all in Hegel's sense, then the whole must be the result of the double transition of its terms into each other. Hegel is explicit on this point: "*It is only through this doubled movement [gedoppelte Bewegung] that the difference gets its due, since each of the two differences, considered in itself, consummates itself in the totality and in this totality works out its unity with the other.*"[39] Double transition is constitutive of a whole or totality that is not external to its members but present and immanent in them as their organizing principle. From the perspective of the whole, double transition names the reciprocal movement whereby a self-organizing whole organizes itself. Such a self-organizing whole does not constitute "the reduction of a pluralized intermediation to a singular self-mediation,"[40] because it requires and depends on double transition. Double transition requires plurality and mutual mediation of whole and parts. The whole is not the elimination but rather the consummation of the differences that it organizes.

Judgment, Double Transition, and the First Category of Logic

Judgment is the form in which understanding (*Verstand*) expresses its truth,[41] but Hegel's complaint is that judgment suppresses the difference. For example, judgments of the form "S is P" typically express only one aspect, the identity and unity, of S and P. This judgment also does not express their difference. The apparent suppression of difference then becomes a matter of concern for the understanding. Of course, difference can be expressed by the negative judgment, "S is not P," but then only difference and not identity is expressed; the identity of S and P is excluded. For this reason Hegel believes that both judgments are inadequate and distortions, as he explains: "Judgment is an identical relation between subject and predicate; in it we abstract from the fact that the subject has a number of determinatenesses other than that of the predicate. . . . Now *if the content is speculative, the non-identical aspect of subject and predicate is also an essential moment, but in the judgment this is not expressed*."[42] Taken by itself, each judgment expresses only one aspect of the content that speculative reason (*Vernunft*) intends while omitting the others. Judgment is for Hegel not incorrect, but misleading, because it expresses identity while suppressing the essential nonidentity or difference, and thus it distorts or even suppresses speculative truth.

As practiced by the understanding, judgment abstracts features of a whole from their context, suppresses the context on which these depend, and interprets the subject and some of its features as absolute in their isolation. Such judgments tend toward dogmatism and call forth a skeptical challenge. The skeptical principle of equipollence holds that to every judgment (thesis) there is an opposite, contradictory judgment of equal validity. The skeptical critique of dogmatism proceeds by constructing oppositions or antinomies that cancel each other out, and lead to the *epoché*, or suspension, of judgment. While Hegel rejects skepticism as incoherent, he nevertheless believes that the skeptical tropes contain rational demands, namely, the demand not to mistake abstractions for concrete realities, the demand not to suppress context or exclude essential aspects, and the demand for the whole truth, not just a partial or one-sided half-truth. Most important, the skeptical strategy raises the issue of the difference and exploits difference not only to the point of contradiction but to the point of cancellation—the skeptical *epoché.* Skepticism exploits difference in a negative dialectic, a dialectic of collapse. This dialectic of collapse undermines not only the opposition, but also the essential difference, namely, the truth-question.[43] In contrast to skepticism's negative dialectic, Hegel maintains that the speculative dialectic preserves rather than suppresses truth and difference. While speculative dialectic also pushes the difference to the point of cancellation and collapse, such cancellation is only a partial or determinate negation and thus can have affirmative significance because it preserves the difference, that is, holds fast to the positive in the negative. Hegel explains:

> The immediate, from this negative side, has been extinguished in the other, but the other is not essentially the empty negative, the nothing, that is taken to be the usual result of dialectic. Rather it is the other of the first, the negative of the immediate; it is therefore determined as the mediated—contains the determination of the first within itself. Consequently the first is essentially preserved and retained even in the other. To hold fast to the positive in its negative . . . in the result, this is the most important feature in rational cognition.[44]

The holding fast to the positive in its negative requires the *Aufhebung,* or determinate negation. Determinate negation differs from abstract or total negation; it is a partial negation that can at the same time preserve aspects of that which is negated. Determinate negation means that opposites enter into relation to each other and become qualified by their relation.

The most widely known, but perhaps least appreciated, example of double transition is found in the first category of the logic. Here Hegel attempts to isolate pure being and shows that the attempt to isolate being in its purity fails. It fails because pure being turns out to be empty featurelessness. Hegel expresses it this way: The determination of being is to have no determination. This empty featurelessness, this absence of determination, is indistinguishable from nothing, for empty featurelessness is also what nothing "is." Thus being is indistinguishable from nothing, and the recognition of this is the transition, the passing of being into its apparent opposite, namely, nothing. Similarly, nothing is a featurelessness that nevertheless *is,* and so it passes over into being. The distinction between being and nothing proves to be without foundation, because both terms turn out to be the same empty featurelessness, thus their distinction turns out to be groundless (*Bodenlosigkeit*), and so it collapses.[45]

Does not the collapse of being into nothing and of nothing into being imply their identity? Indeed it does. "In representation, or for the understanding, the proposition: 'Being and Nothing is the same' appears to be such a paradoxical proposition that it may perhaps be taken as not seriously meant. And it really is one of the most difficult propositions that thinking dares to formulate, for being and nothing are the antithesis in all its immediacy. . . . But . . . they do contain this determination [viz., empty featurelessness]; i.e., the one that is the same in both. . . . *But correct as it is to affirm the unity of being and nothing, it is equally correct to say that they are absolutely diverse too—that the one is not what the other is.*"[46] The collapse of being into nothing and of nothing into being proves to be a double transition: Being and nothing are both absolutely the same and absolutely different. The upshot is that being and nothing can neither be identified nor separated. But if they cannot be separated then they must be related, and the category that relates them is becoming. Becoming names and is the result of the double transition of being into nothing (and nothing into being). Becoming is the unity of being and nothing.

How is this unity to be understood? In his second remark on the defectiveness of the expressions "unity" and "identity," Hegel observes that "unity" is a defective expression of speculative truth because it expresses abstract sameness. He further observes, "The statement: being and nothing are one and the same, is incomplete."[47] It is incomplete because "the sense seems to be that the difference is denied."[48] Moreover, the intention of this proposition "cannot be that abstraction should be made from them and only the unity retained. Such a meaning would self-evidently be one-sided because that from which abstraction is to be made is equally present and named in the proposition. Now insofar as the proposition, "being and nothing are the same," asserts the identity of these determinations but in fact equally contains them both as distinguished, the proposition is self-contradictory and cancels itself out . . . it has a movement which involves the spontaneous vanishing of the proposition itself. But in thus vanishing there takes place in it that which is to constitute its own peculiar content, namely, becoming."[49]

Becoming is not a one-sided or an abstract substantial unity of being and nothing. It is rather the joint and inseparable movement of being and nothing. Becoming, as the result of the *Aufhebung*, is not reducible to an original unity prior to the *Aufhebung*, for that would reduce one term to the other. "Becoming is the unseparatedness of being and nothing; but as the unity of being and nothing it is this determinate unity in which there is both being and nothing. But in so far as being and nothing, each unseparated from its other, is, each is not. They are therefore in this unity but only as vanishing, sublated moments."[50] Becoming names the common feature, namely, the double transition in which both being and nothing vanish into their opposite.

Does this vanishing imply the reduction of the double transition to a single transition and singular self-mediation? Hegel denies any reduction of double transition to single transition here: "Becoming is in this way in a *double* determination. In the one, nothing is immediate, that is, the determination starts from nothing which . . . changes into being; in the other, being is immediate, which changes into nothing: the former is coming to be and the latter is ceasing to be."[51] Being and nothing do not simply vanish in an abstract negation or simple unity; rather, they enter into union with each other as the double movements of becoming. "Being is being and nothing is nothing only in their contradistinction from each other; but in their truth, in their unity, they have vanished as these determinations and are now something else. Being and nothing are the same; but *just because they are the same they are no longer being and nothing*, but now have a different significance. In becoming they [are] coming to be and ceasing to be."[52]

Hegel's exposition of becoming as the first concrete category reveals a double transition whose preservation of the difference constitutes a unity irreducible to singular self-mediation. It is here that Hegel introduces the *Aufhebung*, calling it one of the most important concepts in philosophy.[53] In both versions of his logic, Hegel links the *Aufhebung* to the double meaning of terms. This double meaning not only shows the speculative spirit of language, it is linked to the double transition that "transcends the 'either/or' of mere understanding."[54] In the *Aufhebung* a term undergoes suspension. Hegel observes, "Something is sublated only insofar as it has entered into unity with its opposite."[55] But it also is the case that because each term enters into union with its opposite, both terms are transformed and preserved in a higher unity. Hegel insists that this unity is not adequately conceived or expressed as a reinstatement or restoration of an original unity or identity. "Becoming is the first concrete thought, and hence the first concept, whereas being and nothing, in contrast, are empty abstractions. If we speak of the concept of being, this can only consist in becoming . . . but this being which abides with itself in nothing is becoming.

The unity of becoming cannot leave out the difference, for—without the difference—we would return once more to abstract being."[56]

Similar double transitions also show up in the logic of essence in the discussion of identity and difference. In the logic of essence, Hegel points out that all the categories of essence are relative. What appear initially to be absolute differences and distinctions will break down and subvert themselves. This means that as categories of essence neither identity nor difference can be thought apart from each other but only through and by means of each other. Hegel shows that the attempt to isolate difference from identity fails. Absolute or pure difference must differ from itself, hence, absolute difference "is not itself but its other."[57] (Otherwise it would be identical to itself.) If pure difference differs from itself, then it can differ from itself only by being other than itself. "But that which is different from difference is identity. Difference is therefore itself and identity. Both together constitute difference; it is the whole and its moment."[58]

Critics object that this subordinates difference to identity by thinking it as a negation and contradiction. For example, Deleuze maintains that when difference is pushed to the limit in contradiction, difference becomes one with identity and is therefore eliminated.[59] Deleuze is correct that difference when, pushed to its limit, becomes one with identity, but he is wrong in thinking that this eliminates difference. Everything turns on what this unity of identity and difference is. Like Desmond, Deleuze interprets it one-sidedly as a simple unity that eliminates difference. Hegel corrects this apparent one-sidedness when he writes: "Sublated contradiction is not abstract identity, for that is itself only one side of the contradiction."[60] Hegel continues: "When we say that ground is the unity of identity and difference, this unity must not be understood as abstract identity, for then we would just have another name for a thought that is once more just that identity of the understanding which we have recognized to be untrue. So in order to counter the misunderstanding, we can also say that ground is not only the identity, but equally the difference, of identity and difference."[61] Thus Hegel employs double transition to deconstruct the ordinary language and the propositional forms that distort speculative truth.

Double Transition and Syllogism, Reciprocity

What follows is not a treatment, much less a commentary, on syllogism, reciprocity, and teleology per se but only a highlighting of the presence of double transition in these discussions. We should recall Hegel's assertion that "everything rational is a syllogism."[62] He construes syllogism in a broad, nonformal sense, not confining it to a formal three-proposition structure. Organisms are syllogisms for Hegel and already syllogize in the world prior to philosophical-logical reflection on them. Hegel begins his discussion of syllogism with a plea for the reconciliation of the analytical reason that syllogizes with the intuitive reason that thinks absolute thoughts.[63] The latter's immediate vision of the whole as an immediate unity may appear to suppress otherness and difference. However, its immediate vision is the result of mediation, and those mediations preserve the otherness and difference necessary to the articulation of the whole. Syllogism is the structure of reason that exhibits the full process of mediation as double transition. Anything short of this is incomplete mediation, or one-sided, reductive, single "mediation."

Thus syllogism serves as a corrective to the previously noted one-sidedness of judgments. For Hegel the syllogism structure "makes room" for the second or double transition suppressed by judgment; consequently, syllogism preserves the difference that is suppressed by judgment, without landing in sheer pluralism of external relations, as in atomism or mechanism, and without collapsing difference into abstract identity. Syllogism "works" because it involves the double transition of the extreme terms into the middle and of the middle into the extremes. The preservation of difference is safeguarded and expressed in the double transition and reciprocal mediation of the *relata* constitutive of syllogism. Hegel expressed this point in his 1827 Lectures: "It is not yet correct to say 'the unity of thought and being'. For 'unity' implies that the difference of the two is suspended. Only when thought coincides with itself in a syllogism is it the essence, the concrete thought."[64]

Double transition structures not only syllogism but the entire system insofar as the latter is characterized by Hegel as a threefold syllogism with a threefold mediation:

> . . . everything rational shows itself to be a threefold syllogism and it does that in such a way that each of its members occupies the position both of an extreme and of the mediating middle. This is the case especially with the three "members" of philosophical science, i.e., the logical idea, nature, and spirit.[65]

In Hegel's view, each division or "part" of the system plays both the role of extreme and the role of mediator for the other parts of the system. The complex relation between the middle and the extremes exhibits the double transition. In this way the whole is present in each of the parts and connects them. No part has any absolute priority over the others.

Double transition also is evident in Hegel's treatment of the category of reciprocity, which is the sublation of mechanism and external causality into the higher unity of organic life. Reciprocity is a specification of organic double transition. Namely, in reciprocity, "The terms that appear initially to be bound together are not in fact alien to one another; instead they are only moments of one whole, *each of which, being related to the other, is at home with itself, and goes together with itself*."[66] The whole is the coincidence, the collective double transition, of its members.

Double transition also is exhibited in the category of teleology. Hegel praises Kant's distinction between external and internal purposiveness, because the latter opens up the concept of life and raises it "above the determinations of reflection and the relative world of metaphysics."[67] If mechanism consists in the externality of whole and parts, then Hegel sees this externality already beginning to break down in the "elective affinities" of chemism.[68] Teleology extends the overcoming of externality that begins in chemism. The whole and the parts that, on the level of mechanism, are other to each other undergo a double transition that dissolves their mutual externality. The dissolution of externality becomes evident in the following account of teleological activity:

> It can therefore be said of teleological activity that in it the end is the beginning, the result is the ground, the effect is the cause, that it is a coming to be of what has already come to be, that in it only what already exists comes into existence, and so forth; which means that in general all the determinations of relationship belonging to the sphere of reflection or immediate being have lost their distinction, and that what was spoken of as an *other*, such as end, result, effect, etc. no longer have the determination of being an other in the end-relationship.[69]

The following passage articulates double transition and reciprocity in teleological self-actualization:

> Since the concept here in the sphere of objectivity . . . is in *reciprocal* action with itself, the exposition of its movement is itself *double* and a first is always a second also. In the concept

> taken by itself, that is in its subjectivity, its difference from itself appears as an immediate identical totality on its own account; but since its determinateness here is indifferent externality, its identity with itself in this externality is also immediately again self-repulsion so that what is determined as external and indifferent to the identity is the identity itself; and the identity, as identity, as reflected into itself, is rather its other. Only by keeping this firmly in mind can we grasp the objective return of the concept into itself, that is, the true objectification of the concept—grasp that each of the single moments through which this mediation runs its course is itself the entire syllogism of those moments . . . this reflection that the end is reached in the means, and that in the fulfilled end, means and mediation are preserved, is the *last result of the external end-relation.*[70]

Note that teleology here is described as the end-relation (*Zweckbeziehung*) that preserves means and mediation (to which end is contrasted in ordinary reflection) and breaks down not only these distinctions but also the distinction between the whole and the parts: The whole is present in the parts. What breaks down these distinctions is the double transition.

The realization of the end involves the end's having a negative relation to itself whereby its *positing* is an act that excludes itself from itself but equally *presupposes* what it excludes.[71] Note this terminology. *Positing* is a term associated with idealism, which asserts the primacy of the subject, while *presupposing* is a term associated with empiricism or realism and denotes a passive acceptance of a given. Hegel sides with neither idealism nor empiricism but contends that both are sublated in teleology and organism. He regards both terms as occurring in relation, namely, in a double transition. Both terms have to be taken together; neither idealism per se nor empiricism per se can be regarded as the truth but only both taken together and as qualifying each other. In the negative self-relation of the end in its process of realization, what is posited also is presupposed, and what is presupposed also is either posited or *capable* of being posited. The latter is the principle of idealism, "which asserts that *nothing whatever can have a positive relation to the living being if this latter is not in its own self the possibility of this relation.*"[72]

The reciprocal relation of positing (idealism) and presupposing (realism) is further developed in Hegel's mediation of analysis and synthesis:

> It is just as one-sided to represent analysis as though there were nothing in the subject matter that was not imported into it, as it is one-sided to suppose that the resulting determinations are merely extracted from it. The former view, as everyone knows, is enunciated by subjective idealism, which takes the activity of cognition in analysis to be merely a one-sided *positing*, beyond which the *thing in itself* remains concealed; the other view belongs to so-called realism which apprehends the subjective concept as an empty identity that *receives* the thought determinations into itself *from outside*. Analytic cognition, the transformation of the given material into logical determinations, has shown itself to be two things in one: *a positing that no less immediately determines itself as a presupposing.* Consequently, by virtue of the latter, the logical element may appear as something already complete in the object, just as by virtue of the former it may appear as the product of a merely subjective activity. But *the two moments are not to be separated*; the logical element in its abstract form into which analysis raises it, is of course only to be found in cognition, while conversely it is something not merely posited, but possessing being in itself.[73]

Here is a statement not only of the *Aufhebung* of idealism and realism and empiricism but also of the distinction between positing and presupposing. The logical element of idealism is not a separate ego cogito or transcendental subject in contrast to an empirical subject or to unknowable things in themselves; rather, the logical element of idealism is actual only in cognition. On the other hand, the presupposed content, when posited, is not reducible to the positing activity of the subject but possesses intrinsic being in itself. So what is presupposed has to be capable of being posited by the subject—the partial truth of idealism—while what is posited is not thereby reduced to or made wholly relative to the positing activity of the subject but possesses intrinsic being is an end in itself—the partial truth of empiricism and realism. Again, my concern here is not with the plausibility, success, or failure of Hegel's bold attempt to mediate and correct the one-sided alternatives of idealism and realism but rather to call attention to the double transition in this mediation. It is not an exaggeration to say that double transition is what is unique and distinctive about Hegel's philosophy. The double transition sets Hegel's thought apart from idealism in the usual one-sided sense of that term.[74]

With these examples of double transition drawn from the logic, I hope to have explicated and confirmed Hegel's remark that "the double transition is of great importance throughout the whole compass of scientific method." Double transition is the methodological principle that deconstructs the antinomies and oppositions generated by the analytical understanding (*Verstand*). I do not claim that every transition in the logic is a double transition. I do not pretend to have exhausted the topic of double transition or to have determined whether double transition is successful in all of these examples, or to have shown how it affects the details of particular logical transitions. For example, the ontological import of this methodological principle is not yet fully explicit. But I do claim that since "the double transition is of great importance throughout the whole compass of scientific method,"[75] this undercuts any reading of the logic that regards the logical progression as proceeding by subordinating one term to another or as involving a reduction of double mediation to singular self-mediation. If such were the case, then Hegel would have violated his own standard and failed to meet his own systematic methodological requirement. He would be guilty of the "sin" of one-sidedness. I am convinced that double transition is crucial to understand and appreciate Hegel's thought. That it is important is beyond question, if only because Hegel claims that his whole system can and should be understood as a syllogism of syllogisms.[76] How double transition works out in detail in the matter of syllogisms is a topic for further inquiry and research. It would seem to have implications not only for the various levels and divisions of the logic but also for the relations between the logic and *Realphilosophie* or the empirical disciplines. The double transition holds not only for the relation of logical terms and categories but also for the relation between logic and *Realphilosophie* or between thought and being in the most comprehensive and basic sense. If the logic is related to empirical phenomena through double transition, then it would seem to follow that the logic is both open to and in some sense dependent on empirical phenomena.[77] A discussion of this complex issue lies beyond our present task. I now turn to the question of double transition and syllogism in the concept of recognition.

Recognition and Double Transition

We have seen that for Hegel double transition is transition into an other irreducible to the first. It is a process that is double-sided, which is accomplished only jointly and reciprocally. Without the full double transition, one term, and with that, the difference, would be suppressed. The result would be a possibly forcible, one-sided union in which one term is subordinate to or reduced to another. This would further involve a reduction of mediation to singular self-mediation, and concrete mediated identity to abstract identity. Hegel argues that double transition is necessary if the difference is to be given its due, that is, treated as equal in importance with identity. The difference, which is expressed in the negative moment of the dialectic, is actually the more profound and important, because it discloses the contradiction inherent in existence that has to be overcome.[78] Difference is contradiction implicit,[79] but *felt* contradiction "is the root of all movement and vitality; it is only insofar as something has a contradiction within it that it moves, has a drive and activity."[80]

Similarly, it is an experienced contradiction that propels the struggle for recognition. The contradiction of an immediate encounter—which Hegel expresses in the *Phenomenology* as "a self-consciousness exists for another self-consciousness"—has to be resolved, and the resolution of this contradiction is the process of mutual recognition.[81] But the two parties do not begin in mutual recognition; rather, they engage in a struggle for recognition. In this process both sides have to work off their immediacy, that is, their brittle, exclusive identity. The contradiction in the original encounter can be resolved only if the process of recognition is mutually and jointly constituted—in short, only if recognition is fully reciprocal, for only then is the space of recognition a free space. On the other hand, if the process of recognition were arrested or halted short of reciprocity, such as occurs in master and slave, then the result would be a relationship based on coercion, on a denial of a free and plural space of the between. In master and slave, the original contradiction is displaced by another: "The one subjects himself, gives up the independence of his will; [this is] a resolution of the contradiction which is in itself a further contradiction."[82]

My hypothesis is that mutual recognition is a syllogism of spirit, and that its reciprocity exhibits the double transition. Since I have already discussed Hegel's treatment of recognition elsewhere,[83] I shall offer only a brief sketch here. Hegel begins his analysis with the doubling [*Verdoppelung*] of self-consciousness. "The detailed exposition of the concept of this spiritual unity in its doubling [*Verdoppelung*] will present to us the movement of recognition."[84] Self-consciousness undergoes an "internal" doubling, or an immediate reflection, in which it is "for itself" and an "external" doubling, in which it is "for another." These doublings are correlated and portrayed in an immediate encounter with another self-consciousness. "A self-consciousness confronts another self-consciousness."[85] These two doublings are correlative; this means that the external doubling should not be confused with or collapsed into the "inner." And yet as the struggle for recognition unfolds, each discovers that the other it excludes turns out to be a condition of its own freedom and self-realization; conversely, the freedom that each asserts turns out to be present in and tied to the freedom and independence of the other. The other is capable of both resistance (nonrecognition) and cooperation. However, each can realize its freedom only if the other is allowed to realize its freedom also. As Hegel puts it in a rather dense, complex sentence: "Self-consciousness is in and for itself when and through the fact that it is in and for itself for an other; that is, it exists only as recognized."[86] Mutual recognition means that the self in its "internal" doubling for itself is nevertheless not simply "for itself" but its "for itself" is mediated by another. It is in and for itself for an other.

Hegel outlines and analyzes the doubling of self-consciousness as a series of ambiguities, double meanings, and double significations. We can pass over the details of these, but we must note the central point: The doubling of self-consciousness means that what is done to the other may, by virtue of the doubling, also be done to oneself. As one gives, so shall one usually receive. Hence, doubling implies not merely plurality but two quite different sets of existence possibilities, a negative and an affirmative. There is double transition in both, but one is a self-contradictory double transition, while the other is reciprocal affirmation. On the one hand, to confirm one's immediate, exclusive identity by negating and eliminating the other is to open oneself to the same risk of elimination. As Hegel observes, death is abstract negation; reciprocally carried out, elimination is self-contradictory. Master and slave stop the struggle for recognition short of death, but their unequal recognition merely propounds another contradiction, namely, a relation between free beings founded on coercion. In both of these cases, double transition sustains the contradiction rather than resolves it. Relations frozen in such contradictions are doomed to failure and will pass away.

On the other hand, to recognize and affirm the other and to allow the other to be is not only to break with exclusive immediate identity it is also to create a new set of affirmative, noncoercive existential possibilities ranging from friendship and love to legal recognition and justice. These possibilities are founded in mutual recognition. In these possibilities there is an intersubjectively mediated identity, an enlarged mentality: "If we speak of right, ethical life and love, we know that when we recognize others we recognize their complete personal independence. We know that we don't suffer because of this, but on the contrary that we too count as free and independent; we know that when others have rights, I also have rights. . . . [we know that] love is not the destruction of one's personality."[87]

From Doubling to Double Transition

Doubling is present in the concept of recognition: Doubling is concretely experienced as an internal and external existential contradiction that has to be overcome. The original contradiction in this encounter is between individuals in their one-sided immediacy. The process of recognition is driven by the existential necessity, or need, to overcome this contradiction. Contradiction is here a form of relationship. Immediate individuals exclude each other but nevertheless confront each other, and in spite of their differences, or even because of their differences, they have to deal with and negotiate their relation to each other, hence the doubling of self-consciousness opens up the possibility of a double transition of each term into the other.

Double transition is suggested at the outset in the correlation of being-for-itself and being-for-an-other: "Self-consciousness is in and for itself when and through the fact that it is in and for itself for an other; that is, it exists only as recognized."[88] Double transition is implicit throughout Hegel's analysis of the concept of recognition. Hegel makes the double transition explicit when he reminds his reader of the following:

> This movement of self-consciousness in relation to another self-consciousness has been represented as the doing of the one. But this action of the one has itself the doubled significance of being equally his action as well as the action of the other. The other is likewise independent, self-determining, and there is nothing in the other except what originates through the other. The first does not have a merely passive object before it as in the case of desire. Rather, the other is an independent being existing for itself. Consequently, the first may not use the other for its own ends, unless the other does *for itself* what the first does. *The process [of recognition] is therefore absolutely the doubled action of both self-consciousnesses.* Each sees the other do the same as it does; each does to itself what it demands of the other and therefore does what it does only insofar as the other does the same. *A one-sided action would be useless, because what is supposed*

> *to occur can only come about through both acting together. The action is therefore double signifying [doppelsinnig], not only because it is an action directed towards oneself as well as towards another, but also because it is indivisible, the doing of the one as well as the other.*[89]

This passage presents a clear and forceful statement that the "between" of mutual recognition has to be jointly and reciprocally constituted. A one-sided constitution of the between, the relation, would be useless and would end in failure. The space of mutual recognition is not only jointly constituted by both sides but its constitution is a plural intermediation. The space of mutual recognition is a space of communicative freedom in that a condition of mutual recognition is that both parties must respect each other's freedom and allow each other to be. Each is then for itself through the mediation of the other, and thus at home with self in its other.[90]

From Double Transition to the Syllogism of Recognition

Hegel shows that double transition exhibits a quasisyllogistic structure. In the *Logic*, Hegel maintains that the syllogism is the completely posited concept, and that everything rational is a syllogism.[91] He distinguishes syllogism from the narrow, formal view of it as a collection of three judgments or propositions. He says, "Everything is a syllogism, a universal that through particularity is united with individuality; but it is certainly not a whole consisting of three propositions."[92] We need to keep in mind that Hegel intends a broad sense of syllogism as not only present in the natural world in unconscious living organisms but also present in spirit in the form of mutual recognition.[93] In the *Phenomenology*, recognition mediates the transition from consciousness to self-consciousness; we could say that in recognition the syllogism first becomes explicit, that is, self-conscious. He describes the doubled yet indivisible action of mutual recognition as follows:

> In this movement we see a repetition of the same process exhibited in the interplay of forces, but repeated in consciousness. What in that interplay was *for us* the phenomenological observers, here holds true for the extremes themselves. The middle is the self-consciousness which disintegrates into the extremes. Each extreme is this exchange of its determinateness and absolute transition into its opposite. As consciousness it comes outside

> of itself. However in its self-externality it also retains itself, is for itself; its externality is present to it. It is for consciousness that it immediately is and is not another consciousness. Likewise this other is only for itself, when it cancels itself as being-for-itself and is for itself only in the [independent] being-for-itself of the other [*nur im Fürsichsein des andern für sich ist*]. Each is the mediating term for the other, through which each mediates itself with itself and coincides with itself. Each is for itself and for the other an immediate self-existing being, which at the same time is for itself only through this mediation. They recognize themselves as reciprocally recognizing each other.[94]

For Hegel everything rational is a syllogism. The syllogism of recognition has a middle term, the self-consciousness, which in the original doubling disintegrates into the extremes, each an immediate exclusive self-consciousness. Each extreme must undergo a determinate negation of its immediate, exclusive identity as a condition of transition into its opposite, that is, of entering into relation with its other. When viewed by the self in its exclusive immediacy, such self-externalization is seen and experienced as self-loss. Such self-externality (*Aussersichsein*) is not just there for an external observer, or something external to the selves themselves, as if each remained an invulnerable, abstract "I am I." Rather, each self is conscious of its own self-externality for the other. As Hegel expresses this: It both is and is not another consciousness. This is the existential contradiction that the process of recognition seeks to overcome and resolve.

But a second transition also is evident—the other is likewise only for itself in the other's recognition. It is, Hegel says, only for itself when it suspends its own immediate independent self-existence [*Fürsichsein*] and is for itself only in the independent self-existence of the other. This being-for-self in the other who is also for itself implies a union with other, a union in which each lets the other be (*Freigabe*). Hence, in this union, there is no loss of independence but only a "loss" of immediacy and of relations based on coercion. The free union with other comes about when each is the middle, or mediator, for the other. Each is the mediator for the other; each is the "syllogistic middle" "through which each mediates itself with itself and coincides with itself." In such reciprocal mediation, self-externality acquires a different sense from simple loss of self before the other; self-externality now comes to mean being recognized by the other. Self-externality thus becomes equivalent to self-recognition in other.

The double transition and double-sided process of recognition are starting to become clear: As extreme, each depends on the other to be mediator, to recognize him; conversely, each must play the mediating role for the other. The I that is a We can only arise out of such a double transition, or else there is only the unequal, coerced relation of one by the other, or master and slave. According to Hegel, the self is vulnerable and dependent on the recognition of others. It can be misrecognized, and when that happens, violation and injury are the result. But master and slave represent the failure to achieve mutual recognition. In master and slave there is a double transition, but of a quite different sort from the one that establishes mutual freedom and recognition; it is one in which the truth of mastery is exhibited in the slave who is allowed to think of himself only as a mere tool or commodity, while the coerced, deficient servile recognition of the slave deprives the master of an appreciation of his own dependence, vulnerability, and finitude. For these reasons Hegel believes that master and slave do not resolve the original contradiction but merely propound another contradiction, and are doomed to pass away.

In the syllogism of mutual recognition the apparent contradiction between a one-sided being-for-self and an equally one-sided being-for-other is overcome or reconciled. Each is for itself through the mediation of the other and thus at home with itself in its other. Such mutual recognition means that the contradiction between self-mediation and mediation by other is removed. Self-mediation presupposes and is coconstituted through mediation by other; intermediation presupposes and includes self-mediation. Consequently, the self of self-mediation is no longer an abstract singular, nor is its self-mediation a one-sided, singular self-mediation. They recognize themselves as reciprocally recognizing each other. In the syllogism of recognition, the concept of self-consciousness is completed and sublated in the intersubjective conception of spirit, the I that is We. Spirit names the result of the double transition; it is the overcoming and resolution of the contradiction that the understanding can neither understand nor resolve, the contradiction that generates and drives the process of recognition from desire through the life-and-death struggle, through master and slave, to reciprocal recognition.

Notes

1. Gilles Deleuze, *Difference and Repetition*, trans. Paul Patton (New York: Columbia University Press, 1994), 138.

2. Deleuze, *Difference and Repetition*, 136, 45.

3. See Adriaan Peperzak, *Modern Freedom: Hegel's Legal, Moral, and Political Philosophy* (Dordrecht, Holland: Springer Verlag, 2001).

4. William Desmond, *Beyond Hegel and Dialectic* (Albany: State University of New York Press, 1992), 2.

5. Desmond, *Beyond Hegel*, 7.

6. I cannot do justice to Desmond's wide-ranging, probing analyses of how he believes Hegel's thought shortchanges otherness in philosophy, religion, evil, and art. These are passionate, vigorous, brilliant meditations that do not simply dismiss Hegelian "metaphysics" but seek to correct its alleged distortions. However, the common thread running throughout Desmond's specific critiques is his claim that Hegel reduces mediation by other to singular self-mediation. Accordingly, I confine my attention in this chapter to this central issue.

7. Desmond, *Beyond Hegel*, 7.

8. Ibid.

9. Ibid.

10. Ibid, emphasis added.

11. Desmond, *Beyond Hegel*, 7–8.

12. Ibid., 9.

13. Ibid., 7, emphasis added.

14. Ibid., 11.

15. Ibid., 117.

16. Ibid., 80.

17. Ibid., 185.

18. Ibid., 182.

19. Ibid., 185.

20. G.W. F. Hegel, *The Encyclopedia Logic*, trans. T. F. Geraets, W. A. Suchting, and H. S. Harris (Indianapolis, IN: Hackett, 1991), §99 Zusatz.

21. Ibid., emphasis.

22. Hegel, *Encyclopedia Logic*, §98.

23. G. W. F. Hegel, *Hegel's Science of Logic*, trans. A. V. Miller (Atlantic Highlands, NJ: Humanities Press International, 1989), 684.

24. Hegel, *Science of Logic*, 618.

25. Hegel, *Encyclopedia Logic*, §185; cf. Errol Harris, *An Interpretation of the Logic of Hegel* (Lanham, MD: University Press of America, 1983), 245. This anticipates Desmond's argument that the three terms of the triad reduce to one, and thus Hegel cannot and does not count to two.

26. G. W. F. Hegel, *Elements of the Philosophy of Right*, ed. Allen W. Wood, trans. H. B. Nisbet (Cambridge: Cambridge University Press, 1991), §135. Again, "Where there is nothing there can be no contradiction either" (§135Z).

27. See Errol Harris, *Formal, Transcendental, and Dialectical Thinking: Logic and Reality* (Albany: State University of New York Press, 1987), chap. 8. As Harris

observes, holism and formalism are incompatible, although the latter can be regarded as an abstraction from the former.

28. Hegel, *Science of Logic*, 836.

29. Moreover, Desmond's defense of mediation implies that he too has a stake in overcoming such formalism and externality. Despite his emphasis on plurality, Desmond is not an atomist who precludes or undermines all relation but rather a philosopher who propounds double intermediation.

30. Hegel, *Science of Logic*, 172.

31. Hegel, *Science of Logic*, 172–73. In the *Encyclopedia Logic*, §97Z, concerning the understanding, Hegel notes: "The question arises as to where the many come from. Within representational thinking there is no answer to this question, because the many is there regarded as immediately present."

32. Hegel, *Encyclopedia Logic*, §97Z, emphasis added.

33. It also is found in his account of recognition in the *Phenomenology of Spirit*, not only in the self-consciousness chapter but also in the section on conscience and forgiveness.

34. I am indebted to John Burbidge for bringing this important text to my attention and for extended conversations and correspondence about its significance. I am responsible for its development and application in this article.

35. Hegel, *Science of Logic*, 323, emphasis added.

36. Hegel, *Encyclopedia Logic*, §241, translation, emphasis added. In both texts it is the mature Hegel who underscores and emphasizes the importance of double transition.

37. Hegel, *Science of Logic*, 791.

38. G. W. F. Hegel, *Vorlesungen über die Beweise vom Dasein Gottes,* hrsg. G. Lasson (Hamburg: Meiner Verlag, 1973), 46.

39. Hegel, *Encyclopedia Logic*, §241, emphasis added.

40. Desmond, *Beyond Hegel*, 7.

41. See Kant, *Critique of Pure Reason*, How are *synthetic judgements* a priori possible?

42. Hegel, *Science of Logic*, 91, emphasis added.

43. See note 67 that follows.

44. Hegel, *Science of Logic*, 834.

45. Hegel, *Encyclopedia Logic*, §87Z.

46. Ibid., §88R1. Emphasis added.

47. Hegel, *Science of Logic*, 90.

48. Ibid.

49. Ibid.

50. Hegel, *Science of Logic*, 105.

51. Ibid., 105–106, emphasis added.

52. Ibid., *Science of Logic*, 107–108, emphasis added.

53. Ibid., *Science of Logic*, 106–108.

54. Hegel, *Encyclopedia Logic*, §96Z.

55. Hegel, *Science of Logic*, 107.

56. Hegel, *Encyclopedia Logic*, §88Z, emphasis added.

57. Hegel, *Science of Logic*, 417.

58. Ibid.

59. Deleuze, *Difference and Repetition*; see also his review of Jean Hyppolite's *Logic and Existence, Logic and Existence,* trans. Leonard Lawlor and Amit Sen (Albany: State University of New York Press, 1997), 191–95.

60. Hegel, *Encyclopedia Logic*, §119 Zusatz 2, 187.

61. Ibid., §121Z.

62. Hegel, *Science of Logic*, 664.

63. Ibid. Errol Harris characterizes Hegel's project as an attempt to reconcile analytical philosophy of language with transcendental and existential phenomenology. See Harris, *An Interpretation*, 238.

64. G. W. F. Hegel, *Lectures on the Philosophy of Spirit 1827/8,* ed. and trans. Robert Williams, Oxford University Press, 2007, 273.

65. Hegel, *Encyclopedia Logic*, §187Z.

66. Ibid., §158Z, emphasis added; cf. §§155–59; *Science of Logic*, 569 ff.

67. Hegel, *Science of Logic*, 737. To be sure, Hegel rejects Kant's reduction of mechanism and teleology to merely subjective maxims of judgment such that "I am always to reflect on all natural events according to the principle of natural mechanism alone, but . . . this does not prevent me, *when occasion demands it,* from *investigating* certain natural forms in accordance with *another maxim,* namely . . . final causes; . . . [T]his whole standpoint fails to examine the sole question to which philosophical interest demands an answer, namely which of the two principles possesses truth." (*Science of Logic*, 738–39), emphases in original. Hegel refers to and criticizes Kant's *Critique of Judgment*, §70.

68. Hegel notes that chemism should not be restricted to chemistry of nature; it underlies sexual attraction and "also constitutes the formal basis for the spiritual relations of love, friendship, and the like" (*Science of Logic*, 727). Thus chemism is a higher-level account of the forces of repulsion and attraction in the account of being-for-*self* (*Fürsichsein*) in the logic of being. This challenges Hösle's thesis that the logic provides no categorical foundation for intersubjectivity (*Hegels System: Das ungelöste Problem der Intersubjektivität*). Hösle may be right, but his thesis is not confirmed by Hegel's understanding of the logic.

69. Hegel, *Science of Logic*, 748.

70. Ibid., 752–53, emphasis added.

71. Ibid., 742.

72. G. W. G. Hegel, *Philosophy of Nature*, trans. A. V. Miller (Oxford: Clarendon Press, 1970), §359R, emphasis added.

73. Hegel, *Science of Logic*, 788, emphasis added.

74. See Kenneth Westphal, *Hegel's Epistemological Realism* (Dordrecht, Holland: Kluwer, 1989).

75. Hegel, *Science of Logic*, 323.

76. Hegel, *Encyclopedia Logic*, §187.

77. See John Burbidge, *Real Process: How Logic and Chemistry Combine in Hegel's Philosophy of Nature* (Toronto: University of Toronto Press, 1996). See also David Kolb, "*What Is Open and What Is Closed in the Philosophy of Hegel*," *Philosophical Topics*, 19(2), 29–50. See also the *Owl of Minerva* issue devoted to the problem of "Logic, Nature, and Empirical Science," 34(1), Fall–Winter, 2002–03.

78. Hegel, *Science of Logic*, 439.

79. Ibid., 431.

80. Ibid., 439.

81. Here I follow Hegel's account in the 1827 *Vorlesungen über die Philosophie des Geistes*, 167. "The suspension of the contradiction—for it cannot remain a contradiction—is the process of recognition."

82. Hegel, *Berlin Phenomenology*, ed. and trans. J. Petry (Dordrecht, Holland: D. Reidel, 1981), §432, 83. I have corrected the translation. The material comes from the 1825 Lectures.

83. See Robert R. Williams, *Recognition: Fichte and Hegel on the Other* (Albany: State University of New York Press, 1992); Robert R. Williams, *Hegel's Ethics of Recognition* (Berkeley: University of California Press, 1998).

84. *Phänomenologie des Geistes*, hrsg. Hoffmeister (Hamburg: Meiner 1952), 141; *Phenomenology of Spirit*, trans. Miller (Oxford: Oxford University Press, 1977), §178. Hereafter PhS.

85. PhG, 140; PhS, §177.

86. PhG, 141; PhS, §178.

87. Hegel, *Berlin Phenomenology*, §431, 76–77.

88. PhG, 141; PhS, §178.

89. PhG, 142, emphasis added.

90. The reader should keep in mind that at this stage Hegel analyzes the general concept and relation of recognition; he is not analyzing any particular act of recognition, for example, master and slave, forgiveness, love.

91. Hegel, *Science of Logic*, 664.

92. Ibid., 669.

93. We have already noted that Hegel claims that everything rational is a syllogism. This remark becomes somewhat more intelligible if we recall Hegel's criticism of the formal understanding of syllogism and take note of Ferrarin's observation that "for Hegel the syllogisms as organs, instruments of scientific demonstration, are only interesting to the extent that they express the unconscious syllogisms operating in nature," namely, living organisms. See Alfredo Ferrarin, *Hegel and Aristotle* (Cambridge: Cambridge University Press, 2001), 147. Hamelin writes "The relations on which the logic hinges are natural relations, nature syllogizes like spirit" (O. Hamelin, *Le systéme d'Aristote* [Paris: 1920], 191, cited in Ferrarin, *Hegel and Aristotle*, 147).

94. PhG, 142–43, emphasis in original.

Chapter 3

Identity as a Process of Self-Determination in Hegel's *Logic*

Christopher Yeomans

One of the striking aspects of Hegel's category of identity is that he thinks it involves a process of self-determination: the identical has established its own unity (WL260/SL411).[1] A second striking aspect of Hegel's concept of identity is that it is a relation between semblances or guises of an essence.[2] I will argue that with this concept Hegel grasps identity erotetically, that is, in terms of the kinds of questions and answers that are relevant to identity claims, and that these two aspects of his category are necessary to account for our everyday practice of asking about identity.

A Brief Sketch of Hegel's Category of Identity

As is well known, Hegel's category of identity is not intended as an analysis of a merely formal concept but is instead the basic articulation of what it might mean for something to be an essence (*Wesen*)—where *Wesen* is being used in a sense related to the classical notion of substance.[3] The notion of an essence is just the notion of something that remains self-identical in qualitative change. In this sense even mathematical and logical notions have an essence that can be expressed in various ways, so 'essence' is not equivalent to 'substance' if the latter is taken to involve spatiotemporal continuity. Of the traditional aspects of substance, Hegel's usage of 'essence' involves the notion of a unity remaining the same through change—but a unity of "semblances," not of properties. Hegel's *Wesen* is not Locke's 'something-I-know-not-what' behind or in addition to the semblances. It does not involve active or passive powers, although it does involve tendencies to change in certain ways. Power over attributes is involved in Hegel's category of *Substanz*, which is much richer than that of *Wesen*. *Substanz* involves the notion of an inner essence which manifests its own nature by causal power to create and destroy outer forms of itself. It also involves a relation between inner potential and outer expressed force that is missing in the bare notion of a *Wesen*. *Wesen* is the notion of something that abides in change, whereas the developed notion of *Substanz* brings to bear additional conceptual resources to explain how this abiding actually works.[4] Neither *Wesen* nor *Substanz* can easily be translated by the English philosophical 'substance'—the former because it is more abstract, and the latter because it is more concrete.

Hegel understands the structure of essence to be "the seeming of essence within itself [*das Scheinen des Wesens in sich selbst*]" (WL258/SL409, translation modified).[5] That is, to be an essence is to be the kind of a thing that appears in various guises (semblances) such that no particular guise exhaustively expresses the nature of that thing. The identity of essence is the very process of the guises revealing themselves as *mere* guises. There is no object *behind* these guises, but the guises are not self-sufficient either. Instead of being independent states transformed by outside forces, the guises are dynamic, the very process of transition between themselves and another guise.

For example, the tree appears in one guise in the spring and another in the fall, and although the essence of the tree is present in both guises, neither guise exhaustively expresses that essence. Some guises—for example, leaflessness due to the application of defoliant or even a toy plastic leaf left by a tree-climbing child—need not directly express the essence of the tree, although indirectly the nature of the tree is involved in explaining why the defoliant has the effect that it does or how the toy came to be there. The notion of a guise or semblance is different from the notion of an appearance in that it does not wear its expression of a determinate essence on its face, as it were. Rather, a guise or semblance presents itself problematically as dependent on a process that may constitute a number of different essences. Identity is, however, the resolution of this problem in the connection of the guises together as parts of a determinate process.

The identity of the tree is found in the fact that the differences between its guises do not make a difference to the essence of the tree—this is what it means to be the same tree through change. That is, although they are different guises, the insignificance of their differences expresses the essential identity of the tree. The tree just is the series of these transitions, whether past, present or merely potential.[6] Furthermore, the essence of the tree is the process through which this takes place, that is, the process of development whereby guises are substituted for each other.[7] On pain of circularity, the insignificance of the differences between the guises must be understood in terms of the nature of the process involved, and not in terms of a static essence that would provide the touchstone for the authenticity of each guise.

The tree is self-identical because the process of transformation is governed by coherent and intelligible principles that allow rational reconstruction of the transitions between the guises.[8] The presence of sufficient explanatory regularities is what makes for the (relative) insignificance of the differences and makes the sequences of guises not a series of independent trees but the process of a single tree's development.

This process of development is equally attributable to the tree as such as to the tree at a particular time, but it is attributable to both in an attenuated sense. The minimal self-determination required by identity as such obtains when a change of guises is in some basic sense due to the nature of the guises themselves. This is different from the richer self-determination of activity, which would seem to require in addition that one of the guises *initiate* the change.[9]

The differences between the semblances need not be temporal in addition to being qualitative. We might see a certain shape of leaf on one side of the tree and another shape on the other side. We might then ask whether they were leaves of the same tree or one was the leaf of a vine or another plant growing on the tree. Answering the question—in principle and not just for us—will depend on whether the tree was subject to processes that involve its growing leaves of a different shape and/or subject to the process of being overgrown by vines.

Hegel's notion of identity provides a minimal analysis of the identity of even abstract objects such as logical statements. Consider $(A \rightarrow B)$, $(\neg B \rightarrow \neg A)$, $\neg(A \& \neg B)$, and $(\neg A \vee B)$. On the face of it, all four seem to be different, but one can easily show that they are equivalent and thus intersubstitutable without loss of truth value—and such intersubstitutability *salva veritate* constitutes formal logical sameness.[10] Although we could subjectively establish their unity by deducing each from the others, it is no less natural to say that they entail each other—objectively and on their own regardless of whether any particular logician performs the relevant derivations. This is just to say that the very nature of logical statements is bound up with entailments, whether potential, actual, or past. If one thinks of entailment as the process proper to logical statements—though not of course their activity—then this their mutual identity is a product of their own processes, processes that show their differences to be inessential.

The case of the identity of numbers is a bit more complex, primarily because quantity represents a less developed category than identity. On the one hand, a minimal analysis can be given that parallels the analysis of logical forms. Instead of entailment, calculation is the process that transforms quantitative guises. Thus one can show by addition that '2+3' and '1+4' are insignificantly different guises of '5.' Hegel himself claims that the different forms of calculation can be derived from the concept of number (EL102R). On the other hand, Hegel also claims that quantity is closely associated with sensation, and that this association makes quantity abstract.[11] He further claims that abstract objects are only potential, and not actual. Thus it should not be surprising that Hegel's conception of identity is much more illuminating when applied to concrete objects such as trees.

Quantitative states may take on actuality in virtue of their inclusion in objects that can also be thought through more developed categories (e.g., a quantitative state may be a property of a thing, or a term in a judgment), but part of the deficiency of the pure notion of quantity in the *Logic* is its inability to provide the resources for determinate identifications of numbers. Thus Hegel seems to think that identity conditions for numbers are parasitic on their involvement in more developed categories.

According to Hegel, identity is "the equality-with-self that has brought itself to unity [*sich zur Einheit herstellende ist*], . . . this pure origination from and within itself, *essential* identity" (WL260/SL411, emphasis in original). This means that it is not only the process but also the result of the process, or the process considered as completed.[12] It is self-identity through change, a process whereby the unity of different semblances is established through the undermining of their independence. Hegel claims that this process is the content of the notion of identity, that is, it is equally what we are actually doing when we think about identity, and what essences are actually "doing" when they are self-identical.[13]

An Erotetic Interpretation

Rather than being a set of necessary and sufficient conditions or of criteria for identity, Hegel's discussion of identity presents it as a problem. My suggestion is that we can better understand the nature of this problem if we understand it erotetically. "Erotetic" logic is the logic of questions and answers, and within erotetic logic particular attention is paid to the presuppositions of a question, that is, the conditions under which a question arises or can be meaningfully posed. To understand a notion erotetically is connected to understanding it pragmatically, since one can identify the notion so grasped with our interrogative practice or use of the notion. When I say that Hegel grasps identity erotetically, I mean that he grasps it in terms of the whole complex of presupposition, question, and answer. Now one might think that this is overly broad, and that identity is really just the answer to the question, but on the erotetic analysis, the answer (or at least the direct answer) takes its form from the question.

Furthermore, in answering the question, the answer asserts that the presupposition is true (i.e., that the question is answerable)—otherwise the question is rejected, not answered. On this view, then, the answer includes the structure and content of both the question and the presupposition, so it is a matter of indifference whether we identify the notion of identity with the answer or with the whole complex.[14]

One can see that Hegel grasps identity erotetically by looking at the normal context in which identity is a problem for us, that is, in which the question of identity arises. This is the context in which we have different appearances and want to know whether they are appearances of the same thing or of different things. Differently shaped leaves are on different sides of a tree, or a number of logical statements may have the same truth table or value. Or, yesterday, a white car was parked in my neighbor's driveway, but today a red car of the same make and model is there, and I want to know whether this is the same car repainted or a different car altogether. Although we would usually ask, "Is that the same car as yesterday?," a more perspicuous way of phrasing the question would be, "Were those appearances (or sightings) of the same car?" Expressed in this way, the question determines its own direct, positive answer, namely, "Yes, those are appearances of the same car." The presupposition of the identity question is that there is a plurality of qualitatively different appearances or guises.[15] No one asks if the red car is identical to the red car, unless there is some significant difference.

If faced with such a question without the necessary presupposition, then we would struggle to understand what the questioner meant. In answering a question about identity, then, we assert that the presuppositions are true, that is, that a plurality of guises does obtain. This is part of what we are doing when we assert identity, and thus part of the identity claim itself. The subject matter of the identity claim is primarily the guises, and a positive answer is an identification of the different guises as guises of one essence. To be guises of one essence involves the existence of certain processual pathways from one to the other (e.g., differential growth of leaves, logical derivations, or repainting the car). Hegel's concept of identity, then, is the problem of identity taken as presupposition, question, and answer.[16] In the epistemological mode, this is an articulation of the core of our practice of identification.[17]

So far my argument for attributing an implicitly erotetic concept to Hegel has been grounded on the way in which this erotetic framework organizes the different aspects of Hegel's concept of identity and connects them to the practice of individuation. It is, of course, true that Hegel does not make this connection himself.[18] In the one remark where he does seem to use an erotetic framework, there appear to be two problems for my view. First, he seems to focus on what questions, as opposed to the yes-no questions that I have taken to be paradigmatic. Second, the what question he poses—"What is a plant?"—does not obviously call for an individuation as an answer. How can these be reconciled with the interpretation I have just offered?

The solution to the first problem is to see that yes-no questions are contained in what questions in the sense that each answer to the latter entails an answer to the former.[19] For example, the answer to "What is a plant?" that "A plant is a young tree, vine, shrub, or herb planted or suitable for planting," entails the answer "Yes" to the question, "Is a plant a young tree vine, shrub, or herb planted or suitable for planting," and it entails the answer "No" to the question, "Is a plant a fence?". What questions represent the breadth of identity questions, but yes-no (and whether) questions represent more specific and perspicuous forms of identity questions. This is because in most everyday contexts there is a fairly limited range of possible answers to the what question of identity.

The second problem also is easily solved. "What is a plant?' does not seem to call for an individuation, because we normally associate individuation with the discrimination of physical objects. But if we broaden the notion of individuation to include concepts as well, then "What is a plant?" does call for an individuation, the individuation of the concept "plant." The way we individuate concepts is to define them and thereby differentiate them from other concepts. Hegel objects to the proposed answer "A plant is a plant" because it will not individuate the concept of a plant for the questioner, who legitimately expected a different kind of response, namely, a response that would contrast the topic "plant" with other concepts.

The Value and Necessity of Hegel's Concept of Identity

One important way in which Hegel's concept of identity articulates the core of our practice of identification is to provide a solution to the common puzzle about how questions of identity are possible in the first place. Many philosophers have noted the paradoxical nature of identity. To take two well-known examples, Wittgenstein writes, "To say of *two* things that they are identical is nonsense, and to say of *one* thing that it is identical with itself is to say nothing at all,"[20] and Hume writes, "As to the principle of individuation; we may observe, that the view of any one object is not sufficient to convey the idea of identity. . . . On the other hand, a multiplicity of objects can never convey this idea."[21] For reasons connected to this problem, both the early Wittgenstein and Hume reject identity as either unnecessary or largely fictitious. From a Hegelian perspective, this puzzle is generated by thinking of the identity relation as a relation only between objects, not between states or semblances.[22] If differences between semblances are allowed into the identity relation itself, then both the possibility and importance of identity questions become clear. The greater the difference between the semblances, the more significant the identity is: The identity between the caterpillar and the butterfly is fascinating for the young child, precisely because it expresses an identity relation between very different appearances.[23]

Even more than this, I argue that the specific characteristics of Hegel's category of identity are in fact *required* for an erotetic understanding of individuation. The best way to see this is to explore the consequences of their denial for this project. To begin with, one might think that it is unnecessary to import the presupposition of a question into the very *answer* itself, even if the *answering* implicitly endorses those presuppositions. If one distinguished this presupposition from the pure identity relation between objects (as the answer proper), then one could still account for the practice of individuation without introducing differences between semblances into the identity relation itself. To see why this will not work, consider the consequences of such a maintenance of the absoluteness of identity in the view of Colin McGinn.

McGinn holds a common view that identity is a unitary, indefinable, reflexive, symmetrical, and transitive relation that satisfies Leibniz's

Law (the indiscernibility of identicals).[24] Although McGinn acknowledges that identity is importantly correlated with difference, the unity of identity excludes difference from the identity relation itself. Thus he characterizes identity as "simply the relation x has to y when x is nothing other than y, when there is no distinction between x and y, when x is y."[25] This exclusion of the differences of states results in a conception of identity that is incapable of articulating the structure of our practices of individuation.[26] This exclusion results in a virtual identity (or at least coextension) of identity and objecthood broadly construed: "Whenever we have a subject of predication—existent, merely possible, non-existent—we have an application of the concept of identity to that subject."[27]

Questions about identity arise and are significant "because we don't always *know* the truth about distinctness and identity . . . If we were omniscient about identity, then indeed identity truths would not inform us of anything; but the same could be said of *any* kind of truth."[28] While this is certainly true, there remains an important difference between the problem with identity truths and other truths, namely, that we do not have to know about the *applicability* of other predicates in order to raise the question of their applicability.

On McGinn's view of identity as just the relation of an object to itself, it seems like we cannot raise the question of the applicability of an identity predicate without presupposing the answer. To raise the question we need to have an object that may or may not be self-identical, but once we have the object we know that it is self-identical. And if we have two objects, then the question is already decided in the negative. Every mistake in predication reflects at least some correct comprehension—for we must grasp the subject as a subject even in order to predicate falsely.

But on McGinn's view that identity comes with even the most abstract and tenuous grasp of the subject of predication, it is incomprehensible that we could ever be in doubt, since the knowledge required to raise the question answers it as well. This problem is not primarily temporal but rather arises from the need for a certain gap in our understanding to motivate questions at all. The same problem would arise if we took the question to come after the answer. Thus it appears that Hegel's internalization of the differences between semblances in the identity relation itself is required to account for our practice.

The other distinctive component of Hegel's conception of identity—that it is a process of the self-establishment of unity—is also required for an adequate erotetic analysis of individuation. To see that some sort of process is involved, consider briefly Hume's view of identity. Due to precisely the problem just discussed with respect to McGinn's view, Hume makes a distinction between the *unity* of a thing at any given time as opposed to its *identity* across time. To say that something is identical is to say "that the object existent at one time is the same with itself existent at another," which means to say that it is invariable or unchanged throughout that time.[29] What Hume acknowledges, then, is that some kind of change—namely, temporal change—is required in order to make sense of the identity relation.

In our common practice of individuation, however, more than mere temporal change is required in order to raise the question of identity. In order to avoid Hume's rejection of this practice of individuation, it is necessary to see identity itself as the process of remaining the same through qualitative and not merely temporal change.[30] Once one allows qualitative diversity, the issue of temporality becomes secondary. This is true whether one takes identity in the epistemological mode (i.e., as the process of connecting diverse representations) or in the metaphysical (i.e., as the process of the essence staying the same through change). But this only shows that identity has to involve some process of change. To see the necessity of specifying that the process is the self-establishment of unity through change, consider David Wiggins's neo-Aristotelian view of identity.

Wiggins thinks that we individuate objects according to principles of the normal activity, behavior, or functioning of kinds of objects. When we identify things, we say that "a is the same F as b," where F is a sortal or kind term that specifies such a principle of activity for a and b. On Wiggins's view, if we did not have such a principle then we would be unable to specify what changes an object could undergo and nonetheless remain self-identical, and so we would be unable to individuate objects either in the world or across possible worlds.[31] For example, even the individuation of a rock across possible worlds or qualitative changes within a world requires an understanding of what kind of changes in state are consistent with the normal processes of rocks (e.g., that they resist outside pressure but can be broken down gradually, that they cannot transform themselves into donkeys). Like Hegel, Wiggins's view does not essentially involve temporal change but does try to model our everyday practice of individuation in time and space.

Also like Hegel, Wiggins's approach emphasizes the closeness of ontological and logical questions about identity, but there are important differences in how this closeness and the ontological import of identity are construed.[32] First, Wiggins's notion of identity entails essentialism, but identity is not itself the model of essence. The identity of objects does not have even a structural isomorphism to the processes that subjects consider when identifying objects. For Hegel, identity is not just the abstract self-relation of the thing but includes the sortal specification within itself: The identity of a thing is an answer to the question of *what it is*, and so identity essentially includes the processes a thing undergoes (either actually or potentially). I take this to be an interesting though nondecisive advantage for Hegel's view, since it connects the abstract notion of identity to our use of "identity" in social contexts. When we are posing the question of gender or racial identity, for instance, we are asking whether the question "Who is Jane?" has to be answered in terms of race and/or gender.

Second, the terms of Wiggins's identity statements ('x is the same F as y') are objects, substances, or continuants, not Hegel's semblances.[33] Thus although the point of knowing the kind of an object to be individuated is to know what sorts of changes it typically and possibly undergoes, the identity of the object is not the process or result of such change. Identity is not mere continuity, as Hume or McGinn would have it, but it is nonetheless an absolute relation between objects.[34] There are no differences in Wiggins's identity relation, which is crucial to his rejection of relative identity.[35]

These first two points are closely related to a third difference, which is that Wiggins denies that the practice of individuation has any metaphysical equivalent. As Wiggins puts it, "The object does not single itself out. . . . [E]dges [in nature—even causally effective ones] mark out imperfectly or scarcely at all the boundaries that are drawn by the singling out of continuants or substances."[36] Although our tracking of objects requires "a dialectic of same and other," this subjective dialectic must be regulated by an objective principle of identity in the classic sense.[37] Furthermore, Wiggins holds that there is an essentially deictic element in individuation (the *this* of the 'this such') that seems ineliminably subjective.[38]

Hegel, however, thinks that objects individuate themselves in roughly the same way that we individuate them. For Hegel, the activity of an essence is in part the self-establishment of its identity in roughly the same way that *we* would establish its identity for ourselves. For example, in discussing Leibniz, Hegel claims that

> the more intimate sense [of the maxim of the identity of indiscernibles] is, however, that each thing is in itself something

> determined, distinguishing itself from others implicitly or in itself. . . . The difference must be a difference in themselves, not for our comparison, for the subject must have the difference as its own peculiar characteristic or determination, i.e., the determination must be immanent in the individual. Not only do we distinguish the animal by its claws, but it distinguishes itself essentially thereby, it defends itself, it preserves itself.[39] (VGP458/LHP333-34).

Thus the identity of ontological and conceptual structures reaches higher up for Hegel. Although the ontological picture of processes rooted in the nature of the object is similar in Wiggins and Hegel, the conceptual structure of Hegel's category of identity maps onto the structure of those processes, whereas Wiggins's notions of identity and individuation do not. Leaving Hegel's vocabulary for a moment, we might call the common structure of both identical essences and our practices of individuation "discrimination," which is a more complex process than Wiggins's "edges," which are the extent of common structure on his view. I take it that the Hegelian position is that discrimination becomes "singling out" when it is interpreted in terms of the subject and object distinction. Then designation becomes an appropriate, partial way of making the connection between something subjective and something objective. But the Hegelian point must be that this is only possible because the same basic process of discrimination operates objectively as well as subjectively.

Hegel's view is preferable as an analysis of our practice of individuation because it avoids a certain counterintuitive result of Wiggins's view that is at odds with that practice.[40] Specifically, Wiggins thinks that there can be two objects in the same place at the same time, as long as the objects are of sufficiently different kinds. For example, Wiggins thinks that there can be both a tree and a collection of wood cells, with different persistence conditions, in the same location.[41] But Hegel can accommodate our intuition that, in this case, constitution is identity, and there is only one object. To put Hegel's point in a slightly different way, we might say that the conditions of the nonpersistence of the collection of cells are precisely the persistence conditions of the tree. Without the mobility of cells that would eliminate one collection and establish another, the tree could not remain the self-identical entity that it is. Furthermore, a quantitative state of a tree such as a collection of cells does not present itself to us as an independent entity but as dependent on the lifecourse of the tree. Perhaps a better way of expressing this dependence is to say that the collection of cells does not present itself to us at all but is a theoretical abstraction away from the tree that does present itself.[42]

On Wiggins's view, the only way to accommodate our practice of saying that there is only one object there—the tree—is to identify the tree with the collection of molecules. This, however, would require the abandonment of Leibniz's Law, since the two objects have different persistence conditions and thus different properties.[43] As I have suggested, Hegel's ontology need not countenance the object-status of the collection of wood cells. Thus there need not be any violation of Leibniz's Law, since the involvement of the wood cells in the identity of the tree is more complex than simple coincidence as objects. Any given collection is just an aspect of the identity of the tree and subordinate to it.

This is related to the metaphysical status of individuation because the nonself-sufficiency, and thus nonobjecthood, of the collection of cells follows from the objectivity of the process of discrimination as Hegel describes it. Thus what might look like a minor point based on a strange (if not tendentious) understanding of 'identity,' 'discrimination' and 'individuation' does have substantial weight, since it is connected to Wiggins's counterintuitive result and Hegel's avoidance of the same.[44] This is a kind of inference to the best explanation: The best explanation for why we are able to individuate objects the way we do is that objects individuate themselves.

What I think all of this shows is that Hegel's model or *concept* of identity—though it at first seems far-fetched—in fact does a better job than the competition of matching our *conception* of identity, that is, the range of our practice of asking and answering identity questions and the range of the objects identified. To transpose an important Hegelian reminder from another context, one might say that Hegel's category of identity is so complicated precisely because "philosophy does not waste time with . . . empty and unworldly stuff. What philosophy has to do with is always something concrete and strictly present"[45] (EL94Z).

Conclusion

Once Hegel's conception of identity is understood as articulating the problem of identity along with its direct answer, good sense can be made of the notion that identity involves differences between semblances and the tendency of those semblances to undermine the significance of their own differences. Although I will not argue for it here, I think that the erotetic interpretation is confirmed by the fact that the architectonic function of identity in Hegel's *Logic* is to articulate a problem bequeathed to it by the preceding Doctrine of Being. Briefly, the category of identity rephrases the problem left to the Doctrine of Essence by the Doctrine of Being in terms of a new form of determination, namely, "reflection." The remainder of the Doctrine of Essence is, on this view, an attempt to work out exactly how this form of determination must be filled out in order for it to provide the basis of a more substantial solution to the problem of identity, namely, criteria for the concrete identity of essences. For this reason, my argument here has been limited to showing that the characteristics of Hegel's category of identity are necessary for an erotetic understanding. Hegel himself does not think that they are sufficient—the sufficient conditions are only provided in the further development of the *Logic*. In closing, I briefly point out two aspects of this further development. The first is that Hegel immediately turns from the problem of identity to what he calls "Ground" relations, that is, relations in virtue of which one state of an essence is explained by another state on which it is dependent. So the summer state of the tree is dependent on the spring state of the tree, by which it is explained. Hegel thinks that for essences to be independent in any significant sense they have to be *self*-dependent.[46] This points the way to a criterion of identity that involves a richer notion of self-determination.

The second point is that the Doctrine of Essence culminates in just such a notion of self-determination, a real substantial freedom in the reciprocal interaction of substances. This in turn becomes the model for what Hegel calls the "freedom of the concept," which is in turn the model for freedom of the will.[47] The whole *Logic*, then, can be read as a transcendental defense of the inescapability of that form of independence that the human will exemplifies.

Notes

1. Parenthetical references are to be read as follows: (WL#/SL#) refers to Hegel's *Science of Logic*. The first reference is to the pagination of the German critical edition edited by Hogemann and Jaeschke (Hamburg: Meiner, 1984, 1978). References to the Doctrine of Being have the form (WL21,#) to indicate that they come from volume 21; otherwise, references are to volume 11. The (SL#)

reference is to the translation by A.V. Miller (Atlantic Highlands, NJ: Humanities Press, 1969). The (EL#) reference is to Hegel's *Encyclopedia* version of the *Logic*, trans. Geraets, Suchting, and Harris (Indianapolis, IN: Hackett, 1991) and (EN#) to the *Philosophy of Nature* in the *Encyclopedia of Philosophical Sciences*, and the references to these are by section number. Quotations from the *Philosophy of Nature* are from M. J. Petry's translation (New York: Humanities Press, 1970). The (VGP#/LHP#) reference is to page numbers in Hegel's *Vorlesungen über die Geschichte der Philosophie* (*Dritter Band*), (vol. 19 in *Sämtliche Werke* [Stuttgart: Frommanns, 1928]); and vol. 3 of his *Lectures on the History of Philosophy*, trans. E. S. Haldane and F. H. Simson (Lincoln: University of Nebraska Press, 1995).

2. I will use 'appearance,' 'semblance' and 'guise' to translate the German '*Schein*,' and 'to appear [problematically]' or 'to seem' to translate the verb form '*scheinen*.' I do this even though 'appearance' is usually reserved for the translation of '*Erscheinung*,' which receives a more detailed articulation later in the *Logic*. Briefly, the difference between the terms is that '*Erscheinung*' designates a more determinate relation, whereby the appearance expresses the nature of the essence that appears. In the case of a '*Schein*,' however, whether this relation of expression obtains is precisely what is in question. In my exposition, I will mark this difference simply by insisting on the problematic character of '*Schein*' and identity, so that we will not be mislead into thinking that the relation between a '*Schein*' and an essence is more definite than it is. I do not follow A. V. Miller in rendering '*Schein*' as 'illusory being,' because this seems to me to prejudge the question of the relation between *Schein* and essence in the opposite direction.

3. In the *Encyclopedia Logic*, Hegel writes, "Now when we say further that all things have an essence, what we mean is that they are not truly what they immediately show themselves to be. A mere rushing about from one quality to another, and a mere advance from the qualitative to the quantitative and back again, is not the last word; on the contrary, there is something that abides in things, and this is, in the first instance, their essence" (EL112Z). My reconstruction of Hegel's category focuses on his minimal presentation in the section of the greater *Logic*, entitled "Identity" (book 2, section 1, chapter 2, section A). The contemporary formal notion of an object's continuity with itself is perhaps best represented in Hegel's system by the notion of pure quantity, which Hegel describes as "real being-for-self which has turned into itself and which as yet contains no determinateness: a compact, infinite unity which continues itself into itself" (WL173/SL184). In this sense Leibniz's Law gives the formula of what it is to be *one* thing, where differences between characteristics do not represent differences between things. Cf. WL176/SL187: "The *asunderness of the plurality* is still contained in this unity, but at the same time as not differentiating or *interrupting* it. In continuity, the plurality is posited as it is in itself; the many are all alike, each is the same as the other, and the plurality is, consequently, a simple, undifferentiated sameness."

4. This has the practical consequence for the interpreter that good examples of *Wesen* are likely to be good examples of *Substanz* as well, but one need not appeal to richer notions of causation, self-manifestation, or the expression of force in order to show that the examples have the structure described by *Wesen*.

5. Here I am implicitly relying on the identification of essence with "reflection," and thus the fact that identity is an articulation of the nature of reflection. I am eliding reflection here for simplicity's sake.

6. I take it that this is part of what Hegel means when he speaks of essence as "past—but timelessly past—being" (WL241/SL390). John Findlay makes a similar point in writing that the categories of the Doctrine of Essence deal with "what is *virtually, dispositionally* present" in objects, "with what *would* or *could* be in certain circumstances" in addition to what is manifest. This second formulation is more congenial to my view, since it avoids the positing of specifically dispositional properties. Essential identity is a matter of actual or possible transformation (whether temporal or nontemporal), and this need not be understood on the model of immediately present characteristics. See Findlay's *Hegel: A Reexamination* (New York: Oxford University Press, 1976), 220 (a supplementary note to the revised edition).

7. I take it that Hegel's point is not to argue for the ontological priority of either entities or processes, but to say that entities and processes are always understood in terms of each other. That the two come together is one aspect of the significance of the need to unite independence and dynamic determination (i.e., determination in terms of processes), which animates the Doctrine of Being. The task of the argument that follows Hegel's discussion of identity is to show how the elements of these processes have their independence in that process, and not as opposed to or distinct from that process.

8. The criteria for these principles are of course not to be found in Hegel's discussion of identity itself. But it is significant in this regard that the notion of identity ultimately devolves on the notion of ground, which specifies constraints on the connections between guises that could count as explanatory. The rest of the Doctrine of Essence can be read as a series of attempts to specify in more detail what kinds of connections are explanatory (e.g., between wholes and parts, forces and their expressions, substances and their causally produced accidents).

9. See EL122R, where Hegel distinguishes the emergence characteristic of ground processes from active, teleological, and productive processes. Although Hegel is not quite as cautious in the greater *Logic*, I believe that this is because in that work he is more interested in emphasizing the extent to which the category of identity represents an advance over the categories of the Doctrine of Being.

10. Frege writes, "Now Leibniz's definition [of identity] is as follows: 'Things are the same as each other, of which one can be substituted for the other without loss of truth.' This I propose to adopt as my own definition of identity." See *Foundations of Arithmetic*, trans. J. L. Austin (Oxford: Basil Blackwell, 1976), 76.

11. Here Hegel follows Kant in associating magnitudes with sensation and intuition but reverses Kant in claiming that this very association makes them abstract and thus not fully real.

12. See also WL244/SL393.

13. Nonetheless, he does not think that this model is adequate—in fact, he thinks it is the very essence of contradiction itself. The first problem to note is that if the subsistence of the guises is undermined, then the subsistence of the essence seems to be undermined as well, since the essence is not something beyond its guises (on pain of indeterminacy and Platonic difficulties). The problem, then, is to try to understand the nature of the difference involved in this process in such a way that the dependence of the guise on the essence can be maintained without eliminating the subsistence of the essence itself. In the end, Hegel wants to argue that the way to do this is to understand that difference in terms of asymmetrical explanatory relations between the different guises. This self-reflective insufficiency of the category of identity is implied by the structure of the argument and is an aspect of Hegel's presentation that Reynold Siemens misses. As a result, Siemens takes Hegel's explicit discussion of identity to be his last word instead of his first. From this discussion alone it is as yet undecided what form the differences involved in identity must take—nothing in Hegel's argument rules out statements in which the different terms were different occurrences of the same thing. See Siemens, "Hegel and the Law of Identity," *Review of Metaphysics* 42 (September 1988): 103–27. Errol Harris makes this developmental point in responding to Siemens in "Hegel on Identity (A Reply to Siemens)," in *The Spirit of Hegel* (Atlantic Highlands, NJ: Humanities Press, 1993), 82–92.

14. I take this to be the epistemological sense of Hegel's repeated statements that identity is equally the whole and one element of the whole (e.g., WL266/SL417). For a short review of erotetic logic, see Bas Van Fraassen, *The Scientific Image* (Oxford: Clarendon Press, 1980), ch. 5; David Harrah, "The Logic of Questions," in *Handbook of Philosophical Logic*, vol. 2, ed. D. Gabbay and F. Guenthner (Boston: Reidel, 1984).

15. The temporal order of that plurality is not intrinsically relevant to the arising of an identity question, although it may of course be involved in the significance of particular identity questions. Nor does the structure require even that the question come before the answer. Although most often it does, sometimes we are given an answer and a context, and from them we infer the question. The point is just that the conceptual structure of asking questions does not have any inherently temporal dimension, though our experience of asking and answering questions is in time (like all of our experience in the spatial world).

16. Now one might think that this is hardly saying much, since it is also obvious that Hegel has provided us with only the form of an answer. In order to determine and justify the correct answer, we would need to further understand what a thing must be like if it were to be self-identical and appear in different ways. Hegel not only recognizes this point but endorses it, and the rest of the

Logic can easily be read as a regress on the conditions for making such a positive identity claim, culminating with the requirement that one grasp objects in terms of their concept in the Hegelian sense.

17. I say it articulates the core because this practice is temporal and often social, but there is nothing inherently temporal or social in the notions of questions and answers. I can ask and answer my own questions, for example. Also, although the question usually comes before the answer, if we are given an answer and a context we can often determine the question.

18. At other points in the *Logic* Hegel does seem to invoke an erotetic test for the meaning of terms, for example, WL182/SL192 in a discussion of the meaning of 'consisting' ('Bestehen'): "To ask of what something consists is to ask for an indication of something else, the compounding of which constitutes the said something. If ink is said to consist simply of ink, the meaning of the inquiry after the something else of which it consists has been missed and the question is not answered but only repeated."

19. See Harrah, "The Logic of Questions," in Handbook of Philosophical Logic, Vol. II, ed. D. Gabbay and F. Guenther (Boston: Reidel, 1984), 719.

20. *Tractatus* 5.5303, emphasis.

21. *Treatise on Human Nature*, ed. P. H. Niddich (New York: Oxford University Press, 1978), 201 (book 1, part 4, section 2).

22. Siemens misses this innovative feature of Hegel's notion of identity, and this leads him to misinterpret passages in which Hegel says that the identity statement promises a "different *determination*" and a "further *character*" (emphasis added) as requiring that there be numerically different objects. Siemens considers whether Hegel might mean that the linguistic tokens used in making an identity claim are what are identified, a view that Siemens finds absurd. But this is an anachronistic projection of a later formal and linguistic model of identity back onto Hegel's thought; the semblances that Hegel identifies are real aspects of identical essences, not the linguistic forms used to make statements about those essences. See Siemens, "Hegel and the Law of Identity," particularly 110–12, and 119–20.

23. On my view, it is the *significance* of identity statements that is at issue in Hegel's rejection of such statements as 'A plant is—a plant.' Siemens takes Hegel to think that such statements say nothing because they are tautologies, but even a tautology such as 'A bachelor is an unmarried man' has the requisite difference between subject and predicate to allow it to say something. Hegel's point is about the significance, meaningfulness, and motivation of the claim—thus his complaints of boredom in the face of tedious identity statements. See Siemens, 110–11.

24. See his *Logical Properties* (Oxford: Clarendon, 2000), 1–14.

25. Ibid., 2. The first thing to note is this characterization's vulnerability to Hegel's argument that if identity just is a difference from difference, then its nature is defined by difference, and then the whole characterization threatens to collapse: "[Those who say that identity is not difference] do not see that they are themselves

saying that *identity is different*; for they are saying that *identity is different* from difference; since this must at the same time be admitted to be the nature of identity, their assertion implies that identity, not externally, but in its own self, in its very nature, is this, to be different" (WL262/SL413, emphasis in original). There is a strange and perhaps perverse literalism in this argument, but this can be in part explained as Hegel's pragmatism with respect to even abstract notions, which entails an attentiveness to what we are actually thinking when we consider or employ abstract categories. It also is a kind of unwinding of the definition offered to show its consequences. Of course, McGinn does not offer it as a definition, but I take it that Hegel would be unimpressed by this scruple.

26. I should note that reconstructing this practice is not McGinn's aim, although he does claim to show that identity has a fundamental role in our thought and practice. I am primarily interested in McGinn's view as representative of standard views and in showing that their difference from Hegel is fatal to the project of the erotetic reconstruction of our practice of individuation. My own pragmatism is that I take it that a conception that cannot support such a reconstruction is an unhelpful understanding of the notion of identity.

27. Ibid., 10.

28. Ibid., 13, emphasis in original.

29. *Treatise,* 201.

30. Here again I am abstracting away from the fact that Hume thinks that he has good reason to reject our everyday practice, since I am only interested in showing that the specific characteristics of Hegel's category are needed to model this practice.

31. This is what Wiggins refers to as the thesis of the sortal dependency of individuation. See Wiggins, *Sameness and Substance Renewed* (New York: Cambridge University Press, 2001), 21–24. One difference with respect to Wiggins is that Hegel does not explicitly think of an essence as a continuant—because there is officially no notion of temporality in the *Logic*. For Wiggins, however, the subject of individuation seems to be essentially a continuant. Because temporality does not play a role in either view, however, this distinction does not preclude comparison of the two views.

32. For Wiggins's discussion of the relation between ontological and conceptual questions, see ibid., xii.

33. Wiggins, *Sameness and Substance Renewed*, 5.

34. Ibid., xii.

35. See his discussion of relative identity at 24–28 and also his discussion of the "only a and b" rule at 97–98.

36. Ibid., 159.

37. Ibid., 105.

38. Ibid., 125–26.

39. Ingram takes Hegel to endorse the doctrine of the identity of indiscernibles, but Hegel's discussion of Leibniz suggests that he endorses it only in the

peculiar form shown in this passage. He does not endorse the doctrine in the current sense in which the two qualitatively identical spheres are taken to be a counterexample, since he says that "To such sensuous things the maxim has no application, it is *prima facie* indifferent whether there are things which are alike or not; there may also be always a difference of space" (VGP458/LHP333). As I argue later, however, Hegel's position allows him to avoid Wiggins's counter-intuitive result of having two things in the same place at the same time without abandoning the other, more reasonable version of Leibniz's Law, namely, the indiscernibility of identicals.

40. Another potential Hegelian argument against Wiggins is found in Hegel's claim that his view is required to account for activity as such. Since Wiggins's view depends on the category of activity, Hegel's claim would show Wiggins's view to be parasitic on his own. Specifically, Hegel claims that a rudimentary self-establishment of unity through self-differentiation is a prerequisite for activity.

Hegel writes, "Difference is the whole and its own moment, just as identity equally is its whole and its moment. This is to be considered as the essential nature of reflection and as the specific, original ground of all activity and self-movement" (WL266/SL417). The metaphysical meaning of this claim is that it is of the very nature of the self-identical to differentiate itself, and vice versa. Without this, there would be no activity proper. Although Hegel does not go on to offer an explicit argument for this last claim, I think that his idea is that the notion of activity involves that of a change in an object, which change is in some sense internally determined (since a change due to some outside force would be passivity). The first aspect of activity (change in an object) requires that there be identity across this change, that is, that the object that appears at first is the same that appears after the change (where this 'first' and 'after' need not be given a temporal interpretation). But the second aspect (internal determination) requires that it be in the nature of that self-identical essence to differentiate itself in the way that the change represents.

In his discussion of Leibniz, Hegel says of the active monad, "Activity is to be different, and yet to be one, and this is the only true difference. The monad not only represents, it also changes; but in doing so, it yet remains in itself absolutely what it is. This variation is based on activity" (VGP459/LHP335). Of course, it can be in the nature of something to be passively changed in certain ways. Activity proper requires more robust self-determination than mere identity. The self-determination of identity is that change must be due to the nature of the semblances involved. The self-determination of activity requires that one of the semblances initiate the change. The richer form of self-determination depends on the more abstract self-determination of identity, but it does not supervene on the latter, since the richer form is not exhaustively determined by the more abstract. Although Hegel's claim is intriguing, making it into a plausible argument against Wiggins would require more space than I can devote to it in this chapter.

41. See Wiggins, "On Being in the Same Place at the Same Time," in *Material Constitution*, ed. Michael Rea (Lanham, MD: Rowman & Littlefield, 1997), 3–9.

42. Again, it is not the temporality of the order of the trees' transformations that matters but rather the basic pattern of the successive dependence of certain collections of cells on each other.

43. Wiggins, "On Being," 4.

44. I do not want to overemphasize the difference between Hegel and Wiggins. Many things he says suggest that his ontology is quite similar to Hegel's. Consider the following: "Essences of natural things, as we have them here, are not fancified vacuities parading themselves in the shadow of familiar things as the ultimate explanation of everything that happens in the world. They are natures whose possession by their owners is the precondition of their owners being divided from the rest of the reality as anything at all. These natures are delimited by reference to causal or explanatory principles and purposes that are low level perhaps; but they are fully demanding enough for something to count as their being disappointed or frustrated" (Wiggiins, *Sameness and Substance Renewed*, 143). Furthermore, I take my constructed Hegelian response to the tree/collection of cells problem to be similar to Wiggins's rejection of Geach's puzzle of Tibbles the cat on the basis that one cannot arbitrarily define objects into existence (173–76). Also, Hegel glosses necessity of the objective distinctness of identicals as "What is not distinguished *in thought* is not distinguished" (VGP/LHP338, emphasis added). If Wiggins's "nature" is taken to correspond to what Hegel views as perceptions or "sensuous things" (see n. 38), then the two views are much closer than I have represented them. My basic point, however, is that the strange features of Hegel's category of identity are in fact required to account for our practice of identifying objects, and I take Wiggins's acceptance of two objects in the same place at the same time to be at odds with that practice.

45. As Ingram puts it, Hegel's treatment of identity "is the first major attempt to explain identity in a way which accords with our actual experience while yet satisfying the demands of reason for justification" (Ingram, "Hegel on Leibniz and Individuation" in *Kant Studien* 76: 420–35, 1985).

46. "According to this positive side, in which the self-subsistence in opposition, as the excluding reflection, converts itself into a positedness which it no less supersedes, opposition is not only *destroyed [zugrunde gegangen]* but has withdrawn *into its ground*" (WL281-2/SL4334, translation modified, emphasis in original).

47. See EL158–60 and §7 of the introduction to the *Philosophy of Right* (New York: Cambridge University Press, 1991).

Chapter 4

Identity and Difference, Thought and Being

Martin J. De Nys

In *Identity and Difference*, Martin Heidegger notes that "Thinking has needed more than two thousand years really to understand such a simple relation as that of mediation within identity."[1] Western thought, he observes, has always understood identity in terms of unity. "But that unity is by no means the stale emptiness of that which, in itself, without relation, persists in monotony."[2] This has not always received adequate acknowledgment in Western philosophy. But "since the era of speculative Idealism, it is no longer possible for thinking to represent the unity of identity as mere sameness, and to disregard the mediation that prevails in unity. Wherever this is done, identity is represented only in an abstract manner."[3]

Heidegger goes on to comment that in Western philosophy "the unity of identity forms a basic characteristic of the Being of beings. Everywhere, wherever and however we are related to beings, we find identity making its claim on us."[4] This claim is especially pertinent to science and thinking. In its radical form, the claim that identity makes on thinking is expressed through the notion of identity itself, thus the fragment of Parmenides: *tò gàr àutò noeĩn èstín te kaì eĩnei.* This fragment says that Being and thinking are somehow the same, or that Being belongs to an identity to which thinking belongs as well. The fragment does not address the nature of this identity. Nonetheless, "Long before thinking had arrived at a principle of identity, identity itself speaks out as a pronouncement which rules as follows: thinking and Being belong together in the Same and by virtue of this Same,"[5] where this sameness in turn is at least fixed "as the belonging together of the two."[6]

Of the philosophers cited by Heidegger in his comments on identity, none addressed the problems of the nature of identity and of the identity or unity that prevails between thought and being more thoroughly or powerfully than Hegel. But while Hegel labored mightily to attain a concrete notion of identity, he is often accused of invalidly privileging identity over difference in his considerations of the category of identity and of the unity of thought and being. I argue that the most essential principles at work in Hegel's considerations of these matters lead to very different consequences. I certainly believe that the reading that I offer in these pages is textually warranted. But my ultimate aim is philosophical and not exclusively interpretive. I believe that at least many of the key positions that belong to Hegel's understandings of the nature of identity and of the identity of thought and being invite critical development rather than reversal, just because of the contributions that they make to philosophical truth about these essential issues. Thus a statement and defense of those positions serve conceptual as well as interpretive purposes.

I.

Hegel recognizes very explicitly in the *Phenomenology of Spirit* that "Unity, difference, and relation are categories each of which is nothing in and for itself, but only in relation to its opposite, and they cannot therefore be separated from one another."[7] This recognition operates from the very beginning and throughout all of Hegel's phenomenological considerations. Still, one finds Hegel's most radical treatment of the notions of identity and difference in book 2 of the *Science of Logic*. This is the first text to which my argument must turn.

The logical analysis of identity, belonging as it does to the "Doctrine of Essence," begins with the recognition that identity "is not that equality-with-self that *being* or even *nothing* is but equality-with-self that has brought itself to unity, not a restoration of itself from another, but this pure origination from within itself, *essential* identity."[8] Understood in these terms, identity is not the result of a relative and an external negation in which one thing is distinguished from another, identified through its being separated from the other, but in all other respects taken as an immediate determinacy.[9] "On the contrary, being and every determinateness of being has sublated itself not relatively, but in its own self; and this simple negativity of being in its own self is identity itself."[10] For this reason, identity is now self-related; it is "identity-with-self."[11]

The very fact that one conceives identity in terms of self-relation implies difference, as well as the act of distinguishing through which one acknowledges difference. The "identity-with–self" through which one first conceives logical identity is "simple,"[12] insofar as it is a self-relation that entails, initially at least, difference that vanishes immediately upon its arising, and thus a distinguishing that distinguishes nothing and collapses immediately within itself.[13] Because this distinguishing immediately collapses, it is a positing (*Setzen*)[14] of what is other than identity, namely, the difference in terms that self-relation implies, in its nonbeing. But it is just distinguishing, in the immediacy of its collapse, which brings self-relation about. If so, then "distinguishing is present as self-related negativity";[15] the thought of identity requires the positing of the other of identity, difference and distinguishing, in its nonbeing, and the simultaneous preservation of that other. "In other words," Hegel says, "identity is the reflection-into-self that is identity only as internal repulsion, and is this repulsion as reflection-into-self, repulsion that immediately takes itself back into itself. Thus it is identity as difference that is identical with itself."[16] But of course difference is and can be identical to itself just insofar as it opposes itself to identity and presents itself as nonidentity. This means that one needs to understand identity both as self-related difference, "difference that is identical with itself," and as a determination that stands over against difference and that is, along with difference, one determination of itself.[17]

The preceding remarks summarize the core of the first part of Hegel's treatment of the logical category of identity. This treatment allows Hegel to say that identity, which first presents itself as the same as essence and as the entirety of reflection, shows itself upon fuller consideration to be a determination of essence and a moment of reflection,[18] and that the law of identity and even more so the law of contradiction are synthetic rather than analytic in nature.[19] It is as if it were the case that Hegel, having stripped his thought of all problematic Kantian dualisms, is now well on the way toward establishing his version of the claim that Kant makes at the beginning of the B Deduction, that synthesis, which seems opposed to analysis, is nonetheless that which analysis always and necessarily presupposes.[20] But Hegel's own treatment, as the preceding remarks indicate, requires a further consideration of the category of difference itself.

Hegel begins this treatment by saying that difference is "the essential moment of identity itself which, as negativity of itself, determines itself and is distinguished from difference."[21] Difference is the essential moment of identity. Identity determines itself as the negativity of itself through being the other of its essential moment. This is how identity distinguishes itself from difference. We need carefully to examine the reasoning that leads to these claims.

One must understand the sense of difference that emerges in the consideration of identity, Hegel says, as being simple and absolute. It is "not the other . . . of an other, existing outside it but simple determinateness in itself."[22] According to George Di Giovanni, Hegel wants us to bracket fixed terms "and direct attention to the transition from one to the other. We must conceptualize a point which is neither A nor Not-A, that is, not a *point* at all but a transition between the two. And it is such an "in between" situation that we must abstract and consider as an object in itself, as "*einfacher Begriff*," to use Hegel's phrase. Its essence consists in being *other than* any limit one might want to impose upon it."[23] This is the sense of difference that emerges as the opposite of identity in the Doctrine of Essence.

But must not the attempt to conceive of that which is simply without limit and indefinite fail? Once again, Di Giovanni comments that "The language which Hegel uses to express 'otherness as such' seems indeed already to betray this failure. However hard he might try to express the mere lack of all determinations, it is nonetheless always a well-defined object (viz., one which he declares to be neither A nor B, but a situation in between) which he describes."[24] Hegel acknowledges this in saying that "Difference in itself is self-related difference."[25] But that is just the point. Hegel's aim is to conceive of difference and identity without having "to conceive identity first as a mere self-reference devoid of content, and then to add to it a multiplicity of determinations which leave the identity untouched."[26] He fulfills this aim by showing that difference, understood as an essential determination distinct from identity, nonetheless entails self-relation. If simple or absolute difference is self-related, then "as such, it is the negativity of itself, the difference not of an other, but *of itself from itself;* it is not itself but its other. But that which is different from difference is identity. Difference is therefore itself and identity. Both together constitute difference; it is the whole and its moment."[27] Since absolute or simple difference is a whole that includes itself and identity as well as a moment of the same whole, one might say that simple difference obtains only in relation with identity. But, in the context of the analysis of difference at least, "the truth is rather that, as difference, it contains equally identity and this relation itself."[28] In other words, in showing that the consideration of difference reintroduces the category of identity, Hegel shows that identity is "not merely *added* to other and difference, but *derived* from them."[29] Insofar as identity is derived from difference, it has difference as its essential moment. Since identity presents itself as self-related difference, that is, as a category that has difference as its essential moment and that nonetheless stands in contrast with simple difference, identity determines itself as the other of its essential moment and as the negativity of itself. And identity distinguishes itself from difference just by being a moment of a whole that difference itself defines.

These comments register what is to be said about the connection between the categories of identity and difference from the standpoint of an analysis of difference. A fuller consideration of that connection would repeat the analysis of identity and bring the two analyses together. Hegel suggests this when he observes that "Difference is the whole and its own *moment*, just as identity equally is the whole and its moment."[30] Since each is the whole as well as a moment of the whole, each is the essential moment of the other. Still, this is shown only when the analysis of difference succeeds the analysis of identity. One gains the essential elements of a concrete understanding of identity and difference by noting that *difference* "is not transition into an other, not relation to an other outside it; it has its other, identity, within itself, just as identity, having entered into the determination of difference, has not lost itself in it as its other, but preserves itself, is its reflection-into-self and its moment."[31]

I do not intend to carry my discussion forward into the analyses of diversity, opposition, and contradiction. Those analyses are fascinating in their complexity, philosophical substance, and logical significance. Nonetheless, the analyses that I have discussed so far are sufficient for my purposes, insofar as they lay down the essential and radical principles from which all consideration and employment of the categories of identity and difference should follow. Each of these categories is or defines an intelligible whole that includes its other as a moment, and itself as well. On this basis, an adequate consideration or employment of the category of identity proceeds from the concept of self-related difference, just as an adequate consideration or employment of the category of difference proceeds from the concept of differentiated self-relation. In fact, the situation is more complicated in the latter case, and therefore in the former as well. This is because "differentiation," and the sense of self-relation associated therewith, needs to be understood in light of the analyses of diversity, opposition, and contradiction, and then in light of the further logical categories that develop those essential determinations. But the analyses I have discussed at least show that the categories in question need to be understood in terms of the derivation of each from the other, which means, in part but significantly, in terms of the derivation of identity from difference.

The understanding of identity through the notions of unity and mediation that operates and develops, according to Heidegger, throughout the history of philosophy, attains its first fully adequate and warranted expression in the thought of Hegel. This is a stunning moment of progress in the history of philosophy. That philosophers have, for the most part, ignored or misunderstood and opposed Hegel's understanding of identity indicates the extent to which philosophy falls short of the achievements of its own historical past. There is still a need to grasp that understanding in its complexity. This means surpassing the interpretive position according to which Hegel's considerations of identity and difference, while claiming adequately to conceptualize each, finally privilege the former so as to annul the latter. Even Jacques Taminiaux maintains that "from the moment that Hegel takes up the philosophical project, the proper subject matter of this thought lies in the theme of difference, but that the way in which he relates to it entails the elimination of difference," because with regard to the Absolute, "differences and the whole interplay of references connected with it are condemned to elimination."[32] There well may be even key occasions on which Hegel privileges identity over difference in an objectionable manner. But the most radical principles that belong to his thinking, and that determine the canons for dealing with the notions of identity and difference, are themselves objections to those occasions. The position that identity is itself a moment of difference does not present the whole of Hegel's thinking about identity, but it does reside inalterably at the very basis of that thinking. From this position, an argument that interrelates identity and difference in a way that eliminates difference cannot follow.

II.

Considerations of identity, difference, and the connections between those categories are, by themselves, of fundamental philosophical importance. This importance becomes even more evident when other basic philosophical issues are considered in relation to these categories. As already noted, that happens in a significant way when identity is treated as a determination of beings that makes a claim on thinking, a claim that in its most emphatic form asserts the identity or unity of thought and being.

Clearly Hegel asserts such a claim. He does so in the discussion of the reconciliation of consciousness with self-consciousness in the chapter on "Absolute Knowing" in the 1807 *Phenomenology* and in the discussion of the Idea in the last division of the *Science of Logic*. In the latter text he explicitly refers to the Idea as "the unity of the Concept and Reality" (*die einheit des Begriffs und der Realität*).[33] Hegel's assertion of the claim about the unity or identity of thought and being is not uncontroversial. Taminiaux once again holds that because of the way in which Hegel asserts this claim, the difference between thought and being "is absorbed into a conciliation in which it is eliminated and swallowed up in the indivisible unity of self-consciousness."[34] And on William Desmond's reading of Hegel, "The self-surpassing power of thought is not seen as, in part, shaped by a gift from being-other. It is purely within the power of thought's own resources to determine itself as transparently and comprehensively as possible . . . to the point of complete self-determination, wherein all transcendence has been made entirely immanent."[35]

The implications of these criticisms certainly deserve examination, but so does the question of their accuracy. Hegel seems to give his critics fuel for their fires, as when he says, for example, that external material reality, in relation to the Idea, "is not an abstract *being* subsisting on its own account over against the Concept; on the contrary, it exists only as a *becoming* through the negativity of indifferent being, as a simple determinateness of the Concept."[36] But I have suggested, however briefly, that the fundamental principles that determine what, for Hegel, is normative in considerations of identity and difference should never allow for an argument that annuls difference by absorbing it into self-related identity. This suggests the usefulness of another look at the final chapters of the *Logic* and the *Phenomenology*, for the sake of examining just what Hegel claims there about the identity of thought and being.

Hegel's *Logic* presents a systematic exposition of the categories through which one conceives the pure determinations of self-determining thought and of the actuality grasped in self-determining thought. As this science develops, one comes to see that limitations belong to the categories that conceptualize structures of thought in the "Doctrine of Being" and the "Doctrine of Essence," in large part because of "lack of self-consciousness reflected in those structures about the autonomy, the independent spontaneity of thought required for the possibility of their own project," and that the completion of this science requires an account of "the *way* in which the various moments of being and essence are to be seen as moments in that autonomous process."[37] This account reaches completion in the discussion of the "Absolute Idea." This Idea, in turn, is not precisely another logical category. It is more precisely the self-apprehending (*sich zu vernehmen*) outcome that self-determining thought reaches at the conclusion of a systematically complete account of its own pure, categorical determinations.[38] For this reason, the exposition of the Absolute Idea deals not with specific categories but with the intrinsic dynamic or the "method" of self-determining thought.

This method takes as its beginning a content that is "an immediate something *assumed, found already in existence, assertorical.*" Since the beginning in question belongs to thought rather than to sensation or representation, it is simple and abstractly universal, and in its immediacy "has equally the significance of being, for being is precisely this abstract relation-to-self."[39] One progresses from such a beginning by discerning that while it is initially present in an immediate way, it is nonetheless a locus of inner differentiation in which "the absolute method finds and cognizes the *determination* of the universal within the latter itself."[40] The articulation of the differences that comprise this determination is analytic insofar as it restates the content that the abstract universal subsumes into its immediacy, and synthetic in that this articulated content "exhibits itself as an other" to the initial immediacy.[41] The moments of this dialectical determination in one sense amount to a diversity: The differentiated moments are simply different from each other. But it also is the case that the universal, at first in its immediacy, holds them together, occurs in its own self-relatedness as the unity of these differentiated moments.[42] This indicates a third moment in the dynamic of pure, self-determining thought, whose result is "*equally* immediacy *and* mediation," because it attains a grasp of the different moments that belong to the dialectical determination of the abstract universal in their differentiated unity.[43]

Throughout the discussion that I have just summarized, Hegel is very clear that the dynamic conceptualized through the Absolute Idea belongs to "*pure thought*, in which difference is not yet *otherness*, but is and remains perfectly transparent to itself."[44] This is of fundamental importance. The differences that receive articulation and integration within pure thought are not different from pure thought, not other than it. Within the range of logical categories, those differences include terms such as "*other, different, external, particular, objective*" that are "contrasted with and even opposed to *something, identity, internal, universal, subjective,*" but also integrated with the latter.[45] The integration of the two sets of terms refers pure thought to its other but does not bring about the relationship between pure thought and that other. The occurrence of the former set of terms in those integrations indicates, as John Burbidge points out, that any external reality opposed to pure thought "can be represented by these negative, or determining, characteristics," and consequently, "that which is other than thought will not remain impervious to it. . . . Whatever can be characterized as other than thought will yet remain comprehensible."[46] These comments make an important contribution to an account of the connection between pure thought and its other, and of the status of that other in this connection, and I will return to them. But they do not give a complete account of that connection or status.

One can extend that account by turning to the final chapter of the *Phenomenology of Spirit.* The relationship of "Absolute Knowing" to the phenomenological inquiry that this standpoint concludes is not unlike the relation of the "Absolute Idea" to the scientific exposition of pure categories that its discussion completes. The *Phenomenology* aims at providing a warranted conception of knowing in which truth and certainty coincide, through an immanent examination of the content and necessary relations among forms of consciousness, structures constituted by determinate definitions of the object of consciousness, consciousness itself, or the relation between them. Absolute knowing is not another and final form of consciousness because it surpasses the determinate character of such forms. Absolute knowing entails the realization that fully warranted knowledge follows not from any determinate structure of consciousness but from the self-determining activities of self-consciousness, rational thought.

Absolute knowing comes about through a recollection (*Erinnerung*) and gathering together (*Versammlung*)[47] of transformations that determinations of the object of consciousness undergo on account of the activities of conscious and self-conscious thought. Variously throughout the *Phenomenology* "the object is in part *immediate* being or, in general, a Thing . . . in part an othering of itself, its relationship or *being-for-another,*" and in part "*essence*, or in the form of a universal. . . . It is, as a totality, a syllogism or the movement of the universal through determination to individuality, and also the reverse movement from individuality through superseded individuality, or through determination, to the universal."[48] In part, the recollection and gathering together of these determinations of the object is something that *we* do. But those determinations also come together in the experience of consciousness itself, specifically in the community of conscientious selves that concludes the consideration of morality, and of revealed religion.[49] The integrated occurrence of these determinations, along with the insight that they follow ultimately not from any determinate structure of consciousness but from the autonomy of self-conscious thought, enables that same thought to liberate itself from any dependence on determinate structures and to attain a warranted definition of the conditions of the possibility of knowing that refers to its own self-determining activities.

Hegel characterizes absolute knowing as a reconciliation of consciousness and self-consciousness. This reconciliation supersedes any and all epistemic relations between consciousness and an "object" or a determinacy that is given and in at least that sense external to consciousness, and that is supposed to guarantee knowledge on account of its externality. But this reconciliation does not only surpass the externality of the object in relation to the activities of self-conscious thought, it also entails that those activities comprise "the externalization of self-consciousness that posits the thinghood [of the object]."[50] Moreover, this has a negative and a positive meaning. It means that the object belongs to the unity of self-consciousness with itself. And it means that the unity of self-consciousness with itself preserves and does not annul objectivity, so that self-consciousness is "in communion with itself in *its* otherness as such."[51] Heidegger offers an interesting gloss on this understanding. Noting that "the term *absolute* means initially 'not relative,'" he observes that "For knowledge to be qualitatively other than relative knowledge . . . it must remain bound but also liberate and ab-solve itself from what it knows and yet, as so absolved, as absolute, still be a knowledge. To be absolved from what is known does not mean 'abandoning' it, but 'preserving it by elevating it,'"[52] Heidegger later adds, "What is known absolutely can only be that which knowledge knowingly lets emerge and which, only as emerging thus, stands in knowledge; it is not an object, but an emergence."[53] Knowledge that falls short of that standpoint of absolute knowing is, in Hegel's own words, "a disclosure or revelation (*Offenbarkeit*) which . . . is in fact concealment (*Verborgenheit*)," because that which is known "is still *selfless being* and what is disclosed to it is only the certainty of itself" with regard to the capacity of thought to grasp truth.[54] Absolute knowing discloses thought as the power of disclosure, the power that allows what is known to emerge or present itself in the self-determining activity of knowing. For this reason, Hegel can say that the absolute standpoint exhibits knowing as the power "which empties itself of itself and sinks into its substance, and also, as Subject has gone out of that substance into itself, making that substance into an object and a content at the same time as it annuls the difference between objectivity and content."[55] Self-conscious thought grasps intelligibility through its own determination of the categories that conceptualize the radical necessities that determine its own processes and the actuality of things. At the same time it immerses itself in, "sinks" into, considerations of those actualities as they present themselves in order to grasp their intelligibility through its own categorically self-determined considerations.

I am maintaining, in other words, that the standpoint of Absolute Knowing presents an understanding of autonomous rational thought for which autonomy means the capacity to allow the intelligibility of what is real or actual, and in that sense other than thought, to appear and be grasped in and through the self-determined activities of thinking, thus indicating the rationality of what is actual. To employ a Kantian idiom, I am maintaining that the standpoint of Absolute Knowing presents an understanding of autonomous rational thought that interrelates and preserves the notions of spontaneity and receptivity, rather than supposing that receptivity excludes autonomy, or that autonomy requires that spontaneity be maintained to the exclusion of receptivity. The conclusion of the *Logic* refers pure thought to its other through the distinction between differences within thought and the other of thought, and the consequent insight that categories having to do with the other of thought are yet on their own terms only differences within thought, thus directing pure thought beyond its immanent considerations and toward its other. The conclusion of the *Phenomenology* shows that the relation of fully adequate knowing to that which is known is such that the otherness of the other not simply maintained and not simply annulled but surpassed and preserved insofar as knowing in a fully adequate sense means grasping the integral intelligibility of that which is. Intelligible actuality distinguishes itself from thought, presents itself as an other whose intelligibility is realized in self-determining rational processes, offers itself as an other in which thought can "sink" and immerse itself, and as something to be known through the categories that thought itself determines, such that, in knowing its other, thought as it were knows itself.

III.

Of the many questions that suggest themselves at this point, I find that two are most prominent. First, is the reading of Hegel's position on the identity in difference, or the mediated unity, of thought and reality or being that I have offered an accurate account of what he actually does hold? Second, allowing for an affirmative answer to the first question, does this position adequately account for the difference and otherness that arguably obtain in the relation that binds being and thought together, and that needs to be preserved in any understanding of that relation as a mediated unity? Or is difference and otherness, as Taminiaux says, finally swallowed up and eliminated by Hegel's account of the unity of self-consciousness or of pure thought in its final self-comprehension? I want in no sense to deny that there may be a great deal to be said about the first question. Nonetheless, I want to focus on the second. I believe that the textual resources on which I have drawn for my account of Hegel's position on the relevant issue indicate that my account is at least as plausible as its competitors. I want to focus on the second question in order to discuss an important contribution that Hegel, given the reading I have presented, makes to philosophical truth.

William Desmond offers one of the most informed and substantive criticisms of Hegel's position on the mediated unity of thought and being. He says, in a summary of his critique, that because Hegel understands mediation as self-mediation, "being as immediate is completely self-mediated by dialectical self-determination. Autonomous thought, the Idea, is autonomous being, the absolute whole. . . . Being in its otherness is the self-othering of thought thinking itself; this otherness is dialectically overreached by the process of thought completely determining itself. Transcendence is the self-transcendence of the Idea and also its self-return when it knows itself as self-transcendence in otherness."[56] Desmond finds the problem that these statements indicate to be present at the conclusion of the *Phenomenology* and of the *Logic*.

In the case of the *Phenomenology*, dialectical progress follows in all cases from a failure of self-mediation. "The *telos* is the goal of absolutely self-mediating thought. This goal is reached in absolute knowing when the otherness of the immediate is completely mediated, in its being dialectically subsumed in a self-knowing that is absolutely self-mediating."[57] Absolute knowing entails thoroughgoing self-comprehension. This self-comprehension or "Being self-mindful completely overcomes any thinking that thinks the otherness of being as other to mind. Being self-mindful completes being as the pure self-mediating dialectical process of thought determining itself. Being is the pure self-determination of thought thinking itself."[58] With regard to the *Logic*, opposition is progressively understood as a "*self-opposition* or process of *self-othering*. . . . The equivocation of opposites in such a process is identical with one of reciprocal determination, which is really self-determination in the other; and again since the other here is the self's *own other*, it is hence the self itself once again."[59] This means that Hegelian logic traces "the *inclusive* self-transcendence of thought itself, which appropriates the self-development of being-other. It will proceed, Hegel holds, to the all inclusive thought, which is the absolute Idea, the inclusive whole of thought absolutely determining itself. Hence Hegel's *Logic*, like the *Phenomenology*, completes itself in a *telos* answering to the total self-determination of thought thinking itself."[60]

These comments clearly follow from a careful meditation on difference and being-other. But one can still go farther, and Hegel himself indicates how. He points out in a telling passage that being-other "may be taken in the first instance as a simple determination, but in truth it is a *relation* or a *relationship*. . . . It is therefore the other, but not the other of something to which it is indifferent—in that case it would not be an other, not a relation or relationship—rather it is the o*ther in its own self*, the *other of an other*; therefore it includes *its* own other within itself and is consequently, as *contradiction*, the *posited dialectic of itself*."[61] For Hegel, what does it mean for y to be the other of x in its own self, or for x to have y as its own other? This condition obtains if y is not the other "of something to which it is indifferent." If reality or being were not thought's "own other" then it would be something "indifferent" to thought; it would be, at least in part but radically unintelligible. Hegel certainly claims to demonstrate that being is, as such, comprehensively intelligible. So he does not allow that being is the simple, indifferent other of thought. But this is hardly the only or most important sense of being-other. On account of its integral and demonstrated intelligibility, being is the other of thought in its own self, and qua intelligible includes "its own other within itself." Thought also includes its own other within itself, insofar as activity of thought is, again integrally and demonstrably, the power of realizing, that is, rationally comprehending intelligibility through its self-determining activities and through the pure categories that those activities also determine. But these comments, which do specify the integral relationships that bind being and thought together in a mediated unity, do not all entail the denial of the otherness of each from the other, as Hegel's distinction between two senses of being-other shows. One way of indicating this is to say that if rational thought "appropriates the self-development of being-other," then this is still an appropriation that occurs in thought and points to and requires the self-development of "being-other" in being as its counterpart and its genuine other. Burbidge concludes that one should understand Hegel's position about "thought overreaching that which is other than thought," as presenting "an overreaching that must take account of the difference between concept and actuality—of the nasty, broad ditch, as well as their similarity."[62] I can only register my assent.

But still, Hegel requires that one understand thought as thoroughly self-determining. Does this not imply that the mediated unity of thought and reality or being finally amounts to a self-mediated unity of thought with itself that eliminates the otherness of being from thought? I believe that the plausibility of this claim depends on the questionable view that self-determination excludes mediation by the other or receptivity. I have already mentioned the criticism that the Hegelian understanding of self-determining thought entails, that "The self-surpassing of thought is not seen as, in part, shaped by a gift from being-other."[63] But if someone gives me a gift and if I accept it and then use or enjoy it, I am in all of those respects *doing* something, and my actions are *self-determining*. This homely illustration suggests that self-determination need not at all exclude receptivity and mediation by the other. Self-determination may in fact *require* both agency and receptivity and mediation by the other. This is possible only if the other is other in a genuine sense. I believe my discussion of absolute knowing indicates that just this requirement belongs to the mediated unity of thought and being, as Hegel understands this. If so, then even the position that thought is in a thoroughgoing way self-determining does not require that the mediated unity of thought and being be reduced to the self-mediated unity of thought with itself. It is entirely consistent to maintain that a mediated unity interrelates self-determining thought and being, where the latter presents itself as the other of thought insofar as it possesses an integral intelligibility that thinking comprehends through its own activities, and is also something that thinking receives, and is something that, in each of these two respects, mediates the self-determination of thought.

If Western philosophy required two millennia to understand identity as mediated unity, then Hegel represents a culminating moment of that achievement. His most essential principles call for an understanding of identity and difference that determines each with reference to the other and that insistently preserves both in their reciprocal determination. His position on the mediated unity of thought and being defines thought as the self-determining power of comprehension that meets itself in an other that is nonetheless genuinely other. It defines being as determined by an intelligibility in virtue of which it is thought's "own other," and at the same time as that which presents itself to the receptivity of thought and mediates thought in its autonomy. In these respects, as in many others, Hegel presents contemporary philosophy with a resource upon which it draws to its profit, and ignores at its peril.

Notes

1. Martin Heidegger, *Identity and Difference*, trans. by Joan Stambaugh, together with the German text (New York, Evanston, and London: Harper and Row, 1969), 41/106. All notes to this edition will refer to the page of the English translation followed by the page reference to the German text.
2. Ibid., 25/87.
3. Ibid., 25/88.
4. Ibid., 26/89.
5. Ibid., 27/90.
6. Ibid., 28/91.
7. G. W. F. Hegel, *Phenomenology of Spirit*, trans. by A. V. Miller (Oxford: Clarendon Press, 1977), 219 (hereafter *Phenomenology*); Hegel, *Phänomenologie des Geistes*, herausg. Moldenhauer u. Michel (Frankfurt am Main: Suhrkamp, 1970), 273 (hereafter *Phänomenologie*).
8. *Hegel's Science of Logic*, trans. A. V. Miller (London and New York: George Allen and Unwin and Humanities Press, 1969), 411 (hereafter *Logic*); Hegel, *Wissenschaft der Logik II*, herausg/Moldenhauer u. Michel (Frankfurt am Main: Suhrkamp, 1969), vol. 6, 39 (hereafter *Logik*). Throughout this chapter, all terms and expressions italicized in citations also are italicized in the original text.
9. See Hegel, *Logic*, 411–12; *Logik*, 39.
10. Hegel, *Logic*, 412; *Logik*, 39.
11. Hegel, *Logic*, 411; *Logik*, 39.
12. Ibid.
13. See Hegel, *Logic*, 412; *Logik*, 40.
14. Ibid.
15. Hegel, *Logic*, 413; *Logik*, 40.
16. Ibid.
17. See Hegel, *Logic*, 413; *Logik*, 40–41.
18. See Hegel, *Logic*, 412; *Logik*, 40.
19. See Hegel, *Logic*, 416; *Logik*, 45.
20. Kant, *Kritik der reinen Vernunft* (Frankfurt am Main: Suhrkamp, 1968), B 130.
21. Hegel, *Logic*, 417; *Logik*, 46.
22. Ibid.

23. George Di Giovanni, "Reflection and Contradiction: A Commentary on Some Passages of Hegel's *Science Of Logic,*" *Hegel Studien* 8 (1973): 135.

24. Ibid.

25. Hegel, *Logic*, 417; *Logik*, 46.

26. Di Giovanni, "Reflection and Contradiction," 136.

27. Hegel, *Logic*, 417; *Logik*, 46–47.

28. Hegel, *Logic*, 417; *Logik*, 47.

29. Di Giovanni, "Reflection and Contradiction," 136.

30. Hegel, *Logic*, 417; *Logik*, 47.

31. Hegel, *Logic*, 418; *Logik*, 47.

32. Jacques Taminiaux, "Finitude and the Absolute," in *Dialectic and Difference: Finitude in Modern Thought*, ed. James Decker and Robert Crease (Atlantic Highlands, NJ: Humanities Press, 1985), 75.

33. Hegel, *Logic*, 757; *Logik*, 465. In this and all citations of the *Science of Logic* I modify the Miller translation by substituting for "Notion," "Concept" or "the Concept," as appropriate.

34. Taminiaux, "Finitude and the Absolute," 75.

35. William Desmond, *Being and the Between* (Albany: State University of New York Press, 1995), 31.

36. Hegel, *Logic*, 759; *Logik*, 467.

37. Robert Pippin, *Hegel's Idealism: The Satisfactions of Self-Consciousness* (Cambridge: Cambridge University Press, 1989), 234.

38. Hegel, *Logik*, 550. *Logic*, 826.

39. Hegel, *Logic*, 827, 828; *Logik*, 553, 554.

40. Hegel, *Logic*, 830; *Logik*, 556.

41. Hegel, *Logic*, 830; *Logik*, 557.

42. See Hegel, *Logic*, 830; *Logik*, 556.

43. Hegel, *Logic*, 837; *Logik*, 565.

44. Hegel, *Logic*, 825; *Logik*, 550.

45. John Burbidge, *On Hegel's Logic: Fragments of a Commentary* (Atlantic Highlands, NJ: Humanities Press, 1981), 220.

46. Ibid., 220–21.

47. Hegel, *Phänomenologie*, 590–91, 582.

48. Hegel, *Phenomenology*, 480; *Phänomenologie*, 576.

49. See Hegel, *Phenomenology*, 481–85; *Phänomenologie*, 578–82.

50. Hegel, *Phenomenology*, 479; *Phänomenologie*, 575.

51. Ibid.

52. Martin Heidegger, *Hegel's Phenomenology of Spirit*, trans. Pavis Emad and Kenneth Maly (Bloomington: Indiana University Press, 1980), 14, 15.

53. Ibid., 110.

54. Hegel, *Phenomenology*, 487; *Phänomenologie*, 584.

55. Hegel, *Phenomenology*, 490; *Phänomenologie*, 587–88.

56. Desmond, *Being and the Between*, 175.

57. Ibid., 168–69.

58. Ibid., 169.

59. Ibid., 169.

60. Ibid., 172.

61. Hegel, *Logic*, 835; *Logik*, 562.

62. John Burbidge, *Hegel on Logic and Religion* (Albany: State University of New York Press, 1992), 6.

63. Desmond, *Being and the Between*, 30.

Part 2

Identity and Difference in the *Philosophy of Mind*

Chapter 5

Identity, Difference, and the Unity of Mind: Reflections on Hegel's Determination of Psyche, Consciousness, and Intelligence

Richard Dien Winfield

The Modern Controversy in the Philosophy of Mind

Much debate in modern philosophy of mind has revolved around whether awareness of self, awareness of objects, and awareness of others are intrinsically connected. Controversy has raged ever since Descartes examined what could be doubted, found certainty only of "I" as a thinking thing, and then presumed that self-consciousness could be had without consciousness of anything else. Kant contested this solipsism by showing that self-consciousness could not be apart from consciousness of objects in space. Insofar as intuition of time requires awareness of a persisting backdrop that only spatial objectivity provides, the temporality of self-awareness is inseparable from consciousness of nature in space. Kant's transcendental idealism, however, leaves objectivity merely an appearance, relative to consciousness. As a law-governed realm appearing to consciousness in general, phenomena do retain a comparatively nonsubjective character consisting in an intersubjective commonality extending to all conscious selves. Yet this law-governed character of appearance excludes any experience of spontaneity. Given that spontaneity is basic to selfhood, this exclusion renders problematic consciousness of other selves, just as much as self-consciousness. Hence, on his own terms, Kant cannot make any legitimate theoretical claims about intersubjectivity. Moreover, since no distinction can be drawn between what is general and individual if no plurality is knowable, Kant can hardly claim any knowledge about consciousness in general.

These difficulties might seem to be resolved by the reconception of mind following in the wake of Wittgenstein, Sellars, and Davidson. On this view, self-knowledge, knowledge of objects, and knowledge of others are inseparably connected. Their connection is inextricable because of the relation between knowledge and concepts, on the one hand, and concepts and language, on the other. By invoking justification and the appeal to reasons, knowledge involves propositions and the concepts they contain. This is true of self-knowledge as much as of knowledge of other objects, including other selves. Concepts and the propositions they inhabit presuppose language. Because language is not private, the acquisition of the concepts making knowledge possible is bound up with the intersubjective process of learning and using a language. To the extent that words are learned by observing how others employ them in reference to commonly perceived objects, there can be no knowledge that does not rest upon the conjuncture of self-knowledge, knowledge of objects, and knowledge of other speakers. Accordingly, one cannot coherently entertain Cartesian doubt and be certain of one's own existence while being uncertain of everything else, nor be self-conscious and conscious of objects in space without knowing other interlocutors.

By itself, the connection between knowledge, propositions, and language need not bear upon the validity of the knowledge claims made possible by linguistic interaction. The connection can simply mean that any certainty of self cannot be coherently detached from certainty of some objects other than the self, and from certainty of other selves. The followers of Wittgenstein, Sellars, and Davidson, however, accord epistemological significance to the inseparability of self-knowledge, knowledge of objects, and knowledge of others. So treating linguistic conditions of meaning as conditions of truth presents problems. Because communication is contingent upon what interlocutors happen to recognize in common as the objective reference of commonly employed expressions, making this interaction determinative of not just what terms mean but whether they provide knowledge renders knowledge relative to contingent linguistic interaction. Given how meanings are interconnected in the ever-changing web of language, what results is a relativist holism, wherein no concepts or principles have any necessity, and where knowledge claims are justified with conventional standards as contingent and variable as the rules of any game.

Paradoxically, if this were true, then the theory affirming the interconnection of knowledge, concepts, and language would be relative to linguistic convention, leaving it and every other knowledge claim suspect and corrigible. The holistic interconnection of meanings cannot redeem their truth by some principle of charity, for that idea is equally contingent upon shared practices neither infallible nor unwavering.

This difficulty reflects the dilemma of seeking to know before knowing, that is, of specifying determining conditions of cognition as if such conditions could be identified without falling into the circularity of already employing cognition.

Compounding this problem is the accompanying presumption that discursive knowledge and consciousness are inseparable. Their connection is implied by the assumption that consciousness is a *knowledge* of objects and that therefore subjects cannot be conscious without disposing of concepts and propositions and the linguistic engagement that these involve. This view is anticipated by Kant, who makes the objectivity of experience depend upon conceptual determination of intuitions through necessary judgments. Allegedly, because the given content and association of representations may just be subjective, they cannot convey anything objective unless intuitions are necessarily conceptually ordered. Although Kant does not take account of the intersubjective implications of the discursive character of conceptual determination and objective awareness, he hereby paves the way for the linguistic turn.

Needless to say, if consciousness of objects depends upon concepts and propositions and linguistic interaction, then the same will be true of self-consciousness. Then neither dumb animals nor children who have yet to acquire language can be either conscious or self-conscious.

These exclusions might seem benign. If, however, one considers the scenario where individuals acquire knowledge of self, objects, and other selves by becoming conscious, self-conscious, and discursive at one blow, then one must wonder how selves lacking consciousness, let alone self-consciousness, can first perform the triangulation establishing meanings. How can individuals discriminate themselves from commonly given objects let alone discriminate their responses from those of others unless some form of consciousness and self-consciousness is already available?

The Unheralded Challenge of Hegel's Theory of Mind

Hegel's theory of mind is crucial for resolving these difficulties. This has been largely unrecognized due to two circumstances. On the one hand, Hegel's theory has been co-opted by Wilfrid Sellars and such epigones as Robert Brandom, who have presumed that it anticipates the linguistic holism they advance.[1] On the other hand, the details of Hegel's systematic treatment of mind have been among the least discussed portions of his philosophy. A voluminous secondary literature continues to focus upon the *Phenomenology of Spirit*, as if truths about mind could be legitimately culled from its propaedeutic observation of the self-elimination of the standpoint of consciousness. Meanwhile, the Philosophy of Subjective Spirit in the *Encyclopedia*, where Hegel offers his proper philosophy of mind, has hardly been investigated. Symptomatic of this neglect is Charles Taylor's mammoth tome *Hegel*, which allocates not a single page to the doctrine of subjective spirit.[2] *If* one bothers to examine Hegel's analysis of subjective spirit, then it is hard to miss the fundamental departure from the problematics that have plagued modern philosophy of mind from Descartes through Davidson.

To begin with, Hegel does not treat mind as an epistemological foundation that determines the truth of knowledge and thereby must be known before anything else. Instead, Hegel predicates the systematic theory of mind upon the successive investigations of the *Phenomenology of Spirit*, the *Science of Logic*, and the *Philosophy of Nature*. Before mind can be addressed, the *Phenomenology of Spirit* must provide access to systematic philosophy by eliminating as principle of knowing the opposition of consciousness and its appeal to the given. The *Science of Logic* must then furnish a presuppositionless self-development of categories, establishing the determinacies that any account of reality incorporates and further qualifies. Finally, the *Philosophy of Nature* must unfold the idea of physical reality that any other realities contain.

That the investigation of mind presupposes all of these inquiries has decisive ramifications. First, although the account of mind must end up conceiving how real minds can think the truth, in doing so that account will not fall into the foundationalist trap of treating mind as a juridical epistemological principle, mandating what knowledge is valid. The *Phenomenology of Spirit* has unmasked the internal untenability of the whole enterprise of treating knowing as having foundations, as having something given as its standard of truth. For its part, the *Science of Logic* has effected the positive deed of showing how categories are determinable without appeal to any givens. If these efforts be taken seriously, then it is too late for philosophical psychology to retain any epistemological ambitions. Instead, the conception of mind will explain how real individuals can think, leaving undetermined which thoughts are true among those that are thinkable. The philosophy of mind can then escape invoking epistemological foundations and having to know before knowing, which would be unavoidable if true knowledge could only be ascertained by first knowing mind and its foundational role.

Second, by presupposing systematic logic's self-development of categories, the philosophy of mind can escape the self-refuting pragmatic holism that results when all thought is left conditioned by contingent linguistic practice. Instead of making conceptual determination hostage to arbitrary language games, undercutting all universal claims about thought and language, the philosophy of mind can take advantage of an independent determination of categories whose freedom from foundations signifies a liberation from corrigible convention.

Third, by following upon the systematic determination of nature, from the pure mechanics of matter in motion, through physical and chemical reactions, to the life process involving all dimensions of nature, the philosophy of mind can escape the mind-body dualism making so inscrutable self-consciousness, consciousness of others, and action. Instead of setting nature and mind apart as self-contained substances whose relationship becomes inexplicable, Hegel's placement of mind as the outcome of nature leaves mind inherently connected to a physical world in which there is life. Moreover, because results of immanent development contain what they presuppose, Hegel here presents mind not just as a result of the animal organism but as incorporating that organism as a constitutive element of mental life. On this basis, mind is necessarily a living entity, not merely in the world but metabolically interacting with it. Whatever theoretical challenges this point of departure may involve, it precludes the dualist problems of connecting a disembodied mind with nature or bridging an opposition of freedom and determinism. By being in part an animal in the world, mind never faces the dilemma of dealing with an ontologically incommensurate domain. In acting, for example, mind never wields an immaterial agency exerting external causation upon the body. Instead, action is the self-activity of a being that always involves animal physiology.[3]

These implications of the place of the concept of mind within systematic philosophy set the stage for the more thoroughgoing challenge residing in Hegel's actual delineation of mind. Whereas most modern treatments tend to identify mind with consciousness, Hegel conceives mental reality involving three successively determined processes: the psyche, consciousness, and intelligence, all of which involve life but are not reducible to it. These mental realms do not comprise three parts or powers of mind, given independently of one another. If that were the case, then mind would be rendered a thing, whose unity would be problematic. Instead, psyche, consciousness, and intelligence are successive stages in the self-constitution of the totality of mind. Given this order of development, intelligence involves consciousness and psyche, consciousness involves psyche, and psyche comprises the minimal mental process without which no others can function.

Accordingly, it is possible for an animal organism to have a psyche without possessing consciousness or intelligence. This may be true because: (1) The organism by nature never develops these further mental processes; (2) The organism is still immature and will later acquire consciousness and/or intelligence; or (3) The individual has lost consciousness and/or intelligence through injury or disease. Similarly, an individual with a psyche also may possess consciousness without having intelligence. Once more, this can be due to congenital limitations related to species being or impaired prenatal development, immaturity, or loss of intelligence due to some harm. These options in the possible configuration of mind raise important issues regarding the psyche, consciousness, and intelligence.

First, if the psyche can be had without consciousness and intelligence, but not conversely, then it must be possible to identify a mental process that is not conscious or intelligent yet provides some mental activity that consciousness as well as intelligence cannot do without. Further, to the degree that the psyche supervenes upon the most developed form of life, animal existence, there must be some way of distinguishing between the preconscious activity of the psyche and the sensibility and irritability differentiating animals from plants. Unlike Aristotle, for whom the psyche is the principle of life, possessed by plants as well as animals in its minimal form of nutritive process, Hegel here presents the psyche as something that only certain animals will possess, without necessarily having consciousness.

Two important consequences follow from the psyche subsuming animal life and making possible consciousness and intelligence: Machines are precluded from being conscious or genuinely intelligent, and any mind, finite or infinite, involving no animal body is rendered suspect. Consequences no less crucial, especially for the connection of consciousness, self-consciousness, and language, follow from Hegel's determination of consciousness prior to intelligence.

To begin with, the very distinction between these two spheres permits what any conflation of mind with consciousness prohibits—that intelligence can transcend the opposition of consciousness, whose constitutive reference to the given fatally compromises any attempt to transform certainty into knowledge. In this respect, Hegel's differentiation of consciousness and intelligence provides the psychological *enabling* conditions for systematic philosophy, which, as foundation free, has no juridical *determining* conditions.

Further, to the extent that intelligence is developed as the mental domain in which signs become produced and thinking occurs, the consciousness presupposed by intelligence will be both prelinguistic and preconceptual, even if intelligent individuals will be conscious of words and thoughts. This allows consciousness and self-consciousness to be possessed by both dumb animals and children who have yet to speak and think. It also makes it possible for individuals to be conscious of one another and of common objects without yet entering into linguistic interaction, something that may be a precondition of the triangulation in which meaning and thought become baptized. To the extent that knowledge is both conceptual and propositional, the prelinguistic and preconceptual character of consciousness suggests that conscious awareness may not involve knowledge proper, but only certainty.

If the order of development be taken seriously, then every shape of consciousness determined prior to the emergence of intelligence must be understood to function without discourse. This poses significant challenges. Although sense-certainty may readily be impervious to propositional knowledge, the two further stages of consciousness delineated by Hegel, perception and understanding, might seem to involve awareness of concepts and principles, both to perceive things and their properties and to understand the forces and laws in the dynamic relations of objects. This problem appears just as acute in self-consciousness, where, strictly speaking, not only desire but also recognition should not yet involve discourse. If these forms of self-consciousness can be pre-linguistic, then they too can be accessible to certain dumb animals and immature children. The same applicability applies to the reason of universal self-consciousness. If its consciousness of the unity of subjectivity and objectivity need not involve language and thinking, then conscious reason is of broader scope than commonly supposed. Yet can consciousness lay claim to any reason, not to mention understanding, without already containing an awareness of concepts and the words that allow them to be expressed?

This question can be broadened if one takes seriously Hegel's development of intelligence. Although intelligence is that mental process within which words and thoughts arise, Hegel characterizes it more generally as an awareness of reason, where mind relates itself to its own cognizance of what is equally subjective and objective.[4] On Hegel's account, before intelligence relates to reason in terms of language and thinking, the intellect involves intuition and then representation and imagination. This allows for intelligence to have its own prelinguistic region, which means that those individuals who participate in the engendering of language can already have some intelligence as well as consciousness. However crucial this may be to the production of signs and engagement in real speech and thinking, it presents a formidable challenge to the conception of consciousness. To take seriously Hegel's development of stages of intelligence, one must consider how consciousness can sense, perceive, and understand without already engaging in intuition and representation.

A further quandary concerns the role of intersubjectivity. Although the naturally determined life of the psyche bears the imprint of sexuality and the interrelations it implies, the absence of subject-object distinctions precludes intersubjectivity proper from otherwise figuring in the psychic field of feeling. Hegel brings intersubjectivity into consciousness in the recognition process constitutive of the type of self-consciousness from which universal self-consciousness arises. Nevertheless, when Hegel develops intelligence he refrains from explicitly involving intersubjectivity. This is most strikingly the case in his development of intelligence's sign-making activity and verbal memory. These moves, so crucial for the emergence of thinking, are presented without reference to any intersubjectivity, let alone the triangulation in which individuals fix the meaning of signs through their commonly observed reactions to commonly perceived objects. Has Hegel succumbed to a private language conception, compromising his psychology by ignoring the constitutive intersubjectivity of discourse and thinking?

All of these questions call for resolution, not just to test the coherence of Hegel's account of mind but to sort out how mind achieves identity in difference, integrating psyche, consciousness and intelligence.

The Psyche as the Presupposition of Consciousness

The first issue in Hegel's account that must be addressed is how the psyche can involve more than animal physiology, yet be a preconscious mental process on which consciousness and intelligence depend. What can it be that the psyche adds to the animal organism that does not already include the subject-object distinction constitutive of consciousness? For Hegel, this question is equivalent to asking for the minimal determinacy of mind, and the answer is starkly simple. Mind without further qualification immediately supervenes upon nature in its most complete development as the animal organism and, as such, mind is the encompassing unity that contains that reality as its constituent. This means that mind minimally has a nature of its own that is not the product of any mental process and that mind relates to it without any intermediary, incorporating it without yet modifying its content.

Already, animal physiology involves its own self-monitoring organ in the form of the nervous system, regulating both sensibility and irritability. Supervening upon this naturally given self-registering unity, mind as psyche adds a new level of self-relation. Unlike consciousness, however, the psyche does not relate to its content as something from which it is disengaged and confronts as an other, an objectivity with a unity of its own. Nor is the psyche self-conscious, relating to itself as a self opposing an objectivity from which it is extricated. Instead, the psyche registers the neurophysiological totality of the animal organism as its own given being, doing so immediately. The psyche's self-relation immediately registers the animal organism it encompasses, since any mediated registration would presuppose an immediate relation to the mediating factor, reinstalling an immediate self-relation as the minimal form of the life of the psyche. As immediate, the psyche's registrations are singular and contingent, devoid of the further interceding organization that could impart universality and necessity. Although what is registered reflects the organic unity of animal physiology in its interaction with the surrounding biosphere, the immediacy of mind's relation to its natural constituent takes all of this in without any discrimination. The psyche simply feels, and what it feels is itself as immediately given. For this reason, Hegel observes, the psyche is subject to an *anthropological* treatment, where the psyche draws its content from natural processes that are not yet products of its own mental activity.[5] Instead of determining itself ex nihilo, the psyche simply feels what it is by nature, belonging as it does to an animal organism inhabiting a preexisting biosphere.

In so doing, the psyche does not sense something it confronts from a disengaged standpoint, straddling a subject-object divide. The psyche relates to its own nature in feeling. In contrast to the "I" of consciousness, which senses an object with an independent unity, the self of the psyche is what it feels and feels what it is. In feeling, the psyche is related to itself without relating to anything other, and for just this reason the psyche is self-feeling without being conscious or self-conscious.

Accordingly, the psyche can undergo naturally alternating phases of sleep and awakening, without waking necessarily being accompanied by consciousness, self-consciousness, or intelligence. Although the awake psyche distinguishes itself from being asleep, what are opposed are two naturally occurring phases of itself, not subject versus object. Thus before developing subject-object awareness, infants and young children can be awake and self-feeling, just as can animals to which consciousness need never be ascribed.

These distinctions indicate how the psyche can be a mental domain independent of consciousness and intelligence, but more is needed to establish the dependence of conscious awareness upon the psyche. Hegel's account of the psyche's development from self-feeling through habit to emotive expression offers a neglected key.

In order for mind to be conscious, two requirements must be met. Mind must relate to its own determinations as being both for it and as determinations of an object. If mind's own determinations are not for it, then mind lacks the self-relation on which depends the givenness to consciousness of any object. Unless mind's determinations fall within its own field of awareness, mind can hardly have any object before it. On the other hand, mind must treat its own determinations as being of something other to it, possessing an independent unity from which mind has extricated itself. Otherwise, mind only communes with itself, and there is no subject-object relation.

For mind to be conscious without need of any preconscious mental life, these two requirements would have to be immediately satisfied, as the minimal shape of mind. Yet how can what is immediately given to mind have an independent unity without some mediation of its manifold content? And how can mind extricate itself from this manifold without first being in immediate relation to it and then separating itself from it? These questions go together, for the extrication of mind from its own mental determinacy is only possible if that determinacy can acquire an independent unity, leaving mind an abstracted subject, disengaged from the given material of its feelings.

The psyche, immediately registering the given neurophysiology of its animal organism, need not presuppose any other mentality, since self-feeling is an unmediated communing with an immediately given manifold yet unmodified by any further mental activity. The problem that must be resolved to account for consciousness is how the psyche can develop out of its passive receptivity, separate its self-related unity from its own mental content, and enable that content to stand for it as an independently unified opposing objectivity. Since this must be achieved by the psyche without appeal to other mental processes that take it for granted, the genesis of consciousness can no more involve discursive aspects of intelligence than involve sensation, perception, understanding, desire, recognition, or any other form of subject-object relations.

Hegel's account of habit provides the first crucial step in solving the problem. In feeling, the psyche has a formal unity in that the centrality of the feeling self connects all of its feelings without otherwise determining their content. What is felt is immediately given, and that it be felt by the self-same psyche does not add anything to the felt content beyond what the neurophysiology of the animal organism already provides, given its individual realization of its species being and its unique trajectory through its biosphere. Admittedly, by feeling, the psyche does mediate its mental content in that its feelings exist only insofar as the psyche feels them. Mere feeling, however, does not of itself affect the content felt or the psyche's relation to it. The mediation of feeling by the feeling psyche is as yet wholly formal.

How can the psyche overcome its own passivity and modify the content of feeling and the way it feels? Because the psyche lacks any activity other than feeling, it has no resources for modifying itself through its own activity. All it does is feel, and every feeling is equally undiscriminating, immediately registering a manifold whose further organization cannot be taken in without more developed mental operations. Consequently, if any modification is to occur, it must both be a result of nothing but given feeling and happen by nature, that is, without any further contribution by mind, which, as a merely feeling psyche, has none to offer.

Habit, as Hegel here delineates it, comprises just such a development, where, by nature, the occurrence of feeling alters the character of further feeling. The alteration in question cannot consist in any qualitative difference in the content of feelings, for each feeling is just as singular and contingent as any other. Nor is there any manner in which the content of one feeling can exhibit the prior occurrence of another feeling. Because feeling as such is immediate, one cannot feel relations between feelings, nor the mediation of feeling by anything else. Consequently, the only way feeling can be altered by antecedently given feeling is in respect to not content but form.

Yet because feeling is immediate in form as much as in content, how mind feels can be qualitatively discriminated no more than can what mind feels. All the psyche can do in relation to its feeling without qualitative discrimination is become indifferent to its content in virtue of past feeling. Becoming indifferent, that is to say, becoming habituated, involves a detachment from the content without producing a specific content alteration. Such content alteration would require a qualitative differentiation demanding more mediation than the psyche has at its disposal. In contrast, acclimatization to a feeling simply leaves its given content be. What enables the detachment to result from a prior feeling rather than be a random numbing is some family resemblance between them. That resemblance is provided by regularities in the neurophysiology of the animal organism and its interaction with the encompassing biosphere. This, rather than any activity of the psyche, allows for repetition of similar feelings, whose tie is not so much felt as reflected in the diminishment of feeling automatically occasioned by it.

Although each feeling remains as singular and contingent as ever, the psyche's involuntarily acquired detachment is mediated by the psyche's own history of feeling. This gives mind an abiding pattern of response distinct from what it feels at any moment, while rendering feeling subject to acclimatization. Generally, such habituation allows mind to withdraw from the immediacy of its feelings, making possible attending to other matters, as any further mental activities require. More directly, the automatic inurement to repeated feelings gives the psyche its first disengagement from its immediate content, rendering the psyche something with an integral character that can begin to be distinguished from the feelings it has.

Such habituation to feeling does not make mind conscious, for the habituated psyche relates to contents that still only count as elements of its field of feeling. The psyche may have gained a relative detachment from some of these, but it is not yet a fully disengaged ego, confronting determinations that not only fit within its awareness but have an independent unity. Hegel acknowledges this limitation by passing to one further development of the psyche, which is presented as the final bridge to the emergence of consciousness. This comprises the so-called actual psyche, which embodies actuality, an existence exhibiting its own essence, by having the psyche express itself in some manifestation of its neurophysiological life.

Since the psyche has no content besides feeling, its actuality here comprises an expression of feeling. Moreover, given the absence of subject-object awareness, the psyche has no desire for objects, let alone any intentions. Consequently, its expression of its own feeling cannot be intentional but can only comprise an involuntary, purely emotive gesture. In order for such gesture to occur, the psyche must, of course, have a feeling to express. That feeling, like any other, involves its own neurophysiological reality, to which it is immediately conjoined. What gesture adds is a further neurophysiological realization, which instead of being immediately one with feeling is now posited by a feeling, as its manifestation. The psyche, which detached itself from given feeling through habit, now disengages itself from its given immersion in its natural physical reality. To gesture, the psyche must figure as the underlying ground of its expression, which manifests a centrality of feeling of which it is the product. In so doing, the psyche does not become a ghost in a machine, for what gesture expresses has its own neurophysiological existence. Nevertheless, by positing a bodily expression, the gesturing psyche produces a realization distinguished from its feeling, which is comparatively inward insofar as it retains a separate existence. The gesture thus comprises a phenomenon that has a unity of its own in contrast to the self-feeling of the psyche that it expresses. All of this still proceeds within the orbit of the neurophysiological life of the psyche, which relates itself to dimensions of its own existence without yet transcending its self-communing field of feeling.

The stage is set, however, for mind to undergo one more transformation that will make it conscious. Through habit, the psyche is already able to detach itself from its feelings, in function of their universal connection with one another, a universal connection consisting in the family resemblance that allows for repetition of similar feelings. That connection is not felt as such by the psyche, which only registers their repetition by becoming detached from them. To become conscious, mind must not just extricate itself from universally connected feelings but externalize them, so that they confront mind as an independent domain. By expressing its feeling in involuntary gesture, the psyche does externalizes itself, making its feeling manifest in a distinct neurophysiological actuality. All that mind must do to be conscious is combine these developments—withdraw from its feelings and externalize them as a connected realm, confronting mind as its other. In habit, mind does withdraw from its feelings, but without externalizing them as an independent domain. In emotive gesture, mind does externalize its feeling, but without connecting its externalized feelings into a united whole. Once both capabilities are mobilized in conjunction with one another, mind is in a position to treat its feelings as the determinations of an otherness with a unity of its own and in so doing relate to itself as a centrality of feeling that is equally extricated from all of these determinations. In this way, mind is an abstracted subject relating to itself as such by externalizing its own determination as psyche, which confronts it as an opposing whole. With this, the opposition of consciousness is at hand. Because it contains the determinations of the psyche, consciousness cannot be without their preconscious mental life.

Consciousness without Intelligence

Hegel underscores the dependence of consciousness on psyche by pointing out that the minimal shape of consciousness, presupposed by all others, consists in nothing but mind relating to the determinations of the psyche as both its own and as other to it. Consciousness is minimally sense-certainty in that mind takes the determinations of feeling provided by the psyche, abstracts itself from them as a disengaged ego, confronting them as an independent whole comprising an object given to it as subject. Although the psyche has already generated universal connections in feeling and the subject of feeling through self-feeling and habit, neither concepts nor judgments play any role in enabling mind to bifurcate itself into subject and object.

Consciousness as sense-certainty relates to a manifold consisting in the psyche's self-feeling, whose singularity and contingency are just as immediately given as the relation in which mind engages in confronting this content as something other. Transformed from self-feeling into sensation, mind's mental determinations are still opaque to thought and language, even though they provide mind with a minimal consciousness of what is given to it. As sensed, the manifold does reflect all of the organization of the living individual's sense organ apparatus, as well as the configuration of the sensed biosphere. Nevertheless, the immediacy of sensation precludes consciousness from yet discriminating any of these relationships. Lacking any resource for registering the conceptual character of tangible reality, sense-certainty comprises a wholly nondiscursive subject-object awareness. It does distinguish what it senses from its sensing, so as not to revert to self-feeling, but in so doing, sense certainty knows nothing determinate about what it senses. Properly speaking, its certainty contains no determinate knowledge claims. This is why, when Hegel observes sense-certainty phenomenologically, he points out that we, the phenomenological observers, must speak for consciousness in delineating what occurs in this its minimal shape.[6]

Both perception and understanding, however, seem to involve knowledge both determinate and propositional. When perception relates to its mental content as a determination of a thing and its properties, consciousness appears to be making a judgment connecting a subject to its predicates. Similarly, when understanding reorders the content of perception through dynamic relations of force and law, consciousness seems to comprehend supersensible concepts and principles that require language and thought to be accessed.

Admittedly, in his *Science of Logic,* Hegel conceives judgment to involve concept determinations, namely, universality, particularity, and individuality. Hegel, however, is careful to distinguish quality and qualitative relations from universality and judgment. Quality involves otherness and differentiation, but not the further relationship that particulars have in participating in the same universal. Moreover, Hegel conceives both the thing and its properties and force and law as categories of the logic of essence. As such, they all lack the self-determined character of the concept and its constitutive elements, the universal, the particular, and the individual. Instead, the thing and its properties, like force and law, involve the two-tiered determinations of essence, where what posits and what is posited remain distinguished. Hence, the thing and its properties do not involve the relation of individual and universal any more than force and law involve judgment. Law may involve regularity in appearance, just as force may manifest itself in appearance, but neither law's relation to what it regulates nor force's relation to its expression involves the relations of universal, particular, and individual that bring the concept into play. A thing and its properties do not present a universal and its particularization insofar as properties contain nothing that manifests the unity of the thing. The thing does not inhere in its properties, which is why they revert to independent matters. Force, for its part, may express itself in its manifestation, but not in a way that allows that manifestation to express itself. In contrast, the universal is self-identical in the particular, which becomes universal once the universal, particular, and individual all exhibit particularity as differentiations of the universal. Finally, what is regulated by law is not a particularization of law, because all that distinguishes it is an unregulated residual content whose connection to law can only be an other, inverted lawfulness.

These logical distinctions imply that perception and understanding bring mediations into conscious awareness that may well transcend the immediacy of sense-certainty but involve neither concepts or judgments nor the discursive intelligence required for the latter's mental representation. Mind can perceive and understand the existence of objects without having to conceive or judge. Accordingly, there is no need to deny prelinguistic children and dumb animals the ability to perceive things and their properties and to understand dynamic relations and regularities among them.

Conversely, there is no need to deny that things have universality and relationships characterized by concepts, even if perceiving and understanding them need not take these concepts in as such. What is conceptually determinate about objects can still require discursive intelligence to be accessed.

By the same token, even though self-consciousness may embody determinations of the concept, as Hegel himself points out in the introduction to the Logic of the Concept, consciousness of self need not involve awareness of concepts or their verbal expression. This becomes evident on examination of the forms of self-consciousness proceeding from the most rudimentary form: self-consciousness as desire.

To confront itself as an object, consciousness must relate to its mental content as having an independent unity that equally manifests the unity of consciousness. This is most minimally achieved in purely negative fashion by consciousness of desire, where the subject, through its own mental content, confronts what is given as something to be made assimilated to the subject, to which it can offer no intractable resistance. Anyone familiar with Hegel's polemics against Kant needs no reminder of how often Hegel points to the satisfaction of animal desire as a refutation of any transcendence of the thing-in-itself. What here matters is that Hegel acknowledges the possession of desire by animals devoid of discursive intelligence. Although this would ordinarily raise few feathers, it becomes more provocative once the connection between desire and self-consciousness is recognized. If dumb animals, not to mention prelinguistic children, can have and fulfill desire, then they can be not only conscious but self-conscious. Desire, after all, involves not just awareness of an object confronting the subject but the certainty that that object can be subsumed to the subject, without any unyielding remain. This would be impossible if consciousness did not contain the psyche and the animal organism it involves. Without that, the subject could not consume any object, let alone perceive it and its relation to its own body.

If desire involves consciousness of self, but not thought, then recognition is open to non-discursive interaction between subjects. The consciousness of self provided by desire and its satisfaction is, of course, ephemeral. The correspondence of subject and object achieved by desire satisfaction is purely negative, since the object of desire gets consumed, leaving behind no tangible objectification of its unification with the subject. To obtain an abiding, positive objectification, the subject must confront an other self that the subject refrains from obliterating yet manages to have reflect its own subjectivity. Can one subject confront another and thereby be reflected back into itself without thinking or engaging in linguistic interaction?

Significantly, Hegel's celebrated account of recognitive self-consciousness makes no direct mention of either thinking concepts or expressing them in language. One self seeks to eliminate the independent otherness of its counterpart, but satisfying this desire initially consists in threatening the life of the other, something hardly requiring conceptualization or language. Given the empty result success would achieve, self-consciousness is better served if the other can be subordinated to fulfilling the desire of the subject in an ongoing manner. Does such subordination, however, require either party to think or communicate in words? Must the dominating individual verbally express his or her desire, let alone formulate it conceptually? And must the subordinated individual show subservience through some verbal acknowledgment, eliciting a conceptual recognition from the master?

If, as Hegel shows, subservience to the desire of another consists in acting to satisfy that desire, then thought and words need not be called upon. The prospective master must indicate what is desired to the individual who will serve that desire. Yet as long as the object of desire is individual and satisfaction requires an individual act, neither concepts nor their verbal expressions are needed. Further, as long as the necessary work is undertaken and the beneficiary observes the other satisfying the former's desire, no inner or outer discourse is required.

Accordingly, recognition need not involve individuals with linguistic intelligence. It can proceed among prelinguistic children, between them and intelligent adults, and conceivably between dumb animals and between them and their intelligent masters. For this reason, the self-consciousness achieved in such recognition must not be confused with the respect and self-respect of individuals as bearers of right accompanying participation in the institutions of freedom. Such recognition involves thinking, linguistic competence, and willing, none of which need be at play in the coordinated desire satisfaction of recognitive self-consciousness.

Even when self-consciousness becomes universal by relating reciprocally to another self-consciousness, no concepts need be thought or communicated. All that is necessary is that two conscious individuals mutually exhibit the desire to satisfy the desire of one another. The psyche's expressive abilities, conjoined with consciousness' awareness and desire of objects, suffice to enable one self-consciousness to be aware of itself confronting another self-consciousness engaging in the same relationship.

The same absence of thought and language applies to consciousness as reason, which is immediately certain of the identity of consciousness and self-consciousness, thanks to universal self-consciousness being conscious of an object equivalent to its own self-consciousness. Although reason proper, that is, reason as intelligence, may need the concept and the idea to *think* this identity in its truth, reason as consciousness can still be *certain* of that identity without employing concepts and language. Hegel makes this manifest in distinguishing consciousness as reason from the intelligence it structurally precedes. As a form of consciousness, reason is aware of the identity of subject and object without removing their opposition. Consciousness as reason is simply certain that its own mental determinations also are determinations of objects as they are independently given. The ego and the non-ego are opposed, but correspond, and this correspondence is what is taken as object by reason as consciousness. Having certainty of this does not involve referral to concepts or propositions as a securing bridge. It is a nonpropositional attitude in which the subject relates to its mental content as both independently given and as matching the subject. The fit is not one between concept and object but merely between the nondiscursive content of the subject and what confronts it.

Experience with children and animals may not indubitably confirm how self-consciousness and consciousness as reason can be preconceptual and preverbal. Two things that help secure this possibility come into focus as Hegel moves from consciousness to intelligence. The first is how certainty and knowledge get distinguished not as elements within conscious awareness but as signposts for differentiating consciousness from intelligence. The second matter is the account of the development in intelligence enabling mind to make and use signs. Whereas the distinction between certainty and knowledge allows for consciousness to operate without thinking concepts and using words, the latter development indicates how mind arrives at the point of thinking and speaking due to prelinguistic consciousness as well as preverbal and preconceptual aspects of intelligence.

Knowledge and Intelligence

What distinguishes the certainty of consciousness from the knowledge of intelligence are limitations underscored by Hegel in characterizing the reason arising from the unity of subjectivity and objectivity achieved in the reciprocity of universal self-consciousness. This reason as consciousness signifies only, Hegel emphasizes, the abstract, formal unity of self-consciousness with its object.[7] The unity is formal in that it in no way determines the content of what is both subjective and objective. Instead of signifying truth, this unity provides merely correctness, a correspondence in which the terms that fit are simply given, without any justification. Consequently, awareness of the correctness of any mental content is no more than certainty, a subjective assurance that mind's disengaged filling corresponds to something given, whose own truth remains undetermined. Correctness mobilizes no reasons to support correspondence, nor does it require conceiving anything universal and propositional.

In contrast, reason as intelligence comprehends the conceptual, that is, universal determination of what is both subjective and objective, which involves both thinking and linguistic competence. The truth of this knowledge will therefore have the conceptual character allowing for propositional relations. Correspondence will now be between concept and objectivity, so that truth will be idea, the unity of concept and objectivity. Unlike the givens that figure in correctness, concept and objectivity both involve self-grounded determinacies that are, as such, intrinsically connected. This enables knowledge of truth to pertain to what is determined in and through itself rather than to something posited by something else to which it is relative. It also is why Hegel can claim that only when true content becomes an object for mind can intelligence become reason in its concrete significance.[8]

Admittedly, intelligent reason takes different forms in which knowledge captures the unity of concept and objectivity with varying degrees of adequacy. In each case, however, reason concretely *theorizes*, that is, *conceives* objectivity, producing mental determinations that are just as conceptual as the object to which they correspond. To do so, mind must employ language, hence, the truth that theoretical knowledge grasps is necessarily discursive. Consciousness, in contrast, can be aware of the correctness of its mental determinations without theorizing, without working them up into a universal, conceptual content and finding that same content in its object. Accordingly, reason as consciousness can be aware of the formal correspondence between what is given in its disengaged mind and what it confronts in the world, without having anything to think or say.

Drawing this hard line between the certainty of consciousness and the knowledge of intelligence does not, however, diminish the role of prelinguistic, preconceptual consciousness and intelligence in the constitution of discursive rationality.

The Production of Signs and the Rise of Thought

Hegel's account of how mind produces and uses signs provides important insights into comprehending why thought and language depend upon processes of consciousness and intelligence involving neither concept nor word.

To begin with, mind is in no position to utilize signs unless it has intelligence, a mental activity in which the disengagement of subject and object has been bridged, without reverting to the self-communing of the psyche. Intelligence is needed, because signs require mind to attend to mental contents that, on the one hand, are externalized, and, on the other hand, signify by being both subjective and objective. Signs are externalized, in that mind signifies only by making something mental its object. Signs involve the identity of subjectivity and objectivity, in that they are at once inward and external, having meaning and reference (*Sinn* and *Bedeutung*).

The bridging broadly enabling this is accomplished via universal self-consciousness. In its reciprocal recognition, the object is another self-consciousness equivalent to the subject. This equivalency renders the object universal, possessing a character encompassing the subject opposing it, while giving the subject a form that encompasses its object.[9] The relation of subject and object is not thereby eliminated. Rather, the opposing sides each overlap their counterpart, each being aware of its unity with the other. Hegel characterizes intelligence (*Geist*) as the resultant truth that is aware of what it is.[10] It is truth insofar as it is the unity of subjectivity and objectivity, and it is aware of what it is because mind here is aware of itself in its unity with what opposes it as object.

This awareness is at work in all three of the successive stages of theoretical intelligence: intuition, representation, and thought. Feelings, which consciousness rendered sensations by treating them as determinations of objectivity confronting the ego, become intuitions when mind attends to sensations as both determinations of objects and mental contents. Intuitions become representations when mind recollects them, rendering them mediated by mind, while still retaining the dual character of being objective and subjective.[11] The image, the form intuition takes upon becoming produced and reproduced by mind, is known by intelligence to be both of something and a fixture in the mind. Concepts and language need not be involved in having and forming images. Unlike habituated feelings, which reflect the psyche, images have intentionality, presenting anew what was immediately at hand in intuition. Moreover, mind can imagine images that represent what is commonly contained in other images without attending to anything transcending the immediacy of images.[12] Representations do possess generality by abstractly subsuming intentional contents as possessions of intelligence, which relate images to one another in associative imagination.[13] But as Hegel emphasizes, this generality falls short of thought by retaining a pictorial matter,[14] derived from intuition.[15] In order for mind to conceive, to be aware of concepts as such, to think the universal, it must liberate itself from the singular content of images and do so without having already to think and converse.

By now Hegel's account has provided the resources for determining the production of signs and the move from image to thought. The psyche with the body it always encompasses allows for minds to have an intuitable reality for themselves and their productions. Consciousness enables selves to be aware of one another as subjects and objects. Lastly, the prelinguistic intelligence at work in intuition and representation enables mind to produce images as well as to relate them to intuitions and other images. Through these relations, the preverbal imagination of intelligence generates general representations,[16] lying in the common content reidentified in recollection.[17] These generalized representations and their relations to other mental contents would be purely subjective *if* mind were unable to give them an intuitable reality. Conversely, nothing worldly could be or be known to be an expression of mind unless contents can be apprehended to be both subjective and objective. To make a sign and be aware of it as such, mind must be able to generate an intuitable content, recognize it as its own product, relate it to a generalized representation that is both something mental and about something else, and recollect that relation as something mind has itself produced. The representation must be generalized, for if it remained merely singular, the intuitable content would just express an incommunicable intuition. The same is true of the relation of the sign to its representation. For communication to be possible, this semiotic relation must become generalized as a repeatable, reidentifiable link of sense and meaning.

As Hegel shows, these requirements of sign production get fulfilled through a complex mental activity in which intelligence operates in conjunction with the psyche and consciousness. Mind via the psyche produces some intuitable appearance. Via consciousness and self-consciousness, mind is aware of this production being its own. Through intelligence, mind recollects a representation, which thereby has a generalized content, common to each reidentifiable apprehension.[18] Mind relates this general representation to the former intuitable appearance. In so doing, mind takes that appearance to refer to its representation, not by anything given in its content but solely by mind setting them in relation. Finally, through verbal memory, mind makes that reference repeatable, generalizing the tie of sense and meaning and rendering the sign itself something general, transforming it from an intuition into a representation that mind can inwardly retain and reproduce.[19]

These operations bring mind to the threshold of word and thought. The contrast between sign production and symbolization is indicative of the new frontier. Because the symbol's given content relates to something in the representation to which it refers, symbolization leaves mind still beholden to imagination, not yet free of image. Intelligence can occupy itself with meanings liberated from the particularity of images only when mind knows its produced appearance to signify a general representation by mental fiat, without connection to the image of that appearance.[20] This knowledge is at hand in the production of the sign. Once verbal memory frees the sign from the immediacy of its own outer intuition by turning it into an inwardly repeatable general representation, mind can then know meaning entirely without intuition or image.[21] Meaning may still be something different from mind's inward representation of it, but through mechanical memory, mind associates represented signs independently of any distinguishable meaning, setting the stage for thought that leaves behind the opposition of consciousness.[22]

Hegel describes these developments arising through activities of intelligence that do not directly involve any relationship between intelligent selves.[23] Yet as he introduces them, sign production and verbal memory are only achievable by a mind embedded in the world and capable of giving its meanings a worldly presence. Moreover, to the degree that intelligence depends upon universal self-consciousness, sign production presupposes recognition. Still, the act of sign production does not involve any triangulation whereby individuals recognize one another fixing meanings in reference to commonly observed objects and commonly observed usage.

Sign production would succumb to problems of private language if that production were identified with language formation. As Wittgenstein would argue, intelligence cannot guarantee the communicability of the meaning of its sign simply through its own singular act of connecting an intuitable produced content with one of its own representations, or through multiple private recollections of that connection.

Although the produced content may be intuitable by others, they can no more determine that it signifies some representation than know which representation it intends.

Hegel shows his awareness of this limitation by expressly noting that sign production is not equivalent to the formation of language.[24] Sign production is not itself an act of communication. Yet can communication and thought operate without a production of signs given independently of linguistic interaction?

The answer to this question has two sides. To begin with, the production of signs cannot be a prerequisite of language and thought unless that production can be achieved without employing words or concepts. Hegel's account of sign production shows how that is the case. All that intelligence need do to produce and know the meaning of a sign is make an intuitable mental content and associate it with a general representation otherwise indifferent to that content. Although this sets intelligence free of imagined content, this freedom is still relative, since the representation signified by the sign does not yet have any positive conceptual filling.

Communicating the sign's meaning is another matter, requiring public recognition of not just the intuitable sign but its connection to some general representation. Because representation is a work of intelligence, at once subjective and objective, these two dimensions must both take public form. This occurs when minds make manifest to one another that some object given to them all is *publicly* associated with some subjective manifestation that they publicly share. Here enters the triangulation in which individuals simultaneously experience the correlation of shared semiotic behavior with commonly observed objects of representation. This shared behavior cannot communicate meaning unless each participant is producing an intuitable expression that she or he independently mentally associates with her or his own mental representation of what is commonly confronted. Otherwise, the correlation of observable behavior and observable object lacks the internal connection that allows that behavior to *signify* the general, repeatable *representation* of the object. Because this internal association is partly constitutive of communication, it does not already comprise language nor the thinking requiring language for its expression. Sign production can therefore occur apart from and prior to linguistic interaction, of which it is a necessary constituent.

In this connection, it is important to note that communication, which involves sign production and use, is not itself equivalent to language. Dumb animals may be imputed communication through signs without yet exercising the syntactical employment of signs by which communication becomes linguistic.[25]

Although Hegel does not address the formation of language, the antifoundationalism of the *Phenomenology of Spirit* and the *Science of Logic* would be contradicted if the triangulation fixing meanings determined their truth. Communication may depend upon common observation of objects and common usage of correlated signs, but this does not decide whether what is communicated is true. Massive uncertainty about reference may be precluded by the conditions of communication, but shared certainty is not equivalent to shared knowledge.

To overcome the limitations of the standpoint of consciousness, mind must use its communicable signs to think without foundations. In so doing, mind does not cease to feel, sense, or desire. Mind can and must exercise intelligence without jettisoning psyche and consciousness, both because psyche and consciousness are its enabling conditions and because both leave undetermined the truth of what intelligence thinks.

By outlining how this is so, Hegel's neglected account of the unity and difference of the psyche, consciousness, and intelligence has paved the way for comprehending the mental reality of thought with neither self-defeating dualisms nor incoherent appeals to epistemological foundations. Recovering, confirming, and elaborating the details provide an abiding agenda for the philosophy of mind.

Notes

1. See Wilfrid Sellars, *Empiricism and the Philosophy of Mind*, with a study guide by Robert Brandom (Cambridge, MA: Harvard University Press, 1997).

2. See Charles Taylor, *Hegel* (Cambridge: Cambridge University Press, 1975), 361.

3. This provides for the "primitiveness" of what Strawson calls the person, with the caveat that Strawson's nondualist conception relates to the problem of individual consciousness, without addressing that of the individual psyche. See P. F. Strawson, *Individuals: An Essay in Descriptive Metaphysics* (London: Methuen, 1979), 101 ff.

4. G. W. F. Hegel, *Philosophy of Mind*, being *Part Three of the Encyclopaedia of the Philosophical Sciences (1830)*, trans. William Wallace, together with the *Zusätze in Boumann's Text (1845)*, trans. A. V. Miller (Oxford: Oxford University Press, 1971), addition to §440, 180; addition to §441, 181; §445, 188.

5. Hegel, *Philosophy of Mind*, §387, 25; addition to §387, 26.

6. G. W. F. Hegel, *Phenomenology of Spirit*, trans. A. V. Miller (Oxford: Oxford University Press, 1977), 59–60.

7. Hegel, *Philosophy of Mind*, §437, 178.

8. Ibid.

9. Ibid.

10. Hegel, *Philosophy of Mind*, §439, 178.

11. The contrast between intelligence and consciousness is manifest in how representation starts not from objects but from intuitions to which it stands in relation. See Hegel, *Philosophy of Mind*, §451, 201.

12. Hegel, *Philosophy of Mind*, §455, 206.

13. Ibid., §456, 209.

14. See G. W. F. Hegel, *Logic*, being *Part I of the Encyclopaedia of the Philosophical Sciences (1830)*, trans. William Wallace (Oxford: Oxford University Press, 1975), remark to §20, 29–30.

15. Hegel, *Philosophy of Mind*, §456, 209.

16. Just as habit confers a universal character upon feeling and perception renders the object a universal nexus of properties, so remembrance gives intelligence a universal mental content by referring an image to a recollected intuition, rendering that image a representation whose content subsumes that intuition. In this respect, representation proper is already imbued with universality, albeit still conditioned by the image. See Hegel, *Philosophy of Mind*, §454, 205.

17. Hegel, *Philosophy of Mind*, addition to §451, 202.

18. Ibid.

19. Hegel, *Philosophy of Mind*, §461, 219.

20. Ibid., addition to §457, 212.

21. Ibid., addition to §461, 219.

22. Ibid., addition to §464, 223.

23. Ibid., §458, 212.

24. Ibid., §459, 214.

25. See, for example, Karl Popper, who distinguishes the communication of animals from bona fide linguistic competence: Karl Popper, *The Open Universe: An Argument for Indeterminism*, from the *Postscript to the Logic of Scientific Discovery* (Totowa, NJ: Rowman and Littlefield, 1982), 122; Karl R. Popper and John C. Eccles, *The Self and Its Brain: An Argument for Interactionism* (London: Routledge, 1998), 58–59.

Part 3

Identities and Differences: Peoples, Genders, and Nations

Chapter 6

Changing Identities: Dialectical Separations and Resisting Barriers

Angelica Nuzzo

A striking, unsettling feature of the contemporary world order is the falling and rising of separation barriers—walls and defensive fences, material and virtual, and political and symbolic borders. A permanent phenomenon in world history displays today some hitherto unknown characters. Indeed, the present epoch, while priding itself on seeing its inception in 1989 with the fall of the Berlin wall, and of bearing witness to the dissolution of the apartheid regime in South Africa, thrives in the fluid geography in which yet and again new barriers rise, new boundaries are drawn, and borders are increasingly fortified. The latest manifestations of such strategies are the ongoing erection of the Israeli-Palestinian wall and the progressive closing of the U.S. border to "aliens" of all origin-ultimately, the project of a "virtual" wall enclosing the U.S. territory. The politics of fortifying borders reveals that identity in our world has become a threatening and precarious entity—that it indicates indeed a somehow new problem.

The process of drawing boundary lines is, in general, an attempt to establish identity. It is one of the ways in which individuals and peoples seek to affirm their identity, positioning themselves within a territory that without borders would appear indeterminate and hence easily threatened. Identity seems to need separation; it seems to require the creation of difference.[1] This is why barriers and walls and limits and borders are there—material or symbolic marks of difference for the sake of identity. And yet another common experience of our present time reminds us that separation ultimately kills identity, that it underscores the lack of any determinate identity other than the separation line itself. The very need to be enclosed by visible or at least recognizable boundaries betrays the fact that identity itself is not there, that identity is not itself visible or recognizable or felt, and that it is threatened or lost or maybe has simply never existed. Moreover, history teaches us that boundaries, as more or less arbitrary political or social constructions, are there to be crossed, to be moved, to be constantly challenged and redesigned. To be sure, boundaries do not enclose a pre-existing fixed identity; they attempt to create one for the first time. The tale often told about the defensive function of borders is only a retroactive ideological construction—there is no preexisting identity to be defended before the dividing line is drawn. The border is created in order to attain identity; only afterward does the precariousness of such identity seem to justify the ascription of a defensive function to the border.

And yet building walls is not the only strategy through which identity can be established. *Culture*—that, which the Germans since the Enlightenment have called first *Bildung* and then *Kultur*—is another, essentially different way of pursuing identity for peoples and individuals. In general, the cultural way to identity ignores material or political borders, is inclusive of difference instead of exclusive, and appeals to the value of "freedom" instead of self-defense.

Given these two alternative models of identity construction, some of the questions that our contemporary world poses to us philosophers are: What is the logic underlying the process of building walls and erecting fences—separation barriers between individuals and peoples meant to assert, in the first place, the existence, the value, or the right of individuals or peoples *within* in opposition to those *without*? And what is, on the other hand, the logic followed by the cultural way to identity aiming at overcoming borders and separations and establishing an identity inclusive of difference? How do the concepts of identity and difference relate, more precisely, to these processes? And, more pointedly, has Hegel's speculative logic anything to offer to our attempts at a philosophical understanding of this contemporary engineering of identity, one of the most salient traits of the present global age?

This is the background and these are the questions that will be discussed in this chapter in their purely logical and abstract form. I will use the analysis of three crucial moments of Hegel's *Science of Logic*, taken, respectively, from the Logic of Being, the Logic of Essence, and the Logic of the Concept, to indicate three alternative models or strategies through which identity (in relation to difference) can be achieved. The progression instituted by the dialectical movement of Hegel's logic will allow us to assess the limits and flaws of the first two models (identity through construction of borders and merely formal identity) in contrast to the third (identity through freedom and culture). Ultimately, my analysis aims at showing the methodological validity of Hegel's dialectic for an understanding of contemporary political reality. Although the discussion of the contemporary scenario will presently remain in the background, it will nonetheless influence my rendering of Hegel's logical language. My conclusion is, first, that the topic of identity and difference is much more pervasive in Hegel's logic than is generally recognized by an analysis limited to the moment of "identity" as "determination of reflection" in the sphere of Essence, and second, that Hegel's *logical* solution of the problem of identity and difference consists in a dialectical progression of three movements corresponding, respectively, to the spheres of Being, Essence, and the Concept. The reality of subjectivity and spirit—the world of the psychological reality of the individual self as well as the world of the political and historical reality of states and peoples—is the actual instantiation of this complex logic.

Identity and Difference: The "Real" Significance of Hegel's Speculative Logic

On Hegel's view, speculative logic replaces traditional logic, namely, the science of the abstract laws of thinking, and it offers the new and "true" form that metaphysics finally assumes in the aftermath of Kant's transcendental logic.[2] Placed in the aftermath of Kant's critique of metaphysics, speculative logic can no longer be ontology. In the framework of Hegel's dialectic, the traditional ontological inquiry into the forms of *Ens* yields to the immanent development of the spheres of Being and Essence as the dimensions in which truth progressively shapes itself. Speculative logic is logic of "objective truth." It is not concerned with (subjective) thinking in its thinking of something that *precedes* thought and is *independent* of it, namely, an original *Ens* in general or Being as such. Rather, logic is the science of thinking that thinks itself in the pure dimension of truth in which thinking and reality are utterly identical.[3] Thereby, thinking eventually constitutes itself as subjective thinking, namely, as the "subject" that thinks and acts in the world of nature, of collective institutions, and history. Hegel's speculative idea of logic grounds his view of the system of philosophy as comprising an exhaustive reconstruction of the natural and spiritual universe in all of its manifestations. The determinations and forms that thinking successively displays in the different spheres of the logic are, at the same time, essential structures of reality. They constitute the internal framework or the supporting "skeleton"[4] underlying the manifold manifestations of nature and spirit. The pure forms or "determinations" of the logic are the bare bones whose shape and inner constitution are responsible for the direction taken by the development of nature's and spirit's manifold reality.[5] This is a possible reading of Hegel's famous claim of the rationality of the actual.[6]

The treatment that the concepts of identity and difference receive in the *Science of Logic* discloses the ways in which Hegel's dialectic is meant to function as methodological tool for any further investigation and understanding of the real world in its natural and spiritual manifestations. As "determinations of reflection," identity and difference are placed, thematically, at the very beginning of the Logic of Essence—the second division of the Objective Logic. Herein, Hegel takes up again—after the Jenaer writings (in particular after the 1805–1806 *Logic and Metaphysics*) and after the 1807 *Phenomenology of Spirit*—his long-standing critique of the empty tautologies constructed by the understanding in the name of the principle of identity (as well as his attack on Schelling's model of *Identitätsphilosophie*, which swallows all difference into the indistinct night of identity—the famous night in which all cows are black). Thereby, he repeats his critique of the formalism of traditional logic, of its stubborn separation and fixation of identity and difference. Identity cannot be thought independently of difference, since the difference that allegedly separates identity from difference becomes, contradictorily, the fundamental determination of identity itself. In addition, the formal law of identity with its predication of an empty and tautological A = A is unable to provide any content to identity as constituting, synthetically, a thing's "essence." What identity is (or what constitutes the identity of something) must somehow be presupposed (empirically and arbitrarily) in order for it to be declared identical to itself. Thus the *pendant* to those formalistic tautologies is sheer empiricism.[7] This remark holds true for Hegel's construction of the problem of identity in his speculative logic. What is it, in its objective content or determinateness, that constitutes the identity declared by formal logic identical to itself?

Hegel's own dialectical formulation of the notions of identity and difference as determinations of reflection has implications that reach far beyond a speculative revision of formal logic. His idea of identity illuminates the manifold ways in which the inseparable pair of identity and difference shapes the world of nature and in particular the world of spirit taken in its (human) finitude. Hegel's criticism of the formalism of the principle of identity occupies the middle position between the development of the Logic of Being and the Logic of the Concept. It is in light of this middle position that the determinations of identity and difference must be read in order to disclose their full speculative potential.

Hegel's purely logical articulation of the notions of identity and difference provides the "inner simple framework" on which finite spirit or finite subjectivity weaves its manifold real forms and attitudes, thereby becoming "real" subjectivity. The far-reaching—spiritual and even political—implications of Hegel's logical account of identity and difference can be gained only by reconstructing the "genesis" or the prehistory of these determinations within the Logic of Being. In particular, it is important to acknowledge that the first seed of the "essential" notion of identity lies in the dialectic of *Etwas* and *Anderes* and of *Grenze* and *Schranke* that constitutes the movement of the finite. Dialectical identity finds its birthplace in the logic of drawing boundaries and building defensive barriers with which the "One" (or better, the still indeterminate and indefinite "something," the mere *Etwas*) replies to the unavoidable encounter and confrontation with the "Other" (*Anderes*). Identity and difference have their dialectical origin in this very early moment of the Logic of Being; they are, to be sure, the concrete, essential "result" of their *Aufhebung*. As the confrontation between something and other leads to the dialectic of limit and barrier, it secretly or covertly (since we are still at the level of Being which, as such, lacks all reflection) aims at constituting their identity and, at the same time, at defining their difference; hence, Hegel's claim that the "something" is the "beginning"—indeed, "only the beginning"—"of the subject."[8] Such beginning must be superseded by the thematization of both identity and difference in the sphere of Essence, which will disclose their mere empty formality. Ultimately, however, a more advanced strategy of building identity and difference will be at work at the level of the Logic of the Concept. At stake here is one of the fundamental features of (the logic of) subjectivity.

In the following three steps of my argument, I discuss three different logical strategies or modalities through which dialectic constitutes identity and difference as fundamental structures of all finite "objectivity" and "subjectivity." I analyze first the aforementioned moments of the logic of Being (and more precisely of *Dasein*) and then turn to the analysis of the *Reflexionsbestimmungen* in the Logic of Essence. My suggestion herein is not that the former simply anticipate the latter (or that essence truly comes before being). My contention is that the essential notion of identity is constituted through the movement of the logic of the finite up to the determinations of limit and boundary. The identity that first defines for reflection what essence is is nothing other than the *Ge-wesen-sein*—the logical past as it were—of finitude constituted through the process of drawing its limits and overcoming its barriers. Dialectically, boundaries do not defend a preexisting identity but first institute it. Third, I show how in the transition from Essence to the sphere of the "concept" (*Begriff*) and in the immanent articulation of the moments of the concept Hegel offers a thoroughly different model of identity that proposes itself as the real alternative both to the building of barriers and defending walls and to the merely formalistic view of identity. At stake is a logic of identity and difference instituted through freedom and culture—a notion of identity *as* freedom and culture. This final form of identity that truly integrates difference (and no longer opposes it) is the logic of "individuality" as moment of *Begriff*, namely, the logic of "concrete universality."

The Identity of Being:
Drawing Limits and Overcoming Barriers

The initial movement of the Logic of Being aims at securing a first qualitative determination against the unstoppable fluidity of "being" and "nothing" continuously merging into each other in a "becoming" with no direction (whereby they also are absolutely identical to one another in the total absence of a difference separating them). Such movement eventually lands on the notion of *Dasein*. Hegel notices that, "etymologically," *Dasein* alludes to a first spatial determination: Being is saved from the whirling flux of becoming by being rooted or positioned in a "certain place." And yet, since Hegel immediately adds that no "spatial representation"[9] belongs to the present logical stage, we must conclude that the first determination of being is to be rooted in a place with no space. Such is merely logical *Da-sein*. Similarly, as we will see, the beginning of the Logic of Essence will establish *Wesen* etymologically as the recollected "past" of being, that is, its *Ge-wesen*. And yet, Hegel will immediately correct, what we have here is a past with no time.[10] Thus dialectically the issue of identity and difference plays itself out between a place with no space and a past with no time. It will be the task of the "real" (or more precisely *real-philosophisch*) figures of spirit to add space and time and geographical and historical coordinates to its merely logical determinateness, for these are the cornerstones of spirit's "concrete" identity, the tools for the construction of all (geographical and historical) difference. In other words, in the logic Hegel discloses the dialectical rationale of spirit's striving for localization and rootedness in space and time: its need, on the one hand, for appropriating a portion of external reality that it calls its own—first its own body, then its own private property, and finally its belonging to a social and political community—and its need, on the other hand, to indicate its belonging to the continuum of history and tradition. Thus the very beginning of the Logic of Being and Essence brings to the fore respectively the structural ground of spirit's relation to place and history as necessary requisites for any enterprise of building identity and discerning difference. Without the moments of *Dasein* and *Gewesensein,* no "real" determination would be possible but only the indistinct flux of becoming.

Within the nonspatial space of *Dasein,* being emerging from the indistinct becoming is in search of determination. Its subsistence or existence, its "reality" (*Realität*)[11] as it were, or the very possibility of claiming a defining "identity," entirely hinges upon the possibility of being determinate as "something"—*Etwas.* Thus the issue of "determination" dominating the first stage of the Logic of Being is clearly the true "presupposition" of the problem of identity and difference which, as a problem of "reflection," Hegel thematizes only successively, at the level of essence.

Hegel brings our attention to the fact that the type of determinateness that actually confers "reality" to being is not just any determination (e.g., merely empirical features that may contingently be attached to being, such as skin color, sex, or age) but is rather a conceptual reality that, logically, is able to claim a certain defining "value"[12] *in relation to something else* (or to something *other*). Thereby, the issue of *Grenze* comes already to the fore.[13] Beyond the traditional logical problem of individuation and beyond Spinoza's ontological principle of *omnis determinatio est negatio,* at stake for Hegel is the question of what guarantees the "substantiality"—in the sense of the Latin "*subsistere*" as the survival—of the "individual." How is individuality constituted in its individual identity in order to subsist or to survive in its being-there (*Dasein*), that is, in order not to be swallowed back into the indistinctness of becoming? The task is to determine where something *ends,* what its limit is, whereby such limit ultimately retains a privilege over any other defining mark that something may display. "The individual—contends Hegel—is relation to itself insofar as it imposes limits on everything else; but thereby these limits are also its own limits; relations to other"; which means that the individual "does not have its own *Dasein* in itself."[14] Paradoxically, the strategy of gaining identity by drawing limits leads to a sort of eccentric identity—that is, an identity that is not placed in oneself but is somewhere else, namely, in the difference, in the different Other defined precisely by the limit. At this point, however, with an eye to the further development of his Logic, Hegel recognizes that such strategy does not get to the heart of the problem of what the individual in its true assertion of identity, is. "The individual is indeed *more* than that which is enclosed on every side; but this "more" belongs to another sphere of the concept."[15] Thereby, Hegel indicates the way in which the problem of identity runs through the three different spheres of his speculative logic. The strategy proper to the logic and "metaphysics of being"[16] goes only so far as construing individual identity as a fortress completely enclosed by limits and defended on all sides against the different Other. The problem with such an identity, however, is already indicated at this stage by Hegel's dialectic. It is, for one, an eccentric, always displaced or negative identity, and it is, for another, a reductive identity that is unable to express what identity is properly meant to express, namely, true individuality, hence, the merely negative, utterly destructive movement of the understanding that ultimately erases all determination and difference and sinks identity into the sheer formality of an empty tautology, the abstract A = A, the principle of identity that comes to the fore in the Logic of Essence.

When *Dasein* claims itself as "something" existing—namely, as *Daseiendes*—a first "difference" (*Unterschied*) is established as a "difference that can no longer be left out since it *is*."[17] The dialectic of identity and difference is already here in place. The identity of being resides in its being different, in its being a different, discrete *Etwas*, something that has negativity in itself as "posited," not just an abstract determination.[18] To be sure, such negativity of being is the first occurrence of the "negation of negation" proper to dialectic and signals, at the same time, the first emergence of the "subject"—the "beginning of the subject."[19] For "something" is what it is only by negating the (negativity of its) difference to other, that is, by restoring simple self-identity within itself. This is the general logic of the limit—*Grenze*—that characterizes finitude as such. The dialectic of the finite develops through three moments that describe what I previously called the "genesis" or the prehistory of the movement of identity and difference as determinations of reflection. These moments are (1) the dialectic of "something" and "other"; (2) the inner movement of *Grenze* as the strategy of drawing limits and of enclosing oneself in them; and finally (3) the constitution of the finite in the terminal moment of the barrier or *Schranke* and in its inherent open-ended movement of transgression—*Sollen*.

(1) At the level of being, Hegel presents the logic that constitutes individuality (or the subject) by determining its identity to itself through its difference from an alien other. The first step of this strategy is the distinction between "something" and "other."[20] Something receives its identity only in relation to the other as specifically *its own* other. Thus paradoxically the identity of being is the relational being of "*Sein-für-Anderes*"[21]—one's being projected toward the other, immediately and entirely absorbed in the relation to the other as that which constitutes what one is. But if we are what we are only insofar as we are different from the other, then we owe only to the other what we are as distinct and different from the other. The *identity* that is meant to distinguish us from what we call the other comes not from us (internally) but from the other. In this relation to the other, the *difference* between the something and the other is erased. The other is other only for us; what makes it into a distinct other is its being tailored to our own need for identity and, correspondingly, to our own need for difference. The other is as much our own construction as our own identity is the product of the other. Moreover, the something, being what it is only in relation to the other, is ultimately identical to the other. Thereby, the "identity of *Ansichsein* and *Sein-für-Anderes*"—the identity of self-identity and relation to a different other—is posited. On this ground, Hegel claims that the other is the "other of itself"—the crucial dialectical figure of "*das Andere seiner selbst.*"[22] At the very beginning of the Logic, this figure already expresses Hegel's fundamental, seminal critique of the traditional, undialectical separation of identity and difference. In the dialectic of something and other, the identity constituting the subject already displays both a *relational* and a *reflexive* structure. Hegel underscores the fact that the possibility of even seeing the crucial moment of "being-for-other," the real turning point of the relation between something and other, is a discovery of the dialectical presentation of speculative logic, a moment that was entirely lacking in traditional logic and metaphysics.[23] Such moment remains as the basis of all dialectic of spirit and self-consciousness. In this realm, the abstract figure of the "other" in relation to which all spiritual, self-conscious identity needs to measure itself will display a more concrete face (that of the other self-consciousness engaged in the struggle for

recognition: master or slave, or that of the other family member or of the citizen of our same community or of another state). But the relation to the other will either follow the elementary logic of being or grow out of the more complex logic in which the logic of being is superseded.

(2) In the second moment of the dialectic of finitude leading to the constitution of the limit, the distinction between something and other appears as the distinction between an internal and external dimension of self-identity. As such, it determines, more specifically, one's (ethical) behavior and attitudes. It is the moment that Hegel indicates as "*Bestimmung, Beschaffenheit*," and their culmination: "*Grenze*."[24] The "determination" or *Bestimmung* is, Hegel explains, the "affirmative determinateness" (*Bestimmtheit*) that constitutes one's own identity. As such, it appears as the internal *Ansichsein* that we cherish as something to which we "remain faithful" in an existence that sees us constantly and unavoidably entangled (*Verwicklung*) with the other, always compromising with him or her. Although the other is still always determining us (and is indeed changing who and what we are), we consider our determination as something fixed, as that in which we "preserve" our inner integrity, remaining identical with ourselves (*Gleichheit mit sich*) against our changing environment. In our determination we proudly prove our value and make ourselves heard in our relation to the other—in our *Sein-für-Anderes*.[25] However, the determination in which we choose to locate our identity (our human identity in opposition to animals, in the first place)[26] is nothing more than a sort of empty "place" that we constantly need to fill with our action, a mark we need to live up to.

While Fichte proposed under the "*Bestimmung des Menschen*" a lofty ideal of human moral "vocation," Hegel's dialectic uncovers the hidden hypocrisy of such a position. With the idea of man's *Bestimmung*, Fichte meant to lend concrete content and individual determination to Kant's formal moral imperative thereby tying the notion of freedom's realization to the movement of a progressive extension of individuality and its limits. Following one's moral vocation, man extends the domain of his individuality in the world.[27] Hegel suggests instead that the notion of *Bestimmung* is still too distant from that of freedom. What we call our inner vocation is nothing but a way of marking out our alleged identity, drawing a protective boundary between ourselves and the other, thereby reserving an empty place that our action should fill. The gap between the moral "ought to" and the reality of freedom is not closed by the arbitrary vocation that Fichte claims for each individual. The Kantian gap stands still wide open. Moreover, Hegel shows how the very notion of vocation or determination is not sufficient to define who and what we are, for, to our determination is opposed our "*Beschaffenheit*," namely, the external part of ourselves, that part of ourselves that we present to others and to the world. We may certainly (and hypocritically) decide not to count this part of ourselves toward identity as it is subject to the influence of the other and can always change. Our *Beschaffenheit*, however, is still there despite our efforts, *daseiend*. This side of ourselves is the side in which identity is compromised with difference, the self with the other, the ideal with the real. It is that part of ourselves that may change and become completely other.[28] Therefore, Hegel ironically concludes that our *Bestimmung*—if it wants to remain pure and fixed as what we claim it is—must remain "indifferent" to our *Beschaffenheit*.[29] Hegel's suggestion is that the external, changing side of the "something" ultimately threatens its inner determination to the point that the "something" dissolves itself under the external pressure of the other even before its identity is fully constituted. This dissolution, however, is an essential moment within the dialectical process through which true identity is established. Dialectically, to be something is to become other: ultimately, "determination is as such open to the relation to other."[30] In our contemporary multicultural societies, we constantly experience this dialectic of determination and constitution, of inner vocation and external compromise. Ethnical "purity" or segregation becomes unmanageable in a world in which everyday life makes the contact with the other inevitable. Hegel's dialectic shows that negotiation with the other necessarily changes the self in its deepest constitution. Ultimately, in order to gain an identity of its own, the self must consent to negotiate a compromise with the other. Dreams of colonization end up backfiring on the purity of the message that we intend to export and to impose on others. In the process, we become the other of ourselves.

As the separation of inner vocation and external constitution vanishes, the difference between ourselves and the other becomes blurred: We no longer know where our "being" ends and where the other's "being" begins. At this point, we need a different strategy for signaling the point of distinction between ourselves and the other. The further stage of this process of achieving one's identity through distinction from the other is the act of fixing a limit, a boundary, or a border (*Grenze*), whereby that open relation to the other is repealed, and the separation between something and the other is made into a "real" barrier.

Two peoples such as the Israeli Jews and the Palestinians cannot be distinguished and really divided by their respective alleged "vocation," for this ultimately translates into acts of violence that are indistinguishable in their results. Thus in order for the two peoples to be effectively separated, the ideality of the vocation yields to the reality of a material dividing boundary, of a wall erected in order to separate the two peoples. Against the confusing entanglement with the other, a boundary is drawn, a border declared.[31] According to this logic, identity must gain clear-cut limits in order to be "real." The limit, however, dialectically expresses the "ideal"[32] coexistence of identity and difference, that is, the deeper contradictory character of the finite. The limit is the mark that is meant to make the separation—or the difference—between the something and the other a visible, hard one. The limit visibly tells where something ends, where its claims must yield to the other's existence. The limit sets something "against" the other; it defines the zone in which the other is excluded, since its *Nichtsein*—its nonexistence—is posited.[33] In the limit, the presence of the other is, at the same time, sanctioned and erased. The limit not only makes the something different from the other but sanctions this difference in the sphere of *Dasein* (it gives to such difference a place—albeit one without space): The limit is the place where the other cannot dwell nor exist but from which it should be expelled. And yet this exclusion is precisely that which calls the other into existence. This exclusion is necessary to the identity or the subsistence of both the something and the other.

The limit has two sides; the border is a double-edged weapon. When considered from the other side of the border, the excluding something is itself an excluded other. The defensive border is truly a barrier that sanctions the finitude of one's being, namely, its not being admitted to the other side. Existence, in the realm of the finite, is always qualified as existence "within" or "without" the border.[34] Thereby, the limit is the "place" in which an egalitarian "contradiction" is instituted.[35] It is the virtual place where "something and other *both are* and *are not*."[36] The limit is the "middle" and the (mediating) "in between." Ultimately, only the limit exists in this space in between: Both the something and the other "cease to be." Thus the limit or the border is the place where identity—far from being established—is instead *suspended*. Identity lies only in the promise of reaching "beyond" the limit, of having passed it (or transgressed it). And yet the limit is the place where the contradictory situation of a "common differentiation" (*gemeinschaftliche Unterschiedenheit*) is sanctioned; it is a meeting point where a differential "unity" is found. Here "identity" becomes, for the first time, "double." Identity is properly "only in the limit"[37]—it exists only at the border, in the act of showing one's documents, in the act of "declaring" (*aussprechen*) what one's being is.[38] Identity vanishes in its individual discreteness once the border is crossed, once the threat of the other or the possibility of being left "without" disappears. The limit dissolves the independent, separate identity of something and the other (and even that of their reciprocal relation, of their being one-for-the-other) and institutes a common identity—the shared moment of "being-at-the-limit," the shared experience of being "at-the-border."

(3) The movement of *Grenze* specifies the identity of the finite as not simply "determinate" but "limited."[39] In the preceding movement, the structure of the limit has cut so deep within the identity of the something as to become "immanent"[40] within the reality of the finite. Now it defines the general mode of its existence. The finite's identity is provided by what it is not, namely, by what lies beyond its limit, by what the limit negates. The limit, once immanent, becomes "essential" to the subsistence and to the surviving of the something. Thereby *Grenze* becomes *Schranke*.[41] The *Schranke* is the border that becomes a barrier terminating the sphere of one's existence; it is the *terminus* to which one's existence comes to its "end."[42] Thereby, the *Schranke* defines one's negative identity. Hegel claims that the negativity of the *Schranke* "cuts with a double edge (*ist zweischneidig*)," because what it negates is the limit once this has grown immanent into what something is. Once the limit has become an intimate part of one's identity, affecting one's very being, this identity changes and becomes the impulse to—or the "ought to"—transgress the limit. This transgression, this open-ended movement of going beyond the limit, is the *Schranke*. We do not know (reflexively) what our limited identity is—that is, what the identity that we gain by being within the protective boundaries of our *Dasein* is—until we move beyond the limit, until we transgress the border and the mere "indifference"[43] to it and we put ourselves beyond it, until we make of ourselves, once again, the "other of ourselves." Thus it belongs to the dialectical constitution of identity through the strategy of drawing limits to be *changing* identity—that is, contradictorily, exactly the opposite of what the fixation of borders aims at obtaining. To be forced within limits is precisely what instigates one to their transgression, what provokes the impulse—sometimes presented as a moral duty—to free oneself from an imposed identity that is perceived and lived, as it were, as a barrier. In the *Phenomenology of Spirit*, Hegel translated this dialectical situation in terms of the

experience of self-consciousness: "The self-knowing spirit knows not only itself, but also the negative of itself or its limit: to know one's limit is to know how to sacrifice oneself."[44]

Not only the optimism of Fichte's "vocation" fails to liberate individuality from its limits, positing instead the unavoidable reality of the *Grenze*, but Hegel's dialectic of the limit shows that an existence confined into boundaries can no longer liberate itself from them; the limit grows into an immanent qualification of one's own being—into *Schranke*—to the point that transgression of the limit turns into one's own extreme vocation.

The experience of the limit becoming a border or barrier and defining an identity is common in our city life. Think of the role of railroad tracks in our cities. They are classic examples of borders exercising an active influence on the surroundings (and not being merely passive edges), so much so that they came to stand for social borders defining the identity of those who live, as it were, "on the other side of the tracks." In cities, borders represent barriers, dead ends—railroad tracks cannot be crossed except at designated points; they define the limit of neighborhoods because the activity and uses that characterize the neighborhood terminate at the border. Yet the very existence and defining power of the barrier produce the need to cross it—to move to the other side of the tracks.

Thus Hegel's dialectical articulation of the strategy of determining identity in the modality of the ideal space (without real space) of *Dasein*, culminating in the defensive (and indeed offensive) procedure of drawing limits, shows in the transformation of *Grenze* into *Schranke* the inevitable collapse of identity proper to finite being, the *impasse* of a way of thinking identity in terms of the mere qualitative determination of one's being set against the other's. What the limit fixates as one's identity is subject to the (human) impulse—indeed, to the self-imposed moral determination—to go beyond the limit, to radically negate that identity. However, the *liberation* from the limit that Hegel indicates as the very result of the logic of *Grenze-Schranke* is still only a formal, merely negative liberation. The structure of *Sollen*, the "ought to" that leads individuality on to an endless reproduction of the limit, is unable to guarantee the real, achieved actuality of identity. Herein Hegel's criticism of Kant's moral imperative reduces the famous empowering formula "you can because you ought to" to a mere expression of powerlessness: "You cannot precisely because you ought to."[45] As *Sollen* is unable to reach the reality of moral freedom, it becomes for Hegel the weak justification for a task left unaccomplished. In action's striving for an unattainable ideal perfection, identity remains an indefinite postponement. The movement of *Sollen* is only the indistinct, open-ended task of erasing limits producing neither the positive gain of a new identity nor a positive difference. The beginning of the Logic of Essence will further pursue this formalistic dissolution of identity.

The Identity of Essence: Different Identity and Identical Difference

"The truth of being is essence"[46] is the famous beginning of the second sphere of the Objective Logic. Essence is the movement of cognition that in search for the truth of immediate being, of what being is in and for itself, is carried by the assumption that "behind being there is something else than being itself, and that this background constitutes the truth of being." Hegel shows that any attempt to go behind being is nothing but thought's sinking further into it. The movement of "coming out" of the sphere of being is the process that "penetrates deeper into it." This trajectory "behind" being toward the inner depths of (its) essence indicates the way in which identity and difference are now relocated. Thus Hegel declares: "It is only insofar as knowing recollects itself (*sich erinnert*) and penetrates into itself from immediate being that it *finds* essence through this mediation."[47] Thereby two claims are made. First, the identity that dialectic construes at the level of essence develops out of the failure to establish identity at the level of being[48]—it is, logically, its "truth." Second, the attempt to gain identity in the sphere of essence is based on the "recollection" of what the movement of being has been, namely, directly to our point, on the recollection of both the confrontation with the other and the failed movement of erecting defensive borders against it. While being articulates a first semblance of identity in the a-spatial dimension of that logical "place" that is *Dasein*, essence through reflection institutes identity and difference at the heart of the atemporal memory of what is *Ge-wesen*. Such recollection is the only way that reflection has to anchor in reality its theorization of the formal dimensions of identity and difference.

Unlike the movement of *Dasein* in the sphere of being, the development of the "determinations of reflection" does not aim at capturing the determinate identity and difference that, coming from the objective constitution of being, confer to being its subsistence. The movement of the sphere of essence aims rather at isolating identity and difference as essential modes or principles of *reflection*, and then at constituting essence (and existence) accordingly. Being's identity and difference were rooted in its immanent determination. In essence, on the contrary, identity and difference determine what essence is. Herein, it is reflection that formally institutes the objectivity of essence through the ordering, categorizing forms of identity and difference. The world has an order that is reflectively expressed in the principles or forms of identity and difference; individuals are disposed in the world according to those forms (not according to the dividing lines of objective borders and limits). At stake is the problem of *conceptualizing* identity in order to structure reality accordingly. Capitalizing on the collapse of determinate identity proper to the logic of the finite, essence launches a strategy of formalistic, universalizing identity according to which it orders the universe of existing things and events. The strategy of drawing limits yields to the classification according to "principles"—identity and difference: A = A; A differs from B, hence A is also different from itself because it is not "A in general" but a "determinate A."[49] Kant's proposed use of the concept of race as a reflective, regulative concept meant to (teleologically) organize the natural realm is an example in point. No claim is made with regard to the ontological (essential) validity of the concept of racial identity; such identity, however, is not discarded but used reflectively and regulatively to establish essential differences among individuals.

To be sure, the notion of formal identity does represent a step forward with regard to the identity of being insofar as it abandons the qualitative, ontological materiality of determination still exploited by the limit. What remains of it in essence is only its dialectical "memory." Identity is essential form of reflection, not ontological determination engraved in being. Furthermore, the dialectical development of the determinations of reflection shows that any attempt to "posit" or to affirm the monolithic wholeness of essence in the name of an unmoved and unchangeable "identity with itself" or "self-sameness" is truly the beginning of its dissolution in the manifold separation of difference, diversity, opposition, and finally contradiction. Such is, for Hegel, the character of the modern world in opposition to the unity, the true original, yet irrecoverable self-identity of the ancient Greek substance. In the modern world, identity is prey of the multiform diversity of difference.[50] The identity proper to the modern age consists precisely in the way in which difference is allowed to penetrate and to internally constitute it. Ultimately, however, the dualism of essence due to reflection's holding fast to the division between identity and difference marks the failure of the logic of essence to attain the figure of free, "reconciled" (modern) individuality. At the end of essence, difference collapses into Spinoza's indistinct substance. The project of constituting ethnically "pure" societies in the name of abstract principles of identity—the abject project dominating the horrors of the twentieth century from Nazism to ethnic cleansing in Rwanda and Yugoslavia—and its necessary failure can be understood as arising from this contradictory, self-defeating logic of reflection. Difference cannot be kept out of identity. Abstract identity cannot survive.

"Essence," Hegel claims, "is [. . .] simple identity with itself."[51] Identity, as simple self-identity, defines essence, the truth of being. The suggestion of the Doctrine of Essence is that identity is to be found internally, not in relation with the other (and with one's other) but in the inward deeper dimension of (one's) being. This is the dimension that allegedly constitutes one's essence. Simple formal identity with oneself defines what one's essence is. The self-identity of essence embraces two moments. Both "otherness" (*Anderssein*) and "relation to other" developed in being are taken up again, this time as suspended (or "vanished") within the "pure self-sameness (*Sichselbstgleichheit*)"[52] of essence. Accordingly, such self-identity has a fundamentally negative character as it arises from the act of erasing all difference with which negativity relates to itself. This is, on Hegel's account, the result of the dialectic of being.[53] Repeating at the level of reflection the movement of something and other (and of being and nothing), Hegel presents identity as emerging from its "separation" (*Trennung*)[54] from difference and thereby as being inseparably constituted with difference. Identity is always infected with difference, while difference is penetrated by identity, by the temptation to unmoved fixation. The movement of identity as determination of reflection leads from a definition of identity as identical with the whole of essence to the notion of identity as "the difference identical with itself."[55] Given the formalism of essential identity, identity is the identity of anything with itself—even the identity of difference with itself.

Difference is the negativity implied by the meaninglessness of the formalism of identity. It is the "nothing expressed by the identical language" of identity. Arising from the emptiness of its identity with the whole of essence, identity must fill its meaningless nothingness with all of the figures of difference. The modern world dreams of the recovery of a safe, homogeneous identity and yet can achieve meaning (and indeed can survive) only by accepting within itself the destabilizing plurality of difference. In the painful yet necessary movement of separation with which the dream of an original identity is abandoned once and for all, the simple defensive logic of the border is entirely overcome. Difference grows from within, and no barrier or limit can keep it out. Unlike the difference of being, which was generated by the external opposition to a self-subsisting independent other against which or whom barriers could be erected, the "difference of essence"[56] is self-produced, arising out of the *reflection* of essence's mere identity with itself. Difference is the separation that breaks from within the monolithic sameness of essence. Difference and identity are not embodied in existence (*Dasein*); they are produced by and in the movement of reflection and only then "projected" onto objectivity with the pretension of constituting its essence. Identity and difference are constructions of reflection. This, however, makes the specific difficulty of the movement of essence, for the determinations of reflection require to be somehow anchored in the objective constitution of reality. The strategy of essential identity and difference replaces the procedure of drawing limits and resorting to borders with "opposition" and "contradiction." Because of their formality, the reflective determinations of identity and difference fail to grasp the richness of true *individuality* (which was precisely the problem both of Leibniz's monad and of Spinoza's substance). Moreover, identity and difference maintain their opposed interdependence; they cut within essence with no resolution or conciliation. The issue of *free*, reconciled individuality requires us to abandon the sphere of essence and to endorse the fundamentally different strategy of the Logic of the Concept.

The Identity of the Concept: Freedom and Concrete Universality

The Logic of the Concept as the "third"[57] to Being and Essence is presented by Hegel as the "realm of subjectivity or freedom."[58] The movement of being and essence is now disclosed as the "genesis" of the concept, as the history of its "becoming."[59] The logic of drawing limits, with which being tried to reach its subsistence, and the reciprocal, circular production of identity and difference within essence are the steps through which the logical subject achieves "freedom" in the dimension of the concept (*Begriff*). To be sure, what Hegel designates as *Begriff* is nothing else but the logical strategy through which subjectivity first institutes itself in its freedom. The concept's identity consists neither in its difference from its other nor in the formal difference of identity and difference that defines the depths of essence. The concept's identity is rather the dialectical process in which the moments of universality, particularity, and individuality constitute the "reality" of the concept, namely, its "concrete universality."

Hegel argues that the result of the development of essence is the "substance that has liberated itself to concept."[60] The concept is the substance that posits *within itself* the moment of absolute negativity and that "posits itself *through* the moment of absolute negativity."[61] Thereby, the concept manifests itself as "posited identity." This is precisely what Hegel calls "freedom."[62] Freedom is identity that grows from the position of absolute negativity. Hegel expresses this thought in the claim that "freedom is the very identity of the concept." Freedom overcomes both strategies of achieving identity: on the one hand, the strategy that resorts to the separation of what belongs within and what belongs without its borders and, on the other, the strategy that employs the opposition of internal/external (or essential/inessential) proper to the circle of identity and difference in essence. Freedom is the act of "positing" the "*an-und-für-sich-seiende*" identity that constitutes the necessity of substance transposing it, as it were, from the "darkness" (*Dunkelheit*) of mere mechanic and abstract causality to the open "transparency" (*Klarheit*) of an intersubjective public form of activity. Freedom is individual self-determination in the open, public dimension of universality.[63] Herein, "self-sameness" (*Gleichheit mit sich*) necessarily includes the difference generated by absolute negativity. Universality affected with negativity is not just difference but "individuality."[64] The dualistic, unresolved opposition of identity and difference, their fixation in the painful "separation" (*Trennung*) proper to essence, yields to the concept's "*Diremtion*"[65]—the procedure according to which the self-identical totality of the organism immanently differentiates itself in other different and yet identical (sub) totalities *with equal right and value*. Universality and individuality are "moments" of the overarching pluralistic reality of the concept (i.e., of its "totality").

In the sphere of the concept, "determinateness" is the moment of "particularity"—the true speculative alternative both to otherness and limit, and to essential difference. Particularity, Hegel argues, "is not *Grenze*"; it does not behave to another as a separated "beyond." Rather, it is "the proper, immanent moment of the universal."[66] In the universal, difference is not otherness but particularity.[67] There is no violent confrontation with otherness in the relation between universal and particular, no fear of otherness or of loss of one's self, no need for border crossing, no clash of identity and difference. The universal, Hegel contends, in the particular "remains absolutely with itself."[68] This is the logical structure of freedom. Particularity is the universal's immanent self-differentiation.[69] Individuality is gained in a similar way as "determinate universality," that is, as universal self-referential determination.[70] Determining itself through its moments, the universal becomes individual as "concrete universal": It is the self-differentiating, inclusive movement of freedom.

The structure of the concept—the modality of its *Diremtion*, its articulation in moments, and the culminating figure of the "concrete universal"—establishes the dialectical reality of the "system."[71] According to the speculative-dialectical logic of the system, to be an individual is to be an integral part of a "system," that is, of an internally differentiated, pluralistic, and organic totality in which (1) the whole depends on its parts (for its survival as well as for its functioning and flourishing), and (2) the parts depend on each other, namely, on their different position in the whole and on their different capacities and functions (just like the members of an organic body). Thereby, otherness and difference become fundamental ingredients of the constitution of the whole. Moreover, the mutual dependence of the different parts on each other provides the "mediation" essential to freedom. (3) Finally, the "system" is a totality that while "closed" to mere mechanical addition of entities is nonetheless "open" to organic growth and change. In other words, otherness and difference do not simply generate *Veränderung* but immanent transformation—or growth—of self-identity.

The movement of the concept differentiating itself in its moments is the process of *Bildung*.[72] Individuality constitutes itself in its universal, inclusive reality through culture. Culture is respectful appropriation for the sake of growth, the process through which the universal substance (the world, moral values, history) is enacted by the individual and thereby renders the individual truly universal. Culture does not erase otherness or difference—be it by excluding, by colonizing, or by appropriating it. Rather, it changes the attitude toward difference, building a relationship to it that eventuality opens up a vaster horizon (the concrete universal) in which both the self and the other gain a new meaning as being-for-each-other. Culture takes away the need for separating borders and dividing walls as well as the confrontational attitude proper to all unresolved, fixed "opposition." As moment of particularity and ingredient to individuality, difference constitutes the identity of the concrete universal.

Conclusion

In the previous discussion, through an immanent reconstruction of Hegel's argument in the Logic, I have shown, first, that the dialectic of identity and difference is not limited to the "determinations of reflection" but is instead pervasive of the logical process from the Logic of Being, through Essence, up to the Logic of the Concept. The dialectic of identity and difference leads to the constitution of free subjectivity (or "personality")[73] with which the Logic culminates. Second, I have argued that the three models through which identity is attained at the successive logical levels—identity by the defensive practice of drawing borders, identity as formal opposition to difference, and finally identity in difference through freedom and culture—represent three alternative strategies in which the concrete reality of spirit and self-consciousness articulates its identity in relation to otherness. While Hegel's logical argument is indeed abstract and hard to grasp, examples of failures and successes of these strategies can be found everywhere in politics, society, and history, as well as in our personal experience of citizens or, alternatively, of guests of cities and states.

The question that Hegel's Logic leaves open for our reflection and discussion is whether the solution of the problem of identity and difference provided by the structure of the concept can indeed offer a model of free individuality for our contemporary globalized and yet still deeply segregated world. It seems to me that Hegel's crucial suggestion lies precisely in the challenge of thinking identity and difference in terms of the inclusive, integrated structure of a system of mutual interdependence.

Notes

1. Accordingly, we can see the need to draw borders and to reinforce difference as the reaction against an increasingly "globalized" order that threatens with its indeterminacy the need for (local or particular) identity.

2. See Hegel, *Wissenschaft der Logik*, in *Werke in zwanzig Bänden*, ed. E. Moldenhauer, and K. M. Michel (Frankfurt: Suhrkamp, 1971), vol. 5, 61. See also H. F. Fulda, *Spekulative Logik als die "eigentliche Metaphysik"—Zu Hegels Verwandlung des neuzeitlichen Metaphysikverständnisses*, in *Hegels Transformation der Metaphysik*, ed. D. Pätzhold and A. Vanderjagt (Cologne: Dinter, 1991), 9–28.

3. See W. Jaeschke, *Objektiver Gedanke: Philosophiehistorische Erwägungen zur Konzeption und zur Aktualität der spekulativen Logik*, in *The Independent Journal of Philosophy* 3 (1979): 23–37.

4. See Hegel, *Wissenschaft der Logik*, *Werke*, vol. 6, 257.

5. A detailed development of this thesis can be found in A. Nuzzo, *Logica e sistema: Sull'idea hegeliana di filosofia* (Genoa: Pantograf, 1992).

6. See *Philosophy of Right*, preface *Werke*, vol. 7, 24; for Hegel's early position in this regard, see A. Nuzzo, "Sinnliche und übersinnliche Erkenntnis: Das Problem des Empirismus in Hegels *Glauben und Wissen*," in *Wissen und Begründung. Die Skeptizismus-Debatte um 1800 im Kontext neuzeitlicher Wissenskonzeptionen*, ed. K. Vieweg, B. Bowman (Würzburg: Königshausen and Neumann, 2003), 75–92.

7. See *Wissenschaft der Logik*, *Werke*, vol. 5, 42 ff.

8. Ibid., 123.

9. Ibid., 116.

10. See *Wissenschaft der Logik*, *Werke*, vol. 6, 13. See also A, Nuzzo, "Dialectical Memory, Thinking and Recollecting," in *Mémoire et souvenir*, ed. G. Gigliotti (Napoli: Bibliopolis, 2006), 89–120.

11. *Wissenschaft der Logik*, *Werke*, vol. 5, 118 ff.

12. Ibid., 119.

13. Ibid., vol. 5, 121.

14. Ibid.

15. Ibid., emphasis in original.

16. Ibid.

17. Ibid., 123, emphasis in original.

18. Ibid., 122.

19. Ibid., 123.

20. Ibid., 125.

21. Ibid., 127.

22. See D. Henrich's important essay *Andersheit und Absolutheit des Geistes: Sieben Schritte auf dem Wege von Schelling zu Hegel*, in D. Henrich, *Selbstverhältnisse: Gedanken und Auslegungen zu den Grundlagen der klassischen deutschen Philosophie* (Stuttgart: Reclam, 1982), 142–72.

23. *Wissenschaft der Logik*, *Werke*, vol. 5, 131.

24. Ibid., 132 ff.

25. Ibid., 132.

26. Ibid.

27. Fichte employs this Enlightenment notion in this sense in 1794; see *Bestimmung des Menschen*, in *Sämtliche Werke*, vol.6, 167–319, 279. Fichte's intention is to overcome both the formality of Kant's moral law and his separation of nature and freedom within the human being. In Fichte's notion of *Bestimmung des Menschen*, the categorical imperative is always individualized as it expresses one's own vocation through which the individual realizes itself as an individual.

28. *Wissenschaft der Logik*, *Werke*, vol. 5, 133.

29. Ibid.

30. Ibid., 134.

31. By rendering Hegel's *Grenze* alternatively with limit, border, and boundary, I want to underscore, on the one hand, the difficulty in translating this term, while, on the other hand, I want to connect Hegel's logic to the political context discussed at the beginning of this chapter—the context that represents the background of my analysis.

32. *Wissenschaft der Logik*, *Werke*, vol. 5, 136.

33. Ibid. The something "has a limit *against* the other: the limit is the *Nichtsein* of the other, not of the something itself." Emphasis added.

34. Ibid., 137. In addition, there is the intermediary figure of the "existence at the border." See *Wissenschaft der Logik*, *Werke*, vol. 5, 136.

35. At the border, the something and the other are playing the same role.

36. *Wissenschaft der Logik*, *Werke*, vol. 5, 136, emphasis added.

37. Ibid.

38. Ibid., 137.

39. Ibid.

40. Ibid.; see 142, "*immanente Grenze*."

41. Ibid., 138.

42. Ibid., 140.

43. Ibid., 142.

44. G. W. F. Hegel, *Phenomenology of Spirit*, trans. Miller (Atlantic Highlands, NJ: Humanities Press, 1990), 492. Hegel, *Phänomenologie des Geistes*, ed. Wolfgang Bonsiepen and Reinhard Heede, in: *Gesammelte Werke* (Hamburg: Meiner, 1968), vol. 9, 433: "Seine Grenze wissen, heißt sich aufzuopfern wissen"—words that must leave behind a peculiar echo in our contemporary situation.

45. *Wissenschaft der Logik*, *Werke*, vol. 5, 144 ff.

46. *Wissenschaft der Logik*, *Werke*, vol. 6, 13.

47. Ibid., 13, emphasis in original. "Erst indem das Wissen sich aus dem unmittelbaren Sein erinnert."

48. The end of the Logic of Being is the (Schellingian) moment of "absolute indifference," the radical collapse of all difference in an indifferent abstract identity.

49. *Wissenschaft der Logik*, *Werke*, vol. 6, 52.

50. See, for example, in the vast literature on the topic, R. Bodei, *Scomposizioni. Forme dell'individuo moderno* (Turin: Einaudi, 1987).

51. *Wissenschaft der Logik*, *Werke*, vol. 6, 39.

52. Ibid., 38 ff.

53. Ibid., 40.

54. Ibid., 42.

55. Ibid., 40.

56. Ibid., 46.

57. Ibid., 241.

58. Ibid., 245; also 251.
59. Ibid., 245–46.
60. Ibid., 251.
61. Ibid., 251, emphasis added.
62. Ibid.
63. Ibid., 251–52.
64. Ibid., 252.
65. Ibid.
66. Ibid., 280.
67. Ibid., 281.
68. Ibid., 280.
69. Ibid., 281.
70. Ibid., 296.
71. See A. Nuzzo, *System* (Bielefeld: Transcript Verlag, 2003).
72. See, for example Hegel, *Werke*, vol. 3, 13 ff.
73. See, *Wissenschaft der Logik*, *Werke*, vol. 6, 549, 564.

Chapter 7

Hegel's Conception of an International "We"

Andrew Buchwalter

Well known though he is for his arguments supporting notions of collective social and political identity,[1] Hegel is generally presumed to advance no arguments in support of collective identity at the international or global level. Indeed, he appears to suggest that such arguments are entirely without merit. On this view, the international order, to the extent that such a concept is even meaningful, is for Hegel comprised of wholly sovereign and self-sufficient nation-states whose existence renders not only unachievable but unintelligible supranational political structures. Indeed, Hegel is assumed to support an account of interstate relations more typified by Hobbes's war of all against all than the cosmopolitan comity articulated in Kant's idea of perpetual peace. To be sure, not all espousing this view assert that Hegel himself is a Hobbesian.[2] Precisely because assertions of state sovereignty are unintelligible without acknowledgment and respect by others of those assertions, he is recognized to claim that interstate relations depend on processes of cooperation and reciprocity not accommodated in "realist" accounts of international relations, at least those that focus on power alone.[3] But in keeping with the apparent exclusionary and "atomistic" nature of his view of interstate relations, such cooperation and mutuality are largely of an instrumental sort, committed to preserving and consolidating the independence and sovereign prerogatives of self-sufficient national-political units. At most, states, on this view, enter into treaty relations with one another. Yet treaties (*Traktate*) are themselves adopted and accepted only to safeguard strategic self-interest, and, as with Hegel's account of contractual relations generally, will readily be disregarded and even breached as they cease to serve state interest.[4] That international relations may be guided by notions of common purpose or shared transnational identity is a view that appears to occupy little place in Hegel's thought. One distinguished Hegel scholar recently expressed this sentiment when claiming that, for Hegel, "there is no international 'We.'"[5]

In what follows I question this understanding of Hegel's position. My aim, however, is not to dispute that realism plays an important role in Hegel's account of international affairs. I argue instead that Hegel's position is not exhausted by the realist approach. I do so by noting that Hegel's *Äusserstaatsrecht*—the external law of states or the external public law commonly (mis)translated as international law—comprises two separate, though not unrelated, components: *Staatenrecht*, what may be called interstate law, and *Völkerrecht*, the law of peoples or international law proper.[6] Both forms of law forefront nation-state sovereignty; as against Kant, Hegel assigns no place to cosmopolitan law (*Weltbürgerrecht*).[7] Yet the two have decidedly distinct foci. Interstate law addresses nation-states in their *legal-political* dimension, is concerned with the formal and external relation of states, and attends to conventionally realist issues such as power relations, treaty arrangements, and claims to sovereign inviolability. In contrast, the law of peoples—*Äusserstaatsrecht* in its "true actuality"[8]—concerns nation-states in their *cultural* dimension, is focused principally on the internal and substantive relations of nations and peoples, and accommodates structures of cooperation, interdependency, and commonality. While *Staatenrecht* dismisses as unintelligible supranational institutions and other forms of global *governance*, *Völkerrecht*—so it will be here argued[9]—accentuates not only the intelligibility but the necessity of a culturally conceived globality focused on shared purposes and a notion of common or "universal identity" (*allgemeine Identität*).[10]

My discussion is divided into three main sections. First, I explicate Hegel's culturalist notion of the nation-state, noting how claims to identity, far from championing—as with Herder—separatism and uniqueness, actually facilitate notions of global interdependency and shared identity. Special attention is given here to Hegel's rendering of cultural identity in terms of the idea of *self-consciousness*, a move that enables him to construe the interactions of nations or peoples in terms of a notion of reciprocal recognition dedicated not just to ratifying but constituting cultural identity.[11] Second, I delineate the content of Hegel's idea of a global identity, which consists in a global commitment to the *idea of right*. Here I note how Hegel reaffirms features of Kantian cosmopolitanism, but in a way that derives not from abstract principles but from attention to the conditions for the self-realization and mutual recognition of distinct and sovereign peoples. Finally, I note that the notion of right that informs the law of peoples, even as it derives from a variety of distinct cultures, is dependent on processes of interpretive application that reaffirm those differences as well. Here I argue that attention to global interdependency, far from eclipsing consideration of local and particular differences, depends for its reality on their incorporation.

In broader terms this chapter not only seeks to clarify Hegel's insufficiently scrutinized notion of global identity, a notion fully consistent with an understanding of selfhood programmatically defined as the *identity of identity and difference*, but it also aims to contribute to current discussions of such concepts as cultural identity, national sovereignty, globalization, transnationalism, cosmopolitanism, and a global public sphere, indicating how Hegelian thought can be mined to fashion solutions that eschew the rigid dichotomies that continue to beset their contemporary thematization.

I

When Hegel claims that a nation or people must be comprehended culturally, he means this in the widest possible sense—with regard to the conditions and relations that uniquely characterize a community and concretely distinguish it from others. A nation is understood first and foremost not in terms of formal legal-administrative structures. While such considerations are encompassed in the idea of a nation or people, the latter denotes the distinctive ensemble of all of a nation's attributes—"religion, the constitution, the system of justice, . . . industry, trade, arts and science, and the military world, the world of valour."[12] It is for this reason that a people is best conceived as the spirit of the people or the *Volksgeist* and why the components of a law of peoples are *Volksgeister*. Granted, Hegel occasionally employs the terms *state* and *nation* synonymously, going so far as to characterize a people as a state ("*das Volk als Staat*").[13] He does so, however, not because in the end he elects to narrow his understanding of nation but because the institutional structures associated with organized political community most effectively articulate the broader notion of cultural identity he seeks to capture in the concept of nation or people. It is in this regard that he employs the term *state* in the "comprehensive sense" of a cultural totality, one for which the state is construed not just from "the external side" but as a "wholly spiritual entity" (*als*

Geistiges überhaupt), understood as "those spiritual powers that live within the nation and rule over it."[14]

It may seem, however, that a *Völkerrecht* fashioned from the cultural identity of individual peoples is not especially hospitable to notions of transnationalism or global interdependence, let alone global identity. Indeed, it may appear even less hospitable to this end than a theory focused on the relationship of states. In its recognition of abstract claims to existence and territorial integrity, the latter at least makes reference to shared values, including those of independence, autonomy, and even respect and fairness. In contrast, the former, in forefronting the unique values and distinctive forms of life of a particular cultural community, would seem to preclude attention to any cross-cultural commonality in values or identity.[15] Hegel himself seems to suggest as much when characterizing nation-states in their cultural identity as "completely independent (*selbständige*) totalities."[16]

A closer inspection, however, reveals a more nuanced position. While Herder may advance a notion of cultural identity that champions the particularity and irreducible uniqueness of valued forms of life,[17] and while contemporary invocations of cultural identity in a similar manner often culminate in separatism and enclavism,[18] Hegel's position has just the opposite result. Recognition of claims to cultural identity not only challenges claims to complete self-sufficiency on the part of cultural entities but does so in a way that elaborately affirms forms of global interdependence and commonality.[19] The point can be made by noting the centrality of the principle of *self-consciousness* to Hegel's conception of cultural identity.[20]

Self-consciousness is important in this context for at least two reasons. First, it is the principle in virtue of which one can speak of the identity or "spirit" of a people. A nation is comprised of myriad attributes that can be related in myriad ways. It is in the collective self-understanding of a people, its apprehension of itself through these attributes, that the latter are related in the distinctive manner required to speak of a national consciousness, a unified national identity, or, as one might say today, a national imaginary.[21] Second, self-consciousness establishes for a cultural community its particular distinctiveness. In order to account for the uniqueness of a particular culture, it is not enough, according to Hegel, to appeal just to modes of external analysis and observation. While such outside perspective certainly plays a role in an account of cultural identity, the latter itself cannot be comprehensively fashioned in an exogenous manner, but must be construed as a product of a culture's own efforts at definition and comprehension.

In Hegel's language, identity must be conceived not only "in itself" but "for itself" as well. Yet such productive self-positing is just how Hegel understands self-consciousness, a process that not only sustains itself throughout its particular expressions but establishes its specific identity in the awareness of unity as sustained throughout difference. As both a unifying and distinguishing principle, self-consciousness is central to a notion of cultural identity understood as a "completely self-sufficient totality."

Appreciation of the place of self-consciousness in Hegel's notion of cultural identity is for present purposes important, because it demonstrates the degree to which Hegel's concept of national sovereignty is intertwined with a robust notion of reciprocal recognition, one that serves to constitute the identity of a particular community and in so doing global identity as well. It is a basic feature of Hegel's epistemology and his social ontology that self-consciousness and selfhood generally are understood intersubjectively. Against the tradition of Cartesian "privacy," Hegel maintains that the self is conceivable only in relation to another self, and that first self is properly known to itself only to the degree that it finds itself in the consciousness of an other. To recall the celebrated sentence from the *Phenomenology of Spirit*: "Self-consciousness achieves its satisfaction only in another self-consciousness."[22] Regarding the identity of cultural communities, Hegel argues similarly, if not with the same detail.[23] As noted, a community fully affirms its distinctiveness in its self-consciousness—in its consciousness of its own identity. Such consciousness, however, is not achieved introspectively. Given Hegel's claim, derived from Kant, that self consciousness is the identity of identity and difference, self-knowledge must acknowledge and encompass that which is other or alien to itself. It is through conscious reference to another that consciousness shapes and validates its own specific identity. In the present case, self-consciousness of a culture is properly obtained only in relation to other peoples and cultures. As Hegel writes in the *Philosophy of History*, it is in "the relationship of nations to other nations" that a people is able "to perceive itself . . . and to have itself as its own object."[24]

For Hegel, at least three things are meant by this appeal to other cultures. First, a culture must recognize cultures other than its own. Cross-cultural comparison is a basic means by which one culture can appreciate its own distinctiveness.[25] Second, the first or originating culture also must *be recognized by* another culture. If one culture is to gain a proper perspective on its own specific identity, then it not enough that it merely contrasts itself to another cultures. If that perspective is to be distinctive in an expansive way, then it must be furnished by the other culture itself. Third, the original culture must recognize its recognition by the other. With regard to the self-identity of an originating culture, it is not enough that the other simply provides a different or an alternate perspective. That perspective can serve to enrich the original culture—it can enable that culture to fashion an identity based on the identity of identity and difference—only if it is also able to find itself in the other. The originating culture attains comprehensive self-identity—it "becomes what it is"—only when integrating the other's consciousness of itself.

Hence, while proceeding from the reality of national sovereignty, Hegel does not affirm an "atomist," a self-contained, or an exclusionary view of the relationship of peoples and nations. Rather, the very assertion of sovereign self-sufficiency includes a moment of self-transcendence.[26] Although appeal to the concept of self-consciousness is meant to define what is most specific to a cultural community, its actual formulation culminates in an expanded and inclusive consciousness of self, an enlarged mentality that also serves to challenge parochial self-understandings. This is so not only because cultures require for their own identity the recognition of those other than their own; it is also because identity itself depends on incorporating diverse conceptions and self-conceptions. Cultural self-consciousness is not only self-transcending; its very identity includes a plural and even "hybrid" dimension. Nor should it be assumed that the enlargement and differentiation resulting from the recognition process simply supplement an already existing self-identity. Hegel's central point is rather that the self is fully constituted as such only in such recognition. When regarded as strictly legal-political entities, states may confront one another as fully self-contained units. When viewed as cultural entities defined in terms of self-consciousness, however, communities find their realization in recognitive processes. One nation is "completed" (*vervollständigt*) in the recognition of the other.[27] Like Herder in his own day, and with certain identity theorists today, Hegel attends to the "authenticity" of a culture. In his view, however, claims to authenticity eschew appeals to the irreducible uniqueness of cultural experience and accentuate instead that which is alien and other to itself.[28]

Hegel of course does claim that nation-states are "completely self-subsistent totalities." Yet this assertion is not inconsistent with the claim that nations also are mutually constitutive in the manner just described. This would be the case were they regarded only from an external perspective, were they regarded, as Hegel would say, only for us or "*an sich*." It is indeed as "*vollkommen selbständige Totalitaten an sich*" that they are juxtaposed in the atomist manner appropriate to a formal-legal account of their relationship. Yet cultural totalities are not properly understood only from this external perspective. They are properly understood only when also considered internally, when understood from the perspective of their own self-understanding. Indeed, it is in their self-consciousness, in the degree that they construe themselves as objects, that they claim reality and indeed self-sufficiency. The proper objects of international law are indeed "entities that are in and for themselves."[29] As we have seen, though, such self-reflexivity, for Hegel, entails intersubjectivity. Thus to acknowledge the self-sufficiency of cultural forms is also to note the degree not only that they advert to other cultures but depend on the latter's recognition for their own identity.[30] Cultural totalities are self-conscious totalities, autonomous in their consciousness of their self-sufficiency, and therefore, both on ontological and epistemological grounds, depend "on the perception and the will of the other."[31]

From the foregoing it may seem that the process of recognition has a decidedly instrumental character, one at variance with the mutuality presumably required for an account of global interdependence and commonality. That is, it may seem that recognition of or by the other is required merely to enable the originating self to achieve its own realization and fulfillment. Nor does Hegel dispute that instrumentalism is part of the recognitive process. His treatment of the master-slave relationship dramatically demonstrates how struggles for recognition can involve manipulation, coercion, domination, insult, and even annihilation. Properly construed, however, autonomous self-identity depends on a recognition process that eschews such asymmetry, that indeed aspires to reciprocity and mutuality. This is no less the case with communities than with individuals—a point Hegel makes in his unequivocal condemnation of colonialism.[32] If the recognition process is the means by which the originating community attains its identity and self-sufficiency, then this itself presupposes that it should afford the same recognition to the recognizing community. This is so not just because any comparative recognition by one culture of another requires that the other be properly understood on its own terms; nor is it just because the other community can provide a perspective on the originating community different and more expansive than that possible from a monological perspective. Hegel maintains as well that the originating culture can find itself in the other only if prepared to recognize and valorize the other as another autonomous entity. It may be that the identity of one community is completed "by recognition on the part of other states. But this recognition requires a guarantee that the state will likewise recognize those other states, . . . i.e., that it will respect their independence (*Selbständigkeit*)."[33]

Mutual recognition, however, is understood by Hegel as something more than a matter of reciprocal respect. It serves as well to fashion a common interest and a common identity. As in the relation of individuals, so too with communities: The "I" tendentially becomes a "We." Inasmuch as reciprocal recognition serves to transform initial self-conceptions in light of challenges provided by the other, and inasmuch as each is reciprocally transformed in integrating the other's conceptions and self-conception, the recognitive process sets in motion a dynamic that contributes to the formation of an enlarged self, an interpersonal or a corporate self forged in the increasing convergence of individual self-conceptions. The dialectic interchange of national self-consciousnesses contributes to a "trend . . . towards unity"[34] culminating in the universal self-consciousness that Hegel variously calls "inner universality"[35] and "universal identity"[36] The requirements of recognition on the part of particular cultural communities serve to forge a global "universal will,"[37] a common global interest that while rooted in particular notions of identity is more than their mere aggregation.

To say that Hegel is committed to a notion of collective identity at the global level is, to be sure, not to say that he is supportive of supranational political structures, be it a world state or even a world federation. His well-known arguments against forms of global governance,[38] well considered or not,[39] are unambiguous and cannot be gainsaid here. Yet the fact that Hegel puts little stock in structures of global governance does not mean that he rejects the idea of a global community or an international We. What he rejects is only its inappropriate construal. A political or an institutional construal of a global community is indeed inappropriate for a law of peoples focused on nation-states understood as cultural entities. Not inappropriate is its cultural construal, and this is how Hegel proceeds. Characteristic of "the mutual recognition of free national individualities (*Völkerindividuen*)"[40] is precisely the emergence of a shared identity focused on practices, customs, traditions, beliefs, and principles. In a law of peoples, communities are increasingly connected and defined "with respect to the universal principle of their legislation, customs, and culture."[41] What Hegel said of a universal self-consciousness generally applies as well to a universal global identity—it manifests the "cultural essentials" (*wesentlichen Geistigkeiten*) that substantively bind a community.[42] In this regard, Hegel claims that the shared values of nations expressed in a global ethos (*Sitten der Nationen*)[43] represent the principle on which a law of peoples is ultimately based.[44] It is thus unsurprising that the law of peoples culminates in an account of world history that, qua "progress in the *consciousness* of freedom,"[45] is preeminently a cultural category, at least the category in Hegel's "system" effectuating the transition from the legal-political domain of "Objective Spirit" to the more strictly cultural spheres (art, religion, and philosophy) of "Absolute Spirit." The "dialectic of . . . finitude" that governs the reciprocal relations of individual *Volksgeister* results in affirmation of a domain understood not as *Weltstaat* but *Weltgeist*[46]—not a system of global governance but a historically emergent global consensus on values and principles.

II

What, then, is the content of Hegel's culturalist account of a global identity? To answer this question we must again bear in mind the centrality of self-reflexivity to Hegel's notion of culture. The values that Hegel sees individuals and peoples embracing in accepting a law of peoples are just the conditions for their cooperation, indeed, the principles of international sociation itself. Global commonality is sustained, for Hegel, by emphatic commitment to the principle of *right*, the same principle informing Kant's own account of *Völkerrecht*.[47] Appropriate to a "universal identity" is the concept of "universal right," deemed to possess "validity in and for itself."[48] He made the point unambiguously in his *Philosophy of History*, whose relevant passage is here cited in the original: "*Die Volker wollen das Recht an und für sich; nicht bloß die besonderen Traktate gelten, sondern zugleich Grundsätze machen den Inhalt der Diplomatik aus*."[49]

This statement is especially illuminating, for at least two reasons. First, in asserting that peoples will view right as intrinsically valid, Hegel is again demarcating a law of peoples, international law proper, from interstate law. Whereas the latter attends at most to the treaties and conventions a community may embrace in pursuit of its perceived self-interests, a law of people thematizes norms that have independent standing and validity. The commonality sustaining *Völkerrecht* is not the amalgamation or aggregation of communal interests and preferences. Instead, a law of peoples is characterized by a commitment to general principles, to moral norms held to be universally binding. Indeed, consonant with the self-reflexivity appropriate to a notion of right understood as valid in and for itself, a properly construed notion of *Völkerrecht* has as its object the conditions for international comity itself. In fashioning his own account of international justice, John Rawls, who also demarcates peoples from states, writes that the stability of a law of peoples "is not a mere *modus vivendi* but rests in part on an allegiance to the Law of Peoples itself."[50] Hegel could have said exactly the same thing.

Second, the passage cited exemplifies Hegel's contention that right is not understood as a universal norm abstractly juxtaposed to the life-forms and self-conceptions of individual cultures. While Hegel shares with Kant the notion that international law is governed by an emphatic concept of right, his is not understood as a moral postulate or an a priori principle of reason.[51] Against such juxtaposing of normative principles to particular forms of cultural life, Hegel claims that the assertion of such norms is intertwined with particular processes of cultural self-valorization. Central to the idea of right informing a law of peoples is its assertion and adoption by the peoples themselves. This means that the validity, and even the reality, of norms is not separate from the conditions motivating their acceptance. The justification of "deontological" principles goes hand in hand with an account of the conditions of individual self-realization, just as assertion of the universal principle of right is simultaneously explication of what is culturally desirable. The point flows from Hegel's view of the place occupied by the principle of right within a system of recognition. As the concrete articulation of the notion of mutual respect and equality of treatment, right is itself the embodied expression of the idea of achieved recognition. As Hegel already noted in his 1805–1806 Jena writings, right is the principle of *Anerkanntsein*.[52] Thus the process by which peoples come to realize themselves via practices of intersubjective recognition is itself clarification and validation of the "universal principle" of right that Hegel claims must govern a notion of international law.[53] A law of peoples' principle of right "is the presupposed recognition of the several states" (*vorausgesetzte Anerkanntsein der Staaten*).[54]

A comment regarding Hegel's view of cosmopolitanism is in order here. Commonplace assumptions notwithstanding, Hegel is not opposed to cosmopolitanism itself. Such would be inconceivable for one who stresses that "[A] human being counts as such because he is a human being, not because he is a Jew, Catholic, Protestant, German, Italian, etc."[55] What Hegel does reject is the "one-sided"[56] cosmopolitanism—he suggestively calls its comopoliticism (*Kosmopolitismus*)—that abstractly juxtaposes "moral commands" and humanitarian or "philanthropic" precepts to particular conceptions of well-being and to "the concrete life of the state."[57] Such juxtapositions fail to appreciate that appeals to personal dignity mean little without accompanying enforcement mechanisms. They also fail to appreciate that "universal" norms themselves emerge and attain validation only in concrete processes of interaction.[58] It is significant that Hegel thematizes the humanity of the person in his account of civil society, itself constituted through pervasive structures of mutual independency.[59] It is equally significant that the principles of the universality of right and spirit that inform *Völkerrecht* only emerge via the "dialectic" of individual *Volksgeistern.*[60] In Hegel's "situated" or "rooted" cosmopolitanism,[61] world history is the world's court of judgment,[62] its principle of "absolute right."[63] This, too, is a component of the claim that peoples will what is right in and for itself.

III

Hegel's idea of rooted cosmopolitanism is significant not just because it clarifies the nature and origin of norms informing his law of peoples but because it also throws light on the concept of universal identity infusing the latter. This becomes clear when we appreciate that appeal to situated experience not only defines and validates norms but specifies the conditions of their contextual application. Matters of application are essential, since it is only as regards their contextualization that norms assume binding value for those to whom they are addressed. A norm—in this case, universal right—may be generated and validated as a *principle* through processes of recognition; it can claim legitimacy for a particular community, assume the status of an *Idea*, only when interpreted and articulated in terms meaningful to the traditions, values, beliefs, and practices of that community. Hegel makes the point in his account of constitutional law, asserting that a legal system claims binding force for a community only in expressing "the customs and consciousness of the individuals who belong to it."[64] He argues similarly when explicating the law of peoples, whose legitimacy depends, he writes, on a "particular wisdom" able to fashion "universal principles" of conduct with regard to the exigencies of "a particular state in its specific interest and condition."[65]

That a law of peoples thus depends on contexts of application may appear to pose problems for an account of universal identity or global commonality. What characterizes the world's peoples and cultures, for Hegel, is precisely their manifold diversity. The "multifarious actuality" of the world's cultures is reflected in the diversity of their "geographical and anthropological" circumstances,[66] the "plurality" of organizational forms,[67] the enduring power of religious and other particularizing sources of cultural identity,[68] and the ever-changing nature of social circumstances that shape the identity of a community. It is with regard to such diversity that one may rightfully speak of the "Herderian legacy" of Hegel's cultural philosophy.[69] If this is the case, however, how can Hegel meaningfully assert a notion of global commonality? Does not appeal to unity and shared identity founder on the shoals of difference and particularity?

Such questions may be answered by noting that a notion of global community, for Hegel, is not a homogeneous sort that eschews difference and diversity. While a law of peoples finds expression in a shared commitment to the idea of right, it is not one that culminates in a Gadamerian "fusion of horizons," where diverse perspectives are merged and perhaps eliminated.[70] On the contrary, global universal identity is not only compatible with heterogeneity, it is sustained by it.[71] This point is central to Hegel's understanding of genuine totality, a genuine notion of globality. It is a basic tenet of Hegelian thought that a genuine unity is defined not in terms of abstract principles of uniformity juxtaposed to the particulars to which they apply but as a "concrete" unity, or "totality," in which the universal is not only embodied in particulars but exists through them. Hegel's is an organic or a "living" notion of unity, one in which the whole subsists only through the parts, just as parts subsist only through the whole. He makes the point in his account of a political unity, which he characterizes as a "whole articulated into its particular circles."[72] He does so as well when challenging the deficient notion of totality that found expression with the Roman Empire. On the Roman model totality consists in an abstract system of global dominion indifferent to the distinguishing variety of peoples and individuals—in Hegel's words, an "abstract universality . . . in which the individualities of nations perish in the unity of a pantheon," giving rise thereby to "an abstract and arbitrary will of increasingly monstrous proportions."[73] In contrast, a genuinely "concrete whole"[74] is a commonality that not only accommodates the specific diversity of individual cultures but is constituted through them. Not unlike some social theorists today, Hegel's principle of globality is necessarily a "glocal" principle, one based on the thorough and indeed organic permeation of global and local considerations.[75]

The differentiated nature of Hegel's account of globality becomes clearer when we consider the place of subjectivity and reflexive self-awareness in his account of a totality. As a general matter, "self-awareness" (*Selbstgefühl*) plays a central role in a genuine totality, inasmuch as the relationship of parts and whole must be evident not just to an external observer (a state of affairs that undermines claims to *totality*) but to the entities themselves.[76] In line with his general assertion that substance is also to be understood as subjectivity, Hegel maintains that an individual political community is constituted as a whole only to the degree that its members understand the relation of their membership to the whole. "[T]he universality of the end cannot make further progress without the personal knowledge and volition of the particular individuals."[77] He makes the same point when describing a global totality, in a passage that also reaffirms a cultural (rather than political) notion of global identity. No doubt adverting to the Roman experience, he asserts, "[T]he identity of the universal" is not that of "abstract world dominion (*Weltherrschaft*) . . . but the hegemony (*Hegemonie*) of self-conscious thought."[78] As against a one-sided idea of totality that imposes a principle of uniformity on the particulars, a genuine unity, a genuine universal identity, subsists only in the conscious acceptance by individual cultures and peoples of their global membership.

In recent years social theorists also have characterized globalization in such culturally reflexive terms. Roland Robertson, for instance, has called it "the intensification of consciousness of the world as a whole."[79] Hegel is sympathetic to this view, yet his point in stressing the *hegemony* of self-conscious thought is to accentuate the dependence of a global identity on the *differentiated* perceptions and experiences of members of the global commonality. Global identity does not depend on an undifferentiated affirmation of common ends, no more than it does on an undifferentiated fusion of individual horizons. It results instead from the process and practice of the world's peoples and nations asserting, individually and from their own perspective, their own self-identity.[80] This is so not just because any notion of *shared* identity presupposes appreciation as much of how we differ as it does of what we may have in common, a point Hegel makes *inter alia* in his account of political representation.[81] It is also his view, consonant with his intersubjective account of self-identity, that successful processes of cultural self-realization are simultaneously processes acknowledging that culture's dependence on other cultures, fostering thereby a consciousness of general global interdependency. "Universal self-consciousness is the affirmative awareness of self in an other self."[82] And just as a global identity emerges from the reflexive self-understanding of individual cultures, it is sustained by affirming their diversity, above all self-understandings of their diversity. This point is advanced more clearly in Hegel's philosophy of history than in the political philosophy and is illustrated in his treatment of the relationship of *Volksgeister* and *Weltgeist*.[83]

Central to Hegel's account of universal identity (and realized freedom) is that the "restricted" (*beschränkte*) principles of individual *Volksgeister* must give way to the "unrestricted" (*unbeschränkte*) principle of the *Weltgeist*.[84] Yet the relationship of the two principles is one not of opposition but codependency. On the one hand, assertion of a global consciousness results not by repudiating a particular cultural form but through its immanent development and realization. A particular community can be properly recognized as particular or restricted only if—here Hegel differs from Kant and Fichte—it posits itself *as* particular or restricted.[85] Yet such particularizing self-positing is possible, as Hegel argues in his Logic's account of the dialectic of limitation (*Schranke*),[86] only with a concurrent awareness and affirmation of that beyond limit. A complete account of the identity of a particular historical community therefore entails affirmation of the identity of other particular cultures, those past[87] and future[88] included, as well as global commonality itself. It is via the *Weltgeist* that "every people . . . attains its proper self-awareness (*Selbstgefühl*)."[89] Conversely, the "unrestricted" *Weltgeist* likewise has proper standing only when fashioned "as" unrestricted.[90] Yet this is possible only with awareness and affirmation of what is restricted and particular. Not only does the *Weltgeist* subsist through the particular *Volksgeister* but, *qua* "self-apprehending totality,"[91] it depends, in the self-transcending and other-affirming sense just noted, on the latter's self-understanding as particular.

From both perspectives, then, Hegel's universal identity has a decidedly mediated and differentiated character. On the one hand, global consciousness, including openness to the other, proceeds from one culture's reflexive awareness of its own individuality. Anticipating Hannah Arendt, Hegel maintains that appreciation of the perspectival nature of one's own stance preconditions an enlarged mentality.[92] On the other, universal identity itself is predicated on acknowledgment and affirmation of global diversity. Not unlike Anthony Appiah today, Hegel maintains that a global consciousness entails not abstract humanism but, as is appropriate to a conception of universal spirit understood as world spirit, a worldliness or "*Weltweisheit*"[93] committed to affirming "the variety of human forms of social and cultural life."[94] Hegel does advance a globally relevant concept of universal identity—an "international 'we,'" as it were, but one that both presupposes and entails robust commitment to global differences.

IV

Let me conclude by returning to the concept of right informing Hegel's law of peoples. While the recognitive process yields a concept of right serving as an overarching principle of universal conduct, the legitimacy of that concept depends on processes of interpretive adaptation sensitive to the diversity of global cultures. The application process is not a static one, however. It is one in which both poles are subject to transformation, where valid norms are fashioned to express local practices, just as these practices are "modified" to express wider principles.[95] It is in this process of mutual adaptation that an "ethos of nations" (*Sitten der Nationen*) and ultimately a global spirit are constituted. Yet the adaptation process never achieves final resolution. This is barred by the endless variety of circumstances to which norms are applied and reapplied. In line with a concept of *Weltgeist* understood as spirit's "unending struggle with itself,"[96] Hegel sees global culture as a site of ongoing and unceasing contestation about the meaning and application of the concept of right. Yet this lack of closure in no way undermines the idea of global identity. Rather, a world spirit, understood as spirit's "interpretation of *itself* to *itself*,"[97] is constituted in its unity just through its conflicts. Consonant with the higher-level struggles that Hegel claims are appropriate to achieved forms of mutual recognition,[98] it is in the oppositions that the whole is fashioned and sustained.[99] Here, too, Hegel advances a notion of globality understood as the identity of identity and difference.

Notes

1. For instance, see Raymond Plant, "Hegel on Identity and Legitimation," in *The State and Civil Society: Studies in Hegel's Political Philosophy*, ed. Z. A. Pelczynski (Cambridge: Cambridge University Press, 1984), 227–43. See also Jürgen Habermas, "Können komplexe Gesellschaften eine vernünftige Identität ausbilden?," in his *Zur Rekonstruktion des Historischen Materialismus* (Frankfurt: Suhrkamp Verlag, 1976), 92–126.

2. For a recent restatement of the Hobbesian interpretation, see Dudley Knowles: "Hegel's account of international relations is a good illustration of the thesis that Hobbes' state of nature accurately describes the relations between independent nation-states. States recognize each other in the way of independent moral persons but inevitably have an adversarial stance since their primary objective is the welfare of their own citizens." Knowles, *The Routledge Philosophy Guidebook to Hegel and the Philosophy of Right* (London and New York: Routledge, 2002), 341.

3. Thus Robert R. Williams has perceptively called attention to Hegel's critique of Napoleon's seemingly Hobbesian assertion that "the French Republic is no more in need of recognition than the sun is," noting that such absolute claims to sovereign autonomy themselves presuppose, however rudimentarily, the forms of international relations in terms of which alone such claims can be acknowledged. See *Hegel's Ethics of Recognition* (Berkeley: University of California Press, 1997), 350 ff. For the Hegel citation, see G. W. F. Hegel, *Elements of the Philosophy of Right*, ed. Allen Wood, trans. H. B. Nisbet (Cambridge: Cambridge University Press, 1991), §331.

4. Hegel, *Philosophy of Right*, §333.

5. Williams, *Hegel's Ethics of Recognition*, 3.

6. Hegel does not present this distinction as explicitly as would be desirable. Its clearest formulation is presented in his *Philosophy of Mind*, in the one (!) paragraph he there devotes to interstate and international law: "The external law of states (*das äußere Staatsrecht*) rests partly on these positive treaties, . . . partly on so-called international law (*Völkerrecht*)." See *The Philosophy of Mind: Part III of the Encyclopedia of Philosophical Sciences*, trans. William Wallace and A. V. Miller (Oxford: Oxford University Press, 1971), §547. It is elsewhere, in the *Philosophy of History*, that he identifies law focused on positive treaties as *Staatenrecht*. See *Vorlesungen über die Philosophie der Weltgeschichte. Bd 1: Vernunft in der Geschichte* (Hamburg: Meiner, 1994), 147 ff; *Lectures on the Philosophy of World History. Introduction: Reason in History*, trans. H. B. Nisbet (Cambridge: Cambridge University Press, 1975), 123ff. (Hereafter *Reason in History*.)

7. For Kant, see *Perpetual Peace*, where he speaks of *Weltbürgerrecht* "so far as men and nations stand in mutually influential relations as citizens of a universal nation of men (*ius cosmopoliticum*)." Cited in *Perpetual Peace and Other Essays* (Indianapolis, IN: Hackett, 1983), 112n.

8. Hegel, *Philosophy of Mind*, §547.

9. Compare Steve V. Hicks, *International Law and the Possibility of a Just World Order: An Essay on Hegel's Universalism* (Amsterdam: Rodopi, 1999).

10. Hegel, *Philosophy of Right*, §331.

11. Compare Klaus Vieweg, "Das Prinzip Anerkennung in Hegels universalistischer Theorie des äusseren Staatsrechts," in *Metaphysik der praktischen Welt. Perspektiven im Anschluss an Hegel und Heidegger*, ed. Christoph Jamme and Andreas Grossman (Amsterdam: Rodopi, 2000), 23–40. Also instructive is

Robert Williams's *Hegel's Ethics of Recognition*, cited earlier, though this chapter reaches a different conclusion regarding the role of recognition in international law. For one of the first to stress the importance of the concept of recognition in a constructive account of Hegel's internationalism, see Adam von Trott zu Solz's curiously neglected *Hegels Staatsphilosophie und das Internationale Recht* (Göttingen: Vandenhoeck & Ruprecht, 1932), especially 75–87.

12. Hegel, *Reason in History*, 101.

13. Hegel, *Philosophy of Right*, §331.

14. Hegel, *Reason in History*, 96; Hegel, *Philosophy of Right*, §335. In the *Philosophy of Right* he similarly characterizes the state as an "ethical universe" (*sittliche Universum*) and the "spirit of a people" (*Geist des Volkes)*; see preface, 21, §274.

15. Charles Taylor has argued along these lines, contrasting a "politics of difference" focused on the ideal of cultural authenticity to a "politics of equal dignity." See "The Politics of Recognition," in *Multiculturalism: Examining the Politics of Recognition*, ed. Amy Gutman (Princeton, NJ: Princeton University Press, 1992), 25–73.

16. Hegel, *Philosophy of Right*, §330.

17. See again Charles Taylor for a reaffirmation of this Herderian legacy, in "The Politics of Recognition," cited earlier.

18. See Nancy Fraser, "Rethinking Recognition," *New Left Review* 3 (May–June 2000): 113.

19. Against the enclavism associated with some theories of culture identity, Seyla Benhabib has demarcated the idea of cultural identity from processes of recognition. As we shall see, this is close to Hegel's position, with the proviso that, for him, cultural identity, inasmuch as it depends on processes of recognition, itself challenges separatism and enclavism. See Benhabib, *The Claims of Culture: Equality and Diversity in the Global Era* (Princeton, NJ: Princeton University Press, 2002), 49–81, especially 70.

20. Hegel, *Reason in History*, 96.

21. According to H. Setson-Watson, a nation is "a community of people, whose members are bound together by a sense of solidarity, a common culture, a national consciousness." For Hegel, it is the concept of self-consciousness that articulates the notion of a nation qua national consciousness. The citation is taken from Yael Tamir, *Liberal Nationalism* (Princeton, NJ: Princeton University Press, 1993), 60.

22. Hegel, *Phenomenology of Spirit*, trans. A. V. Miller (Oxford: Oxford University Press, 1977), 110. For an instructive discussion of Hegel's account of intersubjectivity from the perspective of self- consciousness, see Hans-Georg Gadamer, "Hegel's Dialectic of Self-Consciousness," in *Hegel's Dialectic: Five Hermeneutical Studies*, trans. P. Christopher Smith (New Haven, CT: Yale University Press, 1976), 54–74. See also Edith Düsing, *Intersubjektivität und Selbstbewußtsein* (Cologne: Jürgen Dinter, 1986).

23. In the *Philosophy of History*, Hegel acknowledges that a proper account of the relationship of self-sufficient states and peoples "would call for a long explanation." For reasons that are not entirely clear or convincing, he claims that such explanation "can well be dispensed with here" (Hegel, *Reason in History*, 123).

24. Hegel, *Reason in History*, 101.

25. As Hegel writes in a different context: "All essential advantage that the learning of foreign languages can grant us is certainly that in this way our concepts are enriched, especially if the culture of the peoples who spoke this language is different from our own." See Johannes Hoffmeister, ed., *Dokumente zu Hegels Entwicklung* (Stuttgart: Frommann, 1936), 169.

26. "[T]he most concrete and the most *subjective*, and that which withdraws itself into the simplest depths, is . . . the most overreaching" (*Übergreifendste*). See G. W. F. Hegel, *Science of Logic*, trans. A. V. Miller (New York: Humanities Press, 1969), 841, amended, in original.

27. Hegel, *Philosophy of Right*, §331. The term *vervollständigt* is emphasized in the original. The constitutive connotation of this term is not adequately captured in the Wood edition of the *Philosophy of Right*, which renders it "supplemented."

28. As Hegel writes in his Encyclopedia logic, "so geht hiermit Etwas in seinem Übergehen in Anderes nur *mit sich selbst* zusammen" (§95). In *The Claims of Culture*, Seyla Benhabib challenges those who understand the politics of recognition in terms of a politics of cultural identity, noting that the former can challenge as well as affirm a group's cultural uniqueness or specificity. Hegel would also reject the notion that recognition involves any undifferentiated affirmation of the identity of a culture. Yet for him this involves no repudiation of a "politics of identity." In his view, cultural identity is itself a highly complex and differentiated category, intertwined with a logic of recognition that challenges any reductionist and narrowly self-contained construal. See Benhabib, *The Claims of Culture*, especially 68–71.

29. Hegel, *Philosophy of Right*, §331, amended.

30. As Hegel writes elsewhere in characterizing universal self-consciousness, a self-conscious subject claims "'absolute' independence" only in the "shape of reciprocity" (*Gegenseitigkeit*) (*Philosophy of Mind*, §436).

31. Hegel, *Philosophy of Right*, §331.

32. "The liberation (*Befreiung*) of colonies itself proves to be the greatest advantage to the mother state, just as the emancipation (*Freilassen*) of slaves is of the greatest advantage to the master" (Hegel, *Philosophy of Right*, §248, addition).

33. Ibid., §331.

34. *Vorlesungen über der Philosophie der Weltgeschichte* (Leipzig: Meiner, 1920), 761, cited in Shlomo Avineri, *Hegel's Theory of the Modern State* (Cambridge: Cambridge University Press, 1972), 207.

35. Hegel, *Philosophy of Right*, §339.

36. Ibid., §331.

37. Ibid., §333.

38. Already in the essay on natural law, Hegel castigated as "empty" or "void" the idea of "a league of nations or a world republic," and this attitude, with only minor variation, continued to infuse his view of international relations. See G. W. F. Hegel, *Natural Law* (Philadelphia: University of Pennsylvania Press, 1975), 132 ff.

39. See Adriaan Peperzak, "Hegel contra Hegel in His Philosophy of Right: The Contradictions of International Politics," *Journal of the History of Philosophy*, 32:1 (January 1994): 241–63.

40. Hegel, *Philosophy of Mind*, §547.

41. Hegel, *Philosophy of Right*, §339, addition.

42. Hegel, *Philosophy of Mind*, §436.

43. Hegel, *Philosophy of Right*, §339.

44. Hegel, *Philosophy of Mind*, §547.

45. Hegel, *Reason in History*, 54, emphasis added.

46. Hegel, *Philosophy of Right*, §340.

47. See Ludwig Siep, "Das Recht als Ziel der Geschichte: Überlegungen im Abschluß an Kant und Hegel," in *Das Recht der Vernunft: Kant und Hegel über Denken, Erkennen und Handeln*, ed. Christel Fricke et al. (Stuttgart-Bad Cannstaat: Frommann-Holzboog, 1995), 355–79.

48. Hegel, *Philosophy of Right*, §333.

49. G. W. F. Hegel, *Werke*, ed. Eva Moldenhauer and Karl Markus Michel (Frankfurt: Suhrkamp, 1970), vol. 12, 418. In English translation: "Peoples will the right in and for itself; regard is not had exclusively to particular conventions between nations, but principles enter into the consideration with which diplomacy is occupied." See G. W. F. Hegel, *The Philosophy of History, With a New Introduction by Professor C. J. Friedrich*, trans. Sibree (New York: Dover, 1956), 346. (Hereafter *Philosophy of History*).

50. John Rawls, *The Law of Peoples* (Cambridge, MA: Harvard University Press, 1999), 45.

51. See Siep, "Das Recht als Ziel der Geschichte."

52. *Hegel and the Human Spirit: A Translation of the Jena Lectures on the Philosophy of Spirit (1805/06) with Commentary*, trans. Leo Rauch (Detroit, MI: Wayne State University Press, 1983), 111. There are, to be sure, significant differences between the Jena writings and the *Philosophy of Right* with regard to the specific relation of right and recognition. In the early writings, *Anerkanntsein* is presented as the definition of right itself, whereas in the *Philosophy of Right*, right is now defined as the "existence (*Dasein*) of the free will" (*Philosophy of Right*, §29). In addition, while in the early writings recognition was invoked both to generate and justify the concept of right, such efforts are not part of the later theory of right. Here he claims that an account both of its origin and justification—what in the Kantian tradition he calls a "deduction"—is "presupposed" (*Philosophy of Right*, §2), having been previously addressed in the section of the *Philosophy of Subjective Spirit* devoted to phenomenology. Yet if in this sense the later Hegel

refuses to reaffirm the conjunction of *Recht* and *Anerkanntsein* presented in the Jena writings, he does affirm it in ways consonant with a notion of right defined as the existence of freedom. For instance, right is normatively linked to *Anerkanntsein*—as is also clear in the account of international law—in the sense that freedom now requires "the form of necessity," understood both as objectively existent organizational mechanisms ensuring the recognition of rights and the forms of subjective disposition required for their acceptance and continued maintenance. See *Philosophy of Mind*, §484.

53. For a recent account of recognition that contraposes, in a way at variance with what is presented here, "deontological" principles of justice to "ethical" notions of cultural self-realization, see Nancy Fraser, "Recognition without Ethics?," *Theory, Culture & Society* 18–2–3 (2001): 21–42.

54. Hegel, *Philosophy of Mind*, §547. Hegel discussed this reflexivity in the account of the struggle for recognition that he presents in the *Phenomenology of Spirit*, noting that the participants there "recognize themselves as mutually recognizing one another" (Miller translation, 112).

55. Hegel, *Philosophy of Right*, §209. Speaking of the principle of personhood as the perspective from which individuals should be regarded, he claims that "a grand and important step was taken when humanity came to regard itself in such large and universal terms, . . . where humanity simply as such comes to merit recognition." See *Philosophy des Rechts: Die Vorlesung von 1819/20 in einer Nachschrift*, ed. Dieter Henrich (Frankfurt: Suhrkamp, 1983), 169.

56. Hegel, *Philosophy of Right 1819/20*, 169.

57. Hegel, *Philosophy of Right*, §209, 337.

58. See Hans Friedrich Fulda, "Geschichte, Weltgeist und Weltgeschichte bei Hegel," *Annalen der Internationalen Gesellschaft für Dialektische Philosophie—Societas Hegeliana* (Cologne: Pahl-Rugenstein, 1983), 67, 71.

59. See also Hegel, *Philosophy of Right*, §109.

60. The attempt to affirm cosmopolitanism in a way that appeals not to abstract principles but to processes of transnational communication is evident in John S. Dryzek, "Transnational Democracy: Beyond the Cosmopolitan Model," in *Deliberative Democracy and Beyond*, (Oxford: Oxford University Press, 2000), 115–39. A transnational construal of cosmopolitanism also can be found in Jürgen Habermas, "Why Europe Needs a Constitution," where he writes that a postnational public sphere will "emerge from the mutual opening of existing national universes to one another, yielding an interpenetration of mutually translated national communications" (*New Left Review* 11 [September–October 2001]: 18).

61. A version of "rooted cosmopolitanism" has been advanced by Kwame Anthony Appiah, whose juxtaposition of cosmopolitanism to humanism parallels a distinction between Weltgeist and philanthropy central to Hegel's position. We return to Appiah's proposal at the conclusion of the next section. See "Cosmopolitan Patriots," in *Cosmopoliticus: Thinking and Feeling beyond the Nation*, Pheng Cheah and Bruce Robbins (Minneapolis: University of Minnesota Press, 1988), 91–114.

62. Hegel, *Philosophy of Right*, §340.

63. Ibid., §345.

64. Ibid., §274.

65. Ibid., §337, §339, addition, §337.

66. Ibid., §341, 346.

67. Ibid., §341, 346.

68. Ibid., §331.

69. See Siep, "Das Recht als Ziel der Geschichte," 371.

70. Gadamer, *Truth and Method*, 2d rev. ed. (New York: Continuum, 1995), 305.

71. For an instructive discussion of these issues with regard to Kant, Habermas, and Taylor, see Thomas McCarthy, "On Reconciling Cosmopolitan Unity and National Diversity," in *Global Justice and Transnational Politics*, ed. Pablo DeGreiff and Ciaran P. Cronin (Cambridge: MIT Press, 2001), 235–74.

72. Hegel, *Philosophy of Right*, §308.

73. Ibid., §357.

74. Ibid., §336.

75. See Ulrich Beck, *What Is Globalization?* (Cambridge, UK: Polity, 2000), especially 42–52.

76. Hegel, *Philosophy of Right*, §147.

77. Ibid., §260, addition.

78. Hegel, *Philosophy of History*, 346, amended.

79. See Robertson, *Globalization: Social Theory and Global Culture* (London: Sage, 1992), especially chapter 6, "The Universalism-Particularism Issue," 97–114.

80. The point has been made by Jonathan Rée, who invokes Hegel in this context: "You cannot have a sense of belonging to the same nation as your neighbors unless you are aware of it as one nation among others and of an imagined totality of nations forming, eventually a kind of world system, perhaps arranged in some order of seniority. . . . Nations exist only in the plural, in other words, and if every nation but one were destroyed, then the last one would cease to be a nation as well. Local sentiments acquire national significance only in the light of an imagined international order. It is essential to the principle of nationality that it presuppose internationality." See "Cosmopolitanism and the Experience of Nationality," in *Cosmopoliticus: Thinking and Feeling beyond the Nation*, 83.

81. Hegel, *Philosophy of Right*, §309 ff. See also Giuseppe Duso, *Der Begriff der Repräsentation und das moderne Problem der politischen Einheit* (Baden-Baden: Nomos, 1990).

82. Hegel, *Philosophy of Mind*, §436.

83. See Fulda, "Geschichte, Weltgeist und Weltgeschichte bei Hegel."

84. Hegel, *Philosophy of Right*, §330; see also *Philosophy of Mind*, §552.

85. Hegel, *Philosophy of Right*, §7.

86. Hegel, *Science of Logic*, trans. Miller, 131–36.

87. As Hegel writes, one historical community "is an incomplete present (*unvollständige Gegenwart*) which cannot understand itself and develop an integrated consciousness without reference to the past" (*Reason in History*, 136).

88. As Hegel writes, one "individual national spirit fulfills itself by effectuating a transition to the principle of another nation . . . a new phase and a new spirit" (*Reason in History*, 56, amended; see also *Philosophy of Right*, §343).

89. Hegel, *Natural Law*, 127, translation amended.

90. Hegel, *Philosophy of Right*, §330.

91. Hegel, *Reason in History*, 65, amended.

92. Margaret Canovan, *Hannah Arendt: A Reinterpretation of Her Political Thought* (Cambridge: Cambridge University Press, 1992), 206 ff.

93. Hegel, *Philosophy of Mind*, §552.

94. "Cosmopolitan Patriots," *Cosmopoliticus: Thinking and Feeling beyond the Nation*, 94, 92.

95. Hegel, *Philosophy of Right*, §339.

96. Hegel, *Reason in History*, 127, amended.

97. Hegel, *Philosophy of Right*, §343.

98. Hegel, *Philosophy of Mind*, § 432.

99. The wider issue concerns the role of war in Hegel's theory of international relations. This cannot be taken up here; an elaboration on the present argument would show, however, that for Hegel war and other forms of strife, however "tragic" (another highly complex and multivalent category in his thought), are, as was already the case with Kant, not incompatible with global commonality or even comity.

Chapter 8

The Power of Particularities: Gender and Nation in the *Phenomenology of Spirit* and the *Philosophy of Right*

Patricia Anne Simpson

While it remains uncontroversial to assert that Hegel's philosophy of identity and difference is highly influential, its meaning must be renegotiated in an era that has long since become suspicious of power disparities in his systematic thought. Recent scholarship, characterized collectively and loosely as cultural studies,[1] exposes, among other things, the problematic politics that would privilege identity over difference; it questions the category of the universal and its power over the particular. Representatives of German idealist philosophy, Kant and Hegel foremost among them, often bear the burden of having invented the category of the "universal," read European bourgeois male.[2]

On the other hand, both philosophers focus on the question of freedom. As Robert B. Pippin notes, the problem of modern philosophy is the "problem of freedom."[3] In the same work, Pippin insists that the inferior "other" as it has been posited is *not* part of Hegel's philosophical argument at all.[4] He refines the focus of the problem of freedom further when he writes: "[. . .] The general notions of autonomy and self-conscious subjectivity have been under steady and, in academic and cultural terms, successful attack for some time now. The notion looks naïve to some, 'gendered' to others (as if a striving for 'autonomy' were inherently a patriarchal aspiration, not a human one) [. . .]."[5] It seems crucial to ask, however, what Hegel means by freedom and its declension, autonomy. Is patriarchy merely a historical contingency, or is there a more motivated relationship between hegemonic politics and dominant philosophical theory?

Gayatri Chakravorty Spivak challenges the assertion of philosophy's fictional "other" (indirectly) when she delineates the subaltern position vis-à-vis the paradigm of European reason from a model of critique largely put into place by Kant, Hegel, and Marx. Her articulation of the "Native Informant" is complex and extremely challenging, in part because she so suggestively problematizes the status of her own critical language.[6] Many have echoed her voice.[7] The dialectic of identity and difference has come to preoccupy the study of culture, insisting on the political critique of identity from the perspective of difference in an effort to address a historically conditioned power imbalance that stacks the deck against "otherness," defined in terms of race, ethnicity, gender, sexual preference, and so on.

In a scrupulous intervention into the debate about universal categories, Judith Butler, Ernesto Laclau, and Slavoj Žižek approach the question from different theoretical perspectives but share a provisional conclusion: that identity can never be fully articulated.[8] In order to advance the debate within the realm of Hegelian discourse, I interrogate in this chapter the asymmetrical power relationships among competing "particularities" in Hegel's work. It is necessary, I argue, to recalibrate the relationship between the universal and particular as categories in order to gain insight into the historically specific aspects of Hegel's theories of identity.

Through a reading of the status of the feminine as particularity, the relationship of particularity to power and the actual, and finally of the historical contingencies of war involved in Hegel's leveraging of nation (*Volk*) as particularity in the *Philosophy of Right*, I demonstrate that particularities are fundamentally historical but resist reading when isolated from their dialectical relationship to the category of universality.

To attribute the priority of identity to Hegel paints a somewhat undifferentiated portrait of him as a theorist of power. Indeed, Rudolf Haym, in his *Lectures on Hegel and His Time* (1857), presides over a scholarly tradition within which Hegel's reputation as "the philosophical dictator of Germany"[9] is perhaps not only apt, but possibly deserved. Yet, as Pippin suggests, the relationship between idealism and modernism must be reexamined around the defining issue of freedom. Terry Pinkard underscores in his masterful biography of the philosopher, that freedom for Hegel (para. 23 of the *Enzyklopädie*) is "freedom from particularity."[10]

Butler concludes, in her reading of Hegel's universality, that "The all-encompassing trajectory of the term is necessarily undone by the exclusion of particularity on which it rests. There is no way to bring the excluded particularity into the universal without first negating that particularity."[11] What does the negation of particularity mean within the context of a contemporary debate about identity, represented by gender, nation, and class? And if we even formulate the question as such, are we intentionally misunderstanding the theoretical nature of Hegel's project? The answer to this question lies within Hegel's theory of power and the role of the particular within it.

First I discuss the status of particularity in the *Phenomenology of Spirit* and the *Philosophy of Right.* Hegel's negotiation between the dialectical progression toward identity and the particularities of gender and nation emerges from a discussion of war as the crucial moment in the ethical life of the nation.[12] For this reason, I analyze paragraphs that invoke war, gender, and desire to establish the role of woman in this context. However, I present a differentiated view of this role; the development of the self is contingent upon interaction with the actual, from which woman is excluded. The actual takes the form of social and political institutions that in turn depend on the support of the individual. In this context, I examine the roles of particularity in relation to power assumed by the figures of the "Lord of the World," followed by noble and ignoble consciousness.

Hegel develops by increments the proper degree of identity between the individual and the institutions of governance, and his final criterion for what amounts to citizenship is the willingness to sacrifice the self to the state. Yet even this sacrifice can constitute an act of particularity—if not made within the context of war. Finally, in the *Philosophy of Right,* Hegel valorizes the sacrifice of the self to the state in war. Only here does Hegel sanction particularity in its articulation as nation.

This itinerary traces a relationship between the necessities of the feminine particular as a negative that propels the dialectic; then masculine figures of unethical speech, those who would unduly influence the realm of political power for personal gain, are effectively feminized for their peculiar particularity. Thus Hegel establishes in the *Phenomenology of Spirit* a connection between the unethical feminine and the unethical masculine, a category that remains unrecuperated until the particularity of nation is introduced in the *Philosophy of Right.* These works have essentially different aims. The intervening major works, the *Lectures on the Aesthetic,* the *Logic,* and the *Encyclopedia,* are highly citational and self-referential. The concepts they generate are not always stable, and their meaning is transferable from one text to the next. Yet the role of the feminine does not evolve, except for the stabilization of desire in the family model familiar from the *Philosophy of Right.* The nation, however, in spite of Hegel's own cosmopolitan identity, does evolve. In these respective categories, the feminine fares poorly, while the particularity of nation ascends. Not all particularities are created equal.[13]

As Pinkard observes, "Hegel apparently could never take women seriously as intellectual equals; the idea of the modern emancipated woman was not one with which—to put the most charitable reading on his behavior—he felt comfortable."[14] Pinkard further notes that Hegel's view of sexual differences remains consistent throughout his career.[15] If we historicize Hegel, then, and attribute this posited otherness merely to historical context, then we overlook the nuanced relationship between gender and thought in the early nineteenth century.

Pinkard points out that even Hegel's friend and associate, Karl August Varnhagen von Ense, complained that Hegel would not discuss ideas with his wife, Rahel von Varnhagen, a writer and an intellectual, as well as the center of Berlin's salon culture.[16] The question remains: What is the relationship between Hegel's historical context, his system, and his theory of identity and difference, specifically with regard to gender and national identity? Seyla Benhabib highlights Hegel's allergic response to Caroline Schlegel-Schelling.[17] She asks, "[. . .] Is Hegel's treatment of women merely a consequence of his conservative predilections? [. . .] Is the 'woman question' one more instance of Hegel's uncritical endorsement of the institutions of his time, or is this issue an indication of a flaw in the very structure of the dialectic itself?"[18]

Hegel's resistance to the particular, however, extends to those who would incorporate sexual difference into abstract thought. The most notorious example of this conflation is Friedrich Schlegel's *Lucinde*,[19] though there were other reasons for Hegel's rejection of the "father of irony," among them Schlegel's later conversion to Catholicism and his involvement in imperial politics, as Pinkard notes.[20] Still, Hegel accords only a transitional status to particularity—it is always already accommodating itself to universality. There is a temporality implicit in the dialectic of particularity and universality, and it is precisely at this point that historical narrative enters the philosophical discourse. Hegel's reservations about forward-thinking and free-loving women, or highly intellectual women who were intimately involved in cultural production, are perhaps particular to the era, but he extends the critique inspired by the feminine to other particularities as well. These particularities are defined by increasing degrees of unwillingness to sacrifice the self for the state.

An association emerges between undialectical thought and the unmasculine.[21] In the *Phenomenology of Spirit*, Hegel defines the role of the feminine in the community as irony, and much scholarship, feminist and otherwise, has noted the subversive nature of this role, and, depending upon one's perspective, it is either destructive or potentially empowering.[22] Benhabib acknowledges the imperative to "restore irony to the dialectic."[23] She specifically calls for closer readings of Hegel's female contemporaries to follow the traces of those who have been lost, repressed, erased.[24]

But is the dialectic at stake? If we refrain from historical or biographical explications and insist on the immanence of the system for an answer, then we must look to the competing particularities in Hegel's thought. Within the logic of his system, the role of the feminine as particularity is telling when compared to the particularity of nation. While Hegel opposed the extreme forms of German nationalism in circulation during his lifetime—indeed, he would be counted among the cosmopolitans[25]—he did endorse in his *Philosophy of Right* an identification with nation as a result of the experience of war, though the historical reference remains abstract. The emergence of national affiliation as a category of identity stabilizes the slippage in transferable gender attributes: Hegel welcomes it, in spite of its particularity.

Particularity and Violence

There is a relationship between particularity, force and violence, and the feminine—these converge with the rhetoric of war in Hegel's description of the dialectic. The progression Hegel erects in the *Phenomenology of Spirit* has as its goal the identity of idea and its object, where there is no remainder in the equation. What drives this dialectic? Theodor Adorno foregrounds the negativity, of which particularity is a subset. Patricia Jagentowicz Mills writes, "Thus, for Adorno the concept of the particular is a concept of the dialectics of non-identity whereas the concept of particularity eliminates the particular *as* particular in order to absorb it into a philosophy of identity dominated by the universal."[26] How, then, is particularity "absorbed"? Hegel offers a provisional answer in the "Introduction." After outlining the educative purpose of his series of configurations (master and slave, etc.), Hegel addresses the question of what propels consciousness, what keeps it moving forward. In distinguishing consciousness from the limits of natural life, he defines it by its self-awareness, the knowledge of its idea of itself. He writes of consciousness:

> Hence it is something that goes beyond limits, and since these limits are its own, it is something that goes beyond itself. With the positing of a single particular the beyond is also established

> for consciousness, even if it is only *alongside* the limited object as in the case of spatial intuition. Thus consciousness suffers this violence [*Gewalt*] at its own hands: it spoils its own limited satisfaction. When consciousness feels this violence, its anxiety may well make it retreat from the truth, and strive to hold on to what it is in danger of losing. But it can find no peace [*keine Ruhe*].[27] (*PS*, 51, para. 80)

Hegel here describes the restless process by which consciousness exceeds its own limits, constantly challenged by the existence of the particular. Violence is implicit and instrumental in establishing identity—its relationship to particularity is intimate. In order to reach beyond the limits of self-imposed consciousness, the self must endure self-inflicted violence, but in this equation violence plays the part of particularity. Violence, it would seem, drives the dialectic. It is important to note that Hegel makes this point within the realm of logic; the topic is consciousness, not selves and others, but the rhetorical force of the passage invokes the figurality of violence and respite, agitation and pause.

I move now to the next stage of my analysis—the status of any relationship between individuality and nation. Part of the process of establishing citizenship is the elimination of particularity. The self necessarily implicates the relationship between Spirit, ethical life, and nation, at a time when there is no geographical or political antecedent for Germany as a nation. Hegel next treats this correspondence in "Spirit. A. The *true* Spirit. The ethical order." Spirit is an expression of consciousness, the essence of which is ethical substance. Spirit is individual, capable of action, and real; it is in possession of reason. Moreover, Hegel defines Spirit in political terms: "Spirit is the *ethical life* of a nation . . . the individual that is a world" (*PS*, 265, para. 441). There is a proportional, rational relationship between individuals and the state, between citizens and the powers that rule them, an insight that leads to a consideration of law in the world. This prelude to the section on "True Spirit" situates the individual in a moral relationship to other individuals and to the state. This aspect of Hegel's argument introduces the ethical motivations for action. Hegel invokes human and divine law as regulators of behavior. Consciousness itself splits into a human and divine law, and so Hegel skirts the issue of whether the order is innate or imposed. This division leads Hegel immediately to gender self-consciousness in the subsection, "The ethical world. Human and Divine Law: Man and Woman" (*PS*, 267 ff., para. 446).

It is important to remember that the divided substance of consciousness splits into universality and individuality, that individuality is not particularity or "contingent consciousness" (*PS*, 267, para. 447). Only that expression of individuality is eligible to be constitutive of the community, the nation, and the state. Hegel further specifies the exclusive status of the male as "individual": "But because it is only as a citizen that he is actual and substantial, the individual, so far as he is not a citizen but belongs to the Family, is only an unreal impotent shadow" ("nur der *unwirkliche* marklose Schatten") (*PS*, 270, para. 451). By extension, women are disenfranchised as noncitizens, excluded from the status of individuality. In other words, the family, appropriate domain of the feminine, while accommodating the masculine and an imperative realm of his being, is not and cannot be the sole locus of his existence. This is not to assert, however, that Hegel has no place for the feminine: he ultimately unites the male and female responsibilities for allegiance to human and divine law, respectively, in the realm of ethical action. These affiliations are not determined by blood kinship in the case of the male, though they govern the realm of the feminine.[28] The question remains: If the feminine is to have agency in any form, within the context of the Family, the community (civil society, more or less), or the nation—hers is, after all, the realm of the ethical, and Spirit is the ethical life of the nation—then what is her source of power?

While mine is not a specifically semantic analysis, the relationship between language and power in Hegel's usage compels me to make an observation about Hegel's philosophical lexicon. He tends to use the term *Macht* to signify the power of state, to designate the masculine sphere; he frequently uses *Gewalt* with relation to the feminine—or other subversive particularities. This usage is exemplified again in the continued discussion of the ethical conflict between realms of right. Hegel names the example of ethical consciousness "Antigone" in an argument about the intentionality of opposition to human law: "But the ethical consciousness is more complete, its guilt more inexcusable, if it knows *beforehand* the law and the power (*Macht*) which it opposes, if it takes them to be violence (*Gewalt*) and wrong, to be ethical merely by accident, and like Antigone, knowingly commits the crime" (*PS*, 284, para. 470).

From the perspective of the sister, the power of state is transformed from *Macht* to *Gewalt*. His subsequent remarks about intentionality imply greater guilt for the "doer" of the deed; they gloss over the radicality of her action. The sister, the victim of violence, realizes that violence is a constitutive moment of state power. Though Hegel will take pains to equalize the influence of the two spheres in subsequent paragraphs, he makes explicit the gendering of the two realms: "Human law in its universal existence is the community, in it activity in general is the manhood of the community, in its real and effective activity is the government" (*PS*, 287, para. 475).

Yet, Hegel maintains, while the community contains the Family, the former exists at the latter's expense. Further, the community identifies womankind (*Weiblichkeit*) as the necessary enemy from within. In a passage frequently cited in feminist critiques of Hegel, he writes:

> Womankind—the everlasting irony [in the life] of the community—changes by intrigue the universal end of the government into a private end, transforms its universal activity into a work of some particular individual, and perverts the universal property of the state into a possession and ornament for the Family. (*PS*, 288, para. 475)

In the discussion of the pathos involved in individual activity, or a coincidence of subject and ethical substance, this argument about the place of the family in the state, about private and public law, develops within a context of the conflictual rights of the dead and the collision between divine and human law. It anticipates Hegel's discussion of tragedy in his aesthetics, for which he uses *Antigone* to illustrate his point. Here, however, Hegel remains firmly in the realm of political theory informed by ethical conflict in the aesthetic, cultural sphere. He derives his politics from the language of ethics and frames this passage on the function of the family unit as the domain of the feminine, a gesture shored up in the later *Philosophy of Right*.

The active expression of human law is, according to the passage, masculinity specifically and the state generally. This power is sustained by the dynamic, which divides the lot into family groupings, where femininity reigns. Hegel sketches a contiguous relationship between the state and its male subjects. The formulations of the next stage are critical. The collective exists then only as a corrective to the family; it finds its existence in the disturbance of the family unit and the dissolution of self-consciousness in the passage from the individual to the collective. And this collective perpetuates itself by positing an other, the inner, repressed enemy, *Weiblichkeit*. This constitutes the eternal irony of collective being in which the individual is negated. Hegel associates irony, therefore, or undisciplined subjectivity, with the realm of the feminine as a public enemy.

Hegel introduces war twice in this context: war as a conscious decision on the part of government to upset an order dominated by Family. In a striking connection, Hegel extends his defining role of Woman in the community to a theory of desire in war. Let me backtrack to the first instance:

> The community may, on the one hand, organize itself into systems of personal independence and property, of laws relating to persons and things; and, on the other hand, the various ways of working for ends which are in the first instance particular ends—those of gain and enjoyment—it may articulate into their own special and independent associations. The Spirit of universal assembly and association is the simple and negative essence of those systems which tend to isolate themselves. In order not to let them become rooted and set in this isolation, thereby breaking up the whole and letting the [communal] spirit evaporate, government has from time to time to shake them to their core by war. (*PS*, 272, para. 455)

This description of these social relationships, extensions of the Family, outlines a theory of civil society. However, in typically demanding prose, Hegel introduces war as a necessary corrective to the gaining power of civil society. After the discussion of femininity and the "eternal irony of the community," civil society itself is gendered; the feminine principle corrupts the power of youth, who still stands within the "power of the whole" (*PS*, 288, para. 475): Individuality becomes a weapon (ibid.). Hegel writes:

> War is the Spirit and the form in which the essential moment of the ethical substance, the absolute freedom of the ethical *self* from every existential form, is present in its actual and authentic existence. While, on the one hand, war makes the individual *systems* of property and personal independence, as well as the *personality* of the individual himself, feel the power of the negative, on the other hand, this negativity is prominent in war as that which preserves the whole. The brave youth in whom woman finds her pleasure, the suppressed principle of corruption, now has his day and his worth is openly acknowledged. (*PS*, 288–89, para. 475)

Whereas in the previously quoted passage, war is visited by the government on civil society, here it seems specifically to target woman for her admiration of youth, which must be sacrificed to the power of negativity. Judith Butler reads this passage as a symmetrical substitution: The desire of woman is displaced by the desire of the state—woman is "left behind for the homosociality of state desire."[29] While war is fought for the redemption of the whole, it is woman, and implicitly her desire, that poses the threat from within in the first place. War forces a confrontation of competing desires, competing negativities before the encounter with any enemy. The ironist (male or female), the heckler, the desiring woman, and the subversive slave, must all be sacrificed to the totality of war. Hegel spins a web of associations between gender, a critique of particularity, and the imperative of war as an urgent type of social regulation.

Power and Particularity

The theory of violence in the *Phenomenology* dwells in the dialectic itself as the driving force that propels consciousness to exceed its limits; the idiom of war is introduced to figure the role of particularity and violence in consciousness. This former force constitutes the opposition to male power and, perhaps most cynically, is expressed as the feminized enemy of and within the community, the woman whose desire becomes culpable at a time of war. Yet Hegel leaves behind the question of the feminine in general; nor does he generalize about masculinity in the same way. Instead, he follows individual symptoms of wayward masculine allegories.

One example occurs in the "Lord of the World." I will also refer briefly to the figures of noble and ignoble consciousness. In these allegories, Hegel provides a transition from "Spirit" to "Culture," indexed by the degree of interaction between the self and the actual, mediated by the encounter with power. Hegel's discourse resembles a public pedagogy, a process by which the interests of the individual are demonstrated to align perfectly with those of the government. The power of the state is dependent on the willing obedience of the subject/citizen. Not accidentally, this citizenship primer comprises the section on *Bildung*, conventionally translated as education, with a significant amount of culture implied. Granted, these allegories are figures of consciousness, as are all such tropes in the *Phenomenology*, but they surface in a discussion of the ways consciousness inscribes itself into and leaves traces on the realm of the actual: they therefore exceed the purely figurative realm.[30] More than figurality is at stake.

The passage about the "Lord of the World" marks the moment in Hegel's treatment of rights and the law (still within the *Phenomenology*) in which the individual and the actual coincide. Hegel moves to a discussion of noble and ignoble consciousness and their relationship to the power of the state. The discussion of these figures culminates in the sacrifice of the (male) self to the state, but not yet in war, but all three demonstrate the role of particularity within the state. We proceed from the section on Spirit (*Geist*) to that about culture (*Bildung*), from the place of ethical substance in the context of custom (*Sitte*), to the definition of the self in the world in which legal right prevails. In the introductory paragraph to this section, Hegel describes the *Herr der Welt des Rechts* (*PS*, 292, para. 481) as a dictatorial consciousness: "He is a person, but the solitary person who stands over against all the rest" (*PS*, 292, para. 481). Important here is the way Hegel characterizes the dialectical relationship between the "titanic self-consciousness" (*PS*, 293, para. 481) and the others: "These constitute the real authoritative universality of that person; for the single individual as such is true only as a universal multiplicity of single individuals" (*PS*, 292, para. 481). Because he is cut off from others, he is an "unreal, impotent self" (*PS*, 292 para. 481). The self, in the process of self-alienation in order to achieve a higher level of consciousness, eventually self-consciousness, must access a realm in which there is an interaction between the individual and the actual. The critical moment in this itinerary is the collision with legal right.

The "lord of the world of right" takes the external world, the real world, as his own; this constitutes his negative work, which "[. . .] obtains its existence through self-consciousness's *own* externalization and separation of itself from its essence which, in the ruin and devastation that prevail in the world of legal right, seems to inflict on self-consciousness from without, the violence of the liberated elements" ["*die äußerliche Gewalt der losgebundenen Elemente*"] (*PS*, 294, para. 484, emphasis added).

Once again, the process of self-externalization, the relentless forward drive of the dialectic, is expressed as power/violence. The external violence of these elements must be tamed, domesticated, ordered; they fall into step by the end of this paragraph, as "the spiritual powers ordering themselves into a world and thereby preserving themselves" ["*zu einer Welt sich ordnenden und sich dadurch erhaltenden geistigen Mächte*"] (*PS*, 294, para. 484, emphasis added). Implicit in this critique of legal formalism is the overcoming of the self by the self in this extremely intricate description of the process through which a subject interacts with the actual. Hegel recuperates each of these shed selves along the way, however: "[. . .] even the departed spirit is present in his *blood*-relationship, in the *self* of the family, and the universal *power* of the government is the *will*, the self of the nation" (*PS*, 295, para. 486). The purpose, then, of culture is to maintain the presence of past selves within the sphere of family and that of the government, and the core of its power is *Wille*. All bonds thus forged are instrumentalized in order to stabilize a process through which individuals pass through the actual in their progress toward the universal. Here Hegel connects the family and the universality of the state, which together comprise the self of the nation. The harmony posited between the will of the self and of the state forms the crux of Hegel's cultural theory: "It is therefore through culture that the individual acquires standing and actuality" (*PS*, 298, para. 489), now within the existence of the nation.

Once the relationship between the self and the state has been posited, in which the self is actualized only as citizen, Hegel allegorizes types of citizens and categorizes them according to their attitude toward the power of the state. These masculine figures take their place next to the subversive feminine. State power expresses itself in law, government, and command (*PS*, para. 498). However, it is only "noble consciousness" (*das edelmütige Bewußtsein*) that sees its own obedience and respect reflected in the forms of government. The mimetic relationship between the good self and the good state is violated by "ignoble consciousness" (*das niederträchtige Bewußtsein*), who views the power of the state, *Herrschergewalt* (*PS*, para. 501), as a form of oppression. According to this theory, state power is contingent upon the obedience of the people who redundantly define themselves in a specular relationship to the nation. Hegel must introduce an ethical vocabulary in order to guarantee the actual power of the state over the individuals who potentially represent the "ignoble consciousness" of the people.

State power, at a stage prior to will, has not yet attained the status of government; for this, the division of classes or estates is required. The conflict of individual will and the interests of the state amounts to an individual's "*particular self-interest*" (*PS*, 307, para. 506): "It means that he has in fact reserved his own opinion and his own particular will in face of the power of the state (*Staatsgewalt*). His conduct, therefore, conflicts with the interests of the state and is characteristic of the ignoble consciousness which is always on the point of revolt" (*PS*, 307, para. 506). The will of the state must supersede all individual will—an echo of communal critique of the feminine. Hegel explains the authority of a higher form of consciousness, based on the willingness to sacrifice one's life for the state, but here the sacrifice is imperfect, for the state and its power to govern are not yet informed by nation, and the sacrifice of ignoble consciousness remains mired in particularity:

> The sacrifice of existence which happens in the service of the state is indeed complete when it has gone as far as death; but the hazard of death which the individual survives leaves him with a definite existence and hence with a *particular self-interest*, and this makes his counsel about what is best for the general good ambiguous and open to suspicion. It means that he has in fact reserved his own opinion and his own particular will in face of the power of the state. (*PS*, 307, para. 506)

Whereas ignoble consciousness survives and acts in his own interests, even in the act of self-sacrifice, his noble cousin preserves his self-consciousness in the renunciation of self-interest: "Without this renunciation of self, the deeds of honour, the deeds of the noble consciousness, and the counsels based on its insight would retain the ambiguity possessed by that private reserve of particular intention and self-will" (*PS*, 308, para. 507). In this assessment of the role of noble and ignoble consciousness, Hegel provides male counterparts to the feminine subversive. Their milieu is the bureaucratizing government, not yet the service of the state to the nation.

However, both feminine desire and masculine self-advancement fall under Hegel's critical gaze. Here the affiliation between the subversive feminine and the unmasculine comes into ascendance. Between the publication of the *Phenomenology* and the *Philosophy of Right*, the German-speaking states, in alliance with Prussia, succeed in driving the French from their soil. In the immensely popular genre of patriotic poetry, Napoleon and the French in general came to represent the weak, shifty, and ethically challenged category of the feminized man. In the poetry and essays of E. M. Arndt and others, the French enemies and their sympathizers preferred cosmopolitan luxury to the hard life of a German soldier, fighting for freedom and the greatness of the Fatherland.[31] War draws thick lines to define gender roles, and the Wars of Liberation are no exception. The enemy included not only the feminized French but the cowardly "boys" who refuse to honor their own masculinity.[32] The rhetoric of sacrifice is fused with the rhetoric of gender and national identity. Sacrifice is crucial to Hegel's concept of war and is homologous with the more widely popularized notions of citizenship. In the *Philosophy of Right,* he leaves behind the turbulence of gendered allegories from the *Phenomenology*; the sacrifice of the self to the state is marred by its particularity. The question of female particularity is deferred; it does not resurface in the *Phenomenology.*[33] The element of sacrifice returns, with attention to gender, and there are poets who acknowledge female sacrifices in a time of war, but this realization does not resonate with Hegel.[34] From the blood-infused mud of German soil to the lofty heights of philosophical discourse, the nation as a category participates in the dialectic of universal aims and individual desire. Particularity intimately linked to the feminine remains suspect.[35] Hegel leverages the dialectic of the particular against the universal, elevating the sacrifice of life in war in the name of the nation, thus in the name of the universal.

Particularity of Nation

In the preceding section, I move perhaps too fluidly between the philosophical concepts of particularity and the more general psychological and political term *individuality* to demonstrate a certain slippage in the *Phenomenology* when Hegel deals with the example of woman and her role in the life of the community. Before I turn to the role of nation in the *Philosophy of Right,* I want to look briefly at a crucial passage in *Enzyklopädie der philosophischen Wissenschaften* from the first section on the Science of Logic. This passage, which grounds textually the claim that freedom for Hegel is freedom from particularity,[36] but also furthers Butler's discussion of the relationship between the universal and the particular, provides a transition from the early text of the *Phenomenology* to the *Philosophy of Right.*[37] Butler concludes, as I cite above, "There is no way to bring the excluded particularity into the universal without first negating that particularity."[38] Butler's concern is a contemporary debate about the inflections of identity, represented by gender, nation, and class: the predicates of being in the political arena in which the voice of the particular must claim universal status in order to attain certain rights.

My concern is the context in which the competing particularities in his system of thought remain unrecuperated or gain ascendance in the dialectical progression. I maintain that there is an asymmetrical relationship between the particular and the universal. The meaning of the concept shifts from text to text, and multiple particularities exist, but the universal is singular. Abstract thought is indeed defined by the ability to think outside the box of particularity. One could object to my reading of the feminine in the earlier text because of its philosophical genre (phenomenology); if figures of consciousness are present in the narrative in order to be overcome, then the discussion of woman, Antigone, and individuality in general can be read as stations of thought on the way to the gallery of images that encompass Absolute Knowledge at the end. However, the status of particularity takes on a different meaning in the *Enzyklopädie*, one that constitutes abstract thought as the basis of freedom in the context of a greater human community. The passage reads:

> Freedom lies immediately in thought, because it is the activity of the general, thereby an abstract self-referentiality, a being-with-itself without predicates, according to subjectivity, which is according to *content* simultaneously only in the *thing* and its conditions. If then there is talk of humility or modesty and of haughtiness with regard to philosophy, and humility or modesty exists therein: to attribute to its subjectivity not the particularity of character and activity, thus philosophy at least will be acquitted of haughtiness in that thought according to content is true insofar as it is immersed in the thing and according to the form is not a *particular* being or activity of the subject, but rather it is this: that consciousness behaves as an abstract I, as an I *freed* from all particularity of other qualities, circumstances, etc. and performs only the general in which it is identical with all individuals.[39]

Within the discourse of the logic, abstract thought defines freedom, which in turn requires the conscious renunciation of all particularity, here expressed as any attributes that bar the path of the general. This definition of abstraction is the prerequisite for any participation in the general process not only of thought but of identity with other individuals. In other words, the participation in abstract thought itself signals membership in a larger community, society, perhaps even the nation, imagined or otherwise. Abstract thought, theory, is the cognitive vehicle to collective identity. Without particularity, the abstract, liberated "I" achieves identity with all other individuals. Universality is attained precisely through emancipating the "I" from its predicates. In another context, Hegel counts abstract thought, this "I" without predicates, as a central criterion for German masculinity.[40] While he does not explicitly abnegate particularity, he makes its sacrifice the condition of any participation in universal, general principles. He also makes one exception: nation.

The status of particularity shifts in the *Philosophy of Right*. In the section of Ethical Life, subsection "External Sovereignty," Hegel continues to outline the relationship between the individual and the state. He assigns individuals the duty of preserving the sovereignty of the state, "[. . .] even if their own life and property, as well as their opinions and all that naturally falls within the province of life, are endangered or sacrificed."[41] Hegel takes pains to remove feminine particularity and desire from war, the willfulness and perversity he attributes to the desiring woman in the *Phenomenology*. It is still a defining ethical moment. In the same philosophical idiom, he recuperates particularity, the individual assertion of will against the greater good of the universal:

> War is that condition in which the vanity of temporal things [*Dinge*] and temporal goods—which tends at other times to be merely a pious phrase—takes on a serious significance, and it is accordingly the moment at which the ideality of *the particular attains its right* and becomes actuality. The higher significance of war is that, through its agency (as I have put it on another occasion), "the ethical health of nations [*Völker*] is preserved in their indifference towards the permanence of finite determinacies, just as the movement of the winds preserves the sea from that stagnation which a lasting calm would produce—a stagnation which a lasting, not to say perpetual, peace would also produce among nations." (*PR*, 361, para. 324)

Jason Smith, in his introductory discussion of Jean-Luc Nancy's work on the negative in Hegel, brings together the concept of the state, war, and individual freedom: "For it is precisely at the moment when the individual submits to the law that it is most free; it is precisely at the moment in which its own rights and freedoms are given up that the individual manifests its true freedom—this moment is called war."[42] Smith's observation is astute: The state and individual are identical at this moment of shared freedom and submission to law. The status of war in the *Philosophy of Right* differs considerably from its discussion in the *Phenomenology*, though its role in representing the moment of ethical life in the community remains the same. What has changed? When particularity is defined by gender, Hegel laments the negativity of woman. Yet she grounds ethical identity in the home. The ethical life of the people or nation must transcend this particularity in order to account for the ethical presence in the public sphere from which the feminine is excluded. What justifies the leap from female desire of the brave youth to this naturalized portrayal of war as a necessary movement in the tide of history? The answers are crucial and complex, and here I can sketch only a provisional response.

Hegel contains desire; in the *Philosophy of Right*, he expands his definition of civil society, the anchor of which is the family.[43] He defines marriage as the elimination of whim and willfulness, circumscribes it in the domestic, and stabilizes gender roles to the extent that any ambiguity in relationships is purged. In other words, Hegel institutionalizes the particularity of woman while the masculine experiences the division between public and private personae. The family circumscribes the feminine:

> Man therefore has his actual substantial life in the state, in learning [*Wissenschaft*], etc., and otherwise in work and struggle with the external world and with himself, so that it is only through his division that he fights his way to self-sufficient unity with himself. In the family, he has a peaceful intuition of this unity, and an emotive [*empfindend*] and subjective ethical life. Woman, however, has her substantial vocation [*Bestimmung*] in the family, and her ethical disposition consists in this [family] *piety*. (*PR*, 206, para. 166)[44]

Only the masculine is dialectical, thus giving it access to the actual, while the feminine is not; elsewhere in Hegel's work, in his critique of irony, for example, the undialectical is harshly criticized. Hegel returns to the figure of Antigone, his private version of Antigone: here piety "[. . .] is declared to be the primary law of woman" (ibid.). Here her particularity is reserved for the family, in which man intuits the unity he does not share. Desire, harnessed by the rational, plays no part in this family romance.

Hegel accommodates the particularity of nation. The historical intervention of Prussia in the Wars of Liberation provides a radically different backdrop to philosophy from that of the Napoleonic advance into German states from the early nineteenth century. While I would not endorse a facile cause-effect relationship between history and Hegel's philosophy, I argue that an attempt to historicize the role of particularities, specifically the feminine and the national, helps decipher the dialectic of identity and difference beyond the "metaphysics of closure" in Hegel's thought. Certainly the historical events that unfolded during the remainder of the nineteenth and throughout the last century underwrite the status of "nation" as a master signifier. Yet there is more than a contingent relationship between the abstracted role of war and its presence in Hegel's discourse on women and the nation. Hegel's philosophical and scientific method, the dialectic, relies on the recuperation of particularity into the universal. Particularity in and of itself is never valorized *except* in this definition of war—which Hegel insists is an extraordinary recourse, to be avoided at all costs, but still imperative. Hegel further nationalizes particularity, gives it rights, and includes it in an acceptable moment in the ethical life of nations. In the metaphoric winds of war, Hegel renaturalizes the occurrence of battle, implicitly critiquing Kant's essay on perpetual peace. Ultimately, the dialectic of identity and difference privileges identity, and consulting the narratives of history reveals how particularities are leveraged in the dialectic with the universal. However, the dialectic itself remains the most appropriate tool with which to critique that asymmetry, that historical imbalance of power among competing particularities.

Notes

*Parts of this chapter appear in chapter 1 of my *The Erotics of War in German Romanticism* (Lewisburg, PA: Bucknell University Press, 2006). I thank Bucknell for permission to reprint.

1. For an overview, see Lawrence Grossberg et al., eds., *Cultural Studies* (New York and London: Routledge, 1992), esp. Cary Nelson, Paula A. Treichler, and Lawrence Grossberg, "Cultural Studies: An Introduction," 1–16. There the editors provide a social, historical, and disciplinary context in which to understand the flexible methodologies, sometimes "counter-disciplinary" (4) approach to knowledge informed by cultural studies. Equally useful is their sketch of cultural studies' major engagements with Marxism and linguistic theory, sociology, subcultures, media studies, feminism, and issues of race, class, and ethnicity (9).

Stuart Hall briefly mentions Hegel in "Theoretical Legacies," where he recounts attempts to engage theory and resists any notion that Marxism and cultural studies "joined hands in some teleological or Hegelian moment of synthesis" (280). In the discussion of his paper on aesthetics, Ian Hunter refers to "'meta-institutional' theories of culture derived from the Hegelian and Marxian traditions" (370), and elsewhere, Hunter traces a certain indebtedness to Romantic aesthetics through an investment in Marxist analytical tools (see Meaghan Morris, 466, in the same reader, for further references).

In a discussion of Henry Louis Gates's early critical work, Michele Wallace observes in "Toward a Black Feminist Cultural Criticism," that "[f]rom an 'Afro-centric' perspective, current trends in critical theory look mighty like an exercise in self-absorption designed to reconsolidate the canon of Western Masters (not just Milton and Shakespeare but Hegel, Marx, and Freud, too!), thus trivializing the analysis of any aspect of Afro-American or African diasporic cultural development" (660). Later work insists on a more direct encounter with Hegel's texts, a closer examination of relationships between theories of hegemony and universality. See note 7.

2. For example, Mary O'Brien writes the following: "Hegelian Universality is essentially a *Brotherhood*, united in creation of a community and in the annulment of the natural, in whose sphere women may chafe only impotently." See "Hegel: Man, Physiology, and Fate," in *Feminist Interpretations of G. W. F. Hegel*, ed. Patricia Jagentowicz Mills (University Park: Pennsylvania State University Press, 1996), 179 ff., here 188. O'Brien is not working within the rubric of cultural studies in this observation. I refer more generally to the use of categories of the universal, the absolute, and identity. See also Lata Mani, "Cultural Theory, Colonial Texts: Reading Eyewitness Accounts of Widow Burning," Lawrence Grossberg et al., eds., *Cultural Studies* (New York, London: Routledge, 1992), 392–405. Considering the institutional possibility of cultural studies, Mani suggests that it will "provide a location where the new politics of difference—racial, sexual, cultural, transnational—can combine and be articulated in all their dazzling plurality" (392). Mani observes, however, that "despite its critique of universalisms and essentialisms, there are ways in which certain forms of Euro-American post-structuralism continue to reproduce both" (ibid.). Referring to arguments made by Trinh T. Minh Ha, Mani warns against a "'separate but equal' notion of difference" (393) that potentially obscures any analysis of power relations. These cautionary words inform my attempt to read the power structure between elements of "difference" within Hegel's own work and to historicize the discrepancies among competing particularities.

3. Robert B. Pippin, *Idealism As Modernism* (Cambridge: Cambridge University Press, 1997), 2. Pippin follows up this argument, specifically with regard to those who characterize Hegel's philosophy as one of "'anti-individualism'," in "Hegel's practical philosophy," in *The Cambridge Companion to German Idealism*, ed. Karl Ameriks (Cambridge: Cambridge University Press, 2000), 180–99, here 181.

4. In note 4 to Pippin's "Introduction," he concedes that Hegel indeed did "[. . .] say many ignorant and proimperialist things about, for instance, India or Africa. [. . .] But the philosophical issue concerns the issue now called 'orientalism,' or whether either the very possibility of the institutions Hegel wishes to defend or the ethical norms he wishes to establish as a matter of reason logically presupposes or entails some fabulous 'construction' of an inferior 'other.' I know of no argument establishing such a philosophical point." See Pippin, *Idealism As Modernism*, 4.

5. Ibid., 16.

6. Gayatri Chakravorty Spivak, *A Critique of Postcolonial Reason: Toward a History of the Vanishing Present* (Cambridge, MA: Harvard University Press, 1999), ix.

7. Others have concentrated on Hegel's designation of India as a "land dominated by imagination rather than reason." See Ronald B. Inden, *Imagining India* (Bloomington: Indiana University Press, 1990), 8.

8. Judith Butler, Ernesto Laclau, and Slavoj Žižek, *Contingency, Hegemony, Universality: Contemporary Dialogues on the Left* (London: Verso, 2000), 2.

9. Haym, quoted in Joachim Ritter, *Hegel and the French Revolution: Essays on the Philosophy of Right*, translated and with Introduction by Richard Dien Winfield (Cambridge, MA, and London: MIT Press, 1982), 35.

10. Terry Pinkard, *Hegel: A Biography* (Cambridge: Cambridge University Press, 2000). Butler also reads this passage, however, as a negation of universal, human attributes on which abstract thought is predicated. See Butler, "Restaging the Universal: Hegemony and the Limits of Formalism," in *Contingency, Hegemony, Universality*, 11–43, here 17–18.

11. Ibid., 24. In different terms, Jean-Luc Nancy argues, "No generality and no universality are worth anything unto themselves, nor can they subsume or sublimate the absolute position of the singular." See Jean-Luc Nancy, *Hegel: The Restlessness of the Negative*, trans. Jason Smith and Steven Miller (Minneapolis: University of Minnesota Press, 2002), 57

12. In his introduction to the *Elements of the Philosophy of Right*, ed. Allen W. Wood; trans. H. B. Nisbet (Cambridge: Cambridge University Press, 1991), Wood points out that in the text, war is a circumstance under which the state requires sacrifice of individuals: "We badly misunderstand Hegel's view if we think it implies that wars are a good thing [. . .]" (xxvi). I would not counter Wood's statement, and it is not my intention to misread Hegel or suggest that he theorizes war as desirable. My aim is to interrogate the conditions of his philosophical argument and how it shifts with regard to the status of particularity.

13. I depart from the argument made by Spivak in *A Critique of Postcolonial Reason*, specifically her attempt to expose the "discontinuity between sex- and race-differentiation." (30). While the reading of Hegel in her first chapter ("Philosophy") dwells on his interpretation of the *Srimadbhagavadgita* in the *Lectures on Fine Art*, her point about Hegel's status as a dominant signifier for the West and Western ideology ("Hegel") is revealing. My intention here is to foreground the role of history within the hierarchy of Hegelian particularities.

14. Pinkard, *Hegel*, 70.

15. Ibid., 191.

16. Ibid., 482.

17. Ute Frevert presents a more complete picture of Caroline Schlegel-Schelling: "Despite the turbulent and unconventional course of her life, she upheld the principles of female duty and utterly condemned those who violated them."

See Ute Frevert, *Women in German History: From Bourgeois Emancipation to Sexual Liberation*, trans. Stuart McKinnon-Evans, with Terry Bond and Barbara Norden (Oxford and New York: Berg, 1989, 1997; first published by Suhrkamp, 1986), 51.

18. Seyla Benhabib, "On Hegel, Women, and Irony," in *Feminist Interpretations*, 27; also in *Situating the Self: Gender, Community, and Postmodernism in Contemporary Ethics* (New York: Routledge, 1992), 243–44.

19. On Schlegel's novel and his further theory of femininity, see Frevert, *Women in German History*, 57 ff.

20. The scholarship on irony in the literature of Hegel's time is vast. See Lilian R. Furst, *Fictions of Romantic Irony* (Cambridge, MA: Harvard University Press, 1984). For a more theoretical reading, see Philippe Lacoue-Labarthe and Jean-Luc Nancy, *The Literary Absolute. The Theory of Literature in German Romanticism*, trans. Philip Barnard and Cheryl Lester (Albany: State University of New York Press, 1988). For a sustained analysis of irony as a "theory" that crosses disciplinary borders, see Uwe Japp, *Theorie der Ironie* (Frankfurt am Main: Vittorio Klostermann, 1983). Some feminist philosophers focus more on the status of irony as a potential for political change in an attempt to reclaim the subversive element in Hegel's definition. Richard Rorty's work follows and departs from this tradition.

21. See my "'Wo die Ironie erscheint': Tieck als Herausgeber in den Jahrbücher-Rezensionen," in *Die "Jahrbücher für wissenschaftliche Kritik": Hegels Berliner Gegenakademie*, ed. Christoph Jamme (Stuttgart: Frommann-Holzboog, 1994), 301–20, for an extended reading of this connection with regard to Hegel's Solger review and H. G. Hotho's Kleist commentary. The explicit connection between irony and a lack of masculinity and Prussian patriotism is specific to Hotho's review of Kleist's work. See also Otto Pöggeler, *Hegels Kritik der Romantik* (Munich: Wilhelm Fink Verlag, 1999), esp. 45 ff. for an overview of the historical and biographical context in which Hegel's critique of Romanticism unfolds and the place of irony in that critique. Pöggeler is largely unconcerned with issues of gender.

22. Richard Rorty takes the high road here and associates irony with the possibility of a liberating consciousness in *Contingency, Irony, and Solidarity* (Cambridge: Cambridge University Press, 1989), though others, Benhabib among them, have profiled a less generous approach, situating Hegel in the contemporary debate about sexuality, philosophy, and women. See "On Hegel, Women, and Irony," in *Situating the Self*, 242–50. Benhabib, too, relies quite a bit on the biographical; on Hegel's antipathy for F. Schlegel and Caroline Schlegel-Schelling, among others, but not without connection to his texts.

23. Benhabib, "On Hegel, Women, and Irony," in *Feminist Interpretations*, 41.

24. In Benhabib's reading, she mentions poet Karoline von Günderrode and that she was in love with Hegel's friend, poet Friedrich Hölderlin (*Situating the Self*, 252). Günderrode shared with her friend Bettina von Arnim a love of the poet's work, but there is no evidence that Günderrode, who committed

suicide in 1806, and Hölderlin, who lapsed tragically into madness the same year, ever met. Benhabib also writes: "It is widely believed that Caroline Schlegel was the model for the heroine in the novel *Lucinde*" (ibid.). The model is Dorothea Veit, F. Schlegel's divorced lover whom he eventually marries. Caroline Schlegel is figured in his *Gespräch über die Poesie*, along with other thinly veiled members of the Jena circle, about which Hegel was deeply ambivalent. I insist here for a reason: The historical context of women remains obscure, even as we heed the call for its close inspection.

25. This was a term of derision in the journalism associated with the Wars of Liberation. See, for example, Ernst Moritz Arndt, *Ausgewählte Werke*, ed. Heinrich Meisner and Robert Geerds (Leipzig: Max Hesses Verlag, 1908), 16 vols. In general terms, E. M. Arndt condemns all cosmopolitans, contrasting them to nationalists (vol.1, 24).

26. Patricia Jagentowicz Mills, "Hegel's *Antigone*," in *Feminist Interpretations*, 59 ff., here 68.

27. I quote throughout from the *Phenomenology of Spirit* (hereafter *PS*), trans. A. V. Miller, foreword J. N. Findlay (Oxford: Oxford University Press, 1977), with reference to the original where noted, ed. Eva Moldenhauer and Karl Markus Michel (Frankfurt am Main: Suhrkamp Taschenbuch, 1973). Further citations will be noted by page and paragraph number.

28. On gender difference and forms of kinship, see Butler, *Antigone's Claim: Kinship between Life and Death* (New York: Columbia University Press, 2000). She writes that kinship "is not yet entered into the social, where the social is inaugurated through a violent supersession of kinship" (3).

29. Butler, *Antigone's Claim*, 37. My reading also is informed by Butler's *Subjects of Desire. Hegelian Reflections in Twentieth-Century France* (New York: Columbia University Press, 1987).

30. Hegel's insistence on the separateness of theory from politics, a stance he maintained throughout his career (Ritter, *Hegel and the French Revolution*, 115) may seem disingenuous, given his eventual status as a civil servant.

31. A closer look at the context from which Arndt's poem emerges brings the relationship between French, foreign, and immoral into sharp focus. These traits are feminized in Arndt's general journalism. Arndt condemns Napoleon for betraying his wife, a popular queen (*Geist der Zeit*, I, *Werke*, IX: 73). He refers to Napoleon as "the little Corsican" ("der kleine Korse" [IX: 195]) and attacks his masculinity: "You are small as you are showy, a bloated oriental, just as your luck and fate were oriental, and an astonished Europe beholds this new miracle" (my translations) (*Geist der Zeit*, I, IX: 25). All the while, Arndt valorizes war: Napoleon's reasons for fighting also are corrupt, a violation of the sacred imperative of war (he fights for wealth and self-aggrandizement). While the French reveal a certain barbarity, Arndt recuperates the "precivilized" German male model: the Teutonic warrior.

32. In Theodor Körner we encounter images of the feminine that exceed the roles Arndt imagines for those of the weaker sex left behind. In his poem *Männer und Buben*, Körner rehearses a variety of scenarios in each stanza, in which real men who fight are compared to the *Buben* (boys) who stay behind. This poem draws a dividing line between the men and the boys—the instruments of separation include the ability to attract women. In the refrain, the *Buben* are further stigmatized: a German girl will not kiss them. In the moment Körner includes national identity in the attributes of masculinity, he also confers agency on German female desire. See *Die Patriotische Lyrik der Befreiungskriege*, ed. Adolf Matthias (Bielefeld and Leipzig: Velhagen & Klasing, 1925), 88-90.

33. Mills writes: "The question of exactly how woman can represent the sphere of particularity while never knowing herself as this particular self is a question never addressed by Hegel" ("Hegel's *Antigone*," 68).

34. Friedrich Rückert was one poet who celebrated female sacrifices during the Wars of Liberation. Also a professor for oriental languages in Berlin, he wrote about the sacrifice of wedding rings as a point of departure for the sacrifice of sons, addressed to the "Women of Prussia" (*Die Patriotische Lyrik der Befreiungskriege*, 119). The sacrifice of boys, or *Knaben*, is ambiguous in terms of affiliation, but the jewelry symbolizes a first step, attesting to the emotional disposition of Prussia's women, willing to sacrifice all they have.

35. For a reading on the recuperation of the particular, articulated as "detail," in aesthetic theory, see Naomi Schor, "Reading in Detail: Hegel's Aesthetics and the Feminine, in *Feminist Interpretations*, 119–47.

36. Terry Pinkard, *Hegel: A Biography* (Cambridge: Cambridge University Press, 2000).

37. Butler also reads this passage, however, as a negation of universal, human attributes on which abstract thought is predicated. See Butler, "Restaging the Universal: Hegemony and the Limits of Formalism," in *Contingency, Hegemony, Universality*, 11–43, here 17–18.

38. Ibid., 24.

39. G. W. F. Hegel, *Enzyklopädie der philosophischen Wissenschaften im Grundrisse* (1830). *Erster Teil: Die Wissenschaft der Logik*, vol. 8 of *Werke in 20 Bänden*, ed. Eva Modenhauer and Karl Markus Michel (Frankfurt am Main: Suhrkamp, 1970), vol. 1, 80, para. 23, my translation, emphasis in original.

40. In the review of Solger's work, Hegel reads the negativity of irony as a misunderstanding of Fichte's philosophy: "In the movement from abstract thought, between the general and the specific: It is in this transition that irony appears" (my translation). From *Berliner Schriften 1818–1831*, *Werke II* (Frankfurt am Main: Suhrkamp Taschenbuch, 1970, 1986), 257.

41. Hegel, *Elements of the Philosophy of Right*, ed. Allen W. Wood, trans. H. B. Nisbet (Cambridge: Cambridge University Press, 1991), 360. Subsequent references appear in parentheses following direct quotations.

42. From Jean-Luc Nancy, *Hegel: The Restlessness of the Negative*, trans. Jason Smith and Steven Miller (Minneapolis: University of Minnesota Press, 2002), Smith's introduction, xx. See also his note on paragraphs 258 and 324, in which Hegel explicitly differentiates the state from civil society in a time of war, n. 26, 112–13.

43. For a sustained reading of Antigone, see Patricia Jagentowicz Mills, "Hegel's *Antigone*," in *Feminist Interpretations*, 59–88, esp. 78.

44. Frevert writes: "The model of the family and marriage that emerged fitted neatly into the new political climate of Restoration, and drew on the strict gender-specific differentiation of roles and characters of the pre-Romantic age without, however, *incorporating the products of the Enlightenment and doctrine of natural laws" (Women in German History*, 63, emphasis added). She refers as well to para. 166 to demonstrate the degree to which the male "personal identity and social position" were located in the realm of the actual, defined as the state (Frevert, *Women in German History*, 65).

Chapter 9

The Return of Africa: Hegel and the Question of the Racial Identity of the Egyptians

Robert Bernasconi

At the end of his scandalous discussion of sub-Saharan Africa, and before beginning his account of world history, Hegel announced in a well-known and yet usually unquestioned sentence that he would leave Africa behind, never to mention it again.[1] This has perhaps led casual readers of the *Lectures on the Philosophy of History* to imagine Hegel's ancient Egyptians as Caucasian, or at least anything but black. There is support for this image of Hegel's Egyptians in the fact that he discussed Egypt within the section on Persia, which had begun with his announcement that the Caucasians were finally on the scene and that the account of world history proper could now begin.[2] Employing Blumenbach's racial categories, Hegel consigned the Chinese and the Hindus to "the strictly Asiatic, namely, the Mongolian race," whereas the nations of the Middle East are said to belong to "the Caucasian, i.e., European stock."[3] However, I shall argue that Hegel's text makes it impossible to ignore the fact that, with Egypt, Africa finds a place in his account of world history, and that its introduction is necessary for the transition from the Persian empire to Greece, precisely because of the role he accords to race in his understanding of history. I will introduce my reading by showing, on historical grounds, that Hegel's auditors would not have doubted that the Egyptians were black.

Hegel delivered his *Lectures on the Philosophy of History* during the height of Egyptomania. Interest in Egypt had grown in Northern Europe as a result of the studies made at the time of Napoleon's invasion and had flourished further as the work of deciphering Egyptian hieroglyphs finally advanced. In consequence, the question of the racial identity of the ancient Egyptians had become a prominent issue. The overwhelmingly dominant view was that although they were not strictly Negro in the narrow sense, they belonged to the black race. At the end of the eighteenth century, Constantine de Volney and, following him, Henri Grégoire presented Egypt as a challenge to the growth of a theoretically articulated racial hierarchy; hence Egypt served as one of the foremost battlegrounds on which the debate about white racial superiority was fought. The problem this posed to white racists was eventually answered both by whitening the ancient Egyptians and by minimizing their contribution, but contrary to a widespread impression, this did not take place in any systematic way until the 1840s.[4] My question here concerns how Hegel's discussion of Egypt reflects the state of this debate in his time. In particular, there is the question of how this discussion relates to the much vexed issue of Hegel's discussion of African identity. I argue in this chapter that Hegel's discussion of Egypt in his *Lectures on the Philosophy of History* reads entirely differently once one recognizes the state of the question on the racial identity of the ancient Egyptians at the time he was delivering his lectures. Furthermore, Hegel's discussion of Egyptian identity can be used to throw light on his conception of race. To understand Hegel's contribution to nineteenth-century race thinking, one should not try to locate his account with reference to the arguments for and against monogenesis, which he dismissed as a fruitless debate, but with reference to world history. To that extent, Hegel's discussion points forward more to the philosophy of history of Gobineau or Robert Knox than back to the natural history of race of Kant, albeit Kant set the framework for Hegel's philosophy of history.

The terms of the debate over the racial identity of the ancient Egyptians had already been established before Hegel entered it, although it should always be remembered that this was a relatively recent debate as the European obsession with racial classification had taken hold only in the last quarter of the eighteenth century. If the people of ancient Egypt were African in a way that attached them to the so-called Ethiopian, black, or Negro race, then the attempt to match the hierarchy of civilizations to the hierarchy of races, which Europeans had already defined in the late eighteenth century, could not be sustained. It was the test case for early nineteenth-century racism, and the stakes were particularly high as the Greeks had been explicit about their debt to the Egyptians. In 1787, Constantine de Volney published his *Travels through Egypt and Syria,* where he declared that the Copts, who were widely thought to be the descendants of the ancient Egyptians, still had largely Negro characteristics.[5] Four years later he published *The*

Ruins, or Meditations on the Revolutions of Empires, some editions of which include the sentence "A race of men now rejected from society for their *sable skin and frizzled hair*, founded on the study of the laws of nature, those civil and religious systems which still govern the universe."[6] However, Europeans were becoming increasingly invested in the idea of their own preeminence, even though the evidence of the depth and persistence of the civilizations of China and India had made that at times a difficult thesis to uphold.[7] Northern Europeans had decided to take a kind of ownership of the ancient civilizations of Greece and Rome, partly as a response to this challenge, but the question of the racial identity of the ancient Egyptians became a matter of urgency only as the classification of the races became more rigorous and more nuanced, a process that began only at the end of the eighteenth century. Volney focused on the contrast between the former preeminence of the Egyptians and their current state of decline, thereby highlighting the problem that gave rise to the philosophy of history, the problem of the rise and fall of civilizations. However, by addressing that question in terms of race, he also was well placed to make a comment on the most urgent ethico-political problem of the day, that of the system of chattel slavery imposed on Africans by whites. He believed that the historical facts about Egypt gave philosophy a great deal to think about:

> How are we astonished when we behold the present barbarism and ignorance of the Copts, descended from the profound genius of the Egyptians, and the brilliant intelligence of the Greeks; when we reflect that to the negroes, at present our slaves, and the objects of our extreme contempt, we owe our arts, sciences, and even the very use of speech![8]

Grégoire took up Volney's argument in the opening chapter of his *De la literature des nègres*.[9] Little wonder, then, that in the face of this challenge the upholders of black inferiority recognized the need to respond by challenging the tradition that assigned the racial identity of the Egyptians to black Africa.

We know that Hegel had in his personal library a French copy of Volney's *The Ruins*, and that he alluded to it when he referred to Egypt as the "land of ruins."[10] We also know that Hegel read Baron Vivant Denon's *Voyage dans la basse et la haute Égypte*, where the African features of the Sphinx were described.[11] Denon described the sphinx as follows:

> The expression of the head is soft, gracious, and tranquil. The character is African; but the mouth, the lips of which are thick, has a sweetness in its drawing and an elegance in its execution which are truly admirable.[12]

Hegel also would have read in Denon's description of the several races living in Rashid in which he expressed his conviction that the same facial features that one saw in the ancient Egyptian sculptures could be recognized in the Copts of his day, and that the old Egyptian stock was a kind of swarthy Nubian. Among the features Denon identified were a flat face, half woolly hair, eyes half open, a nose more short than flat, and large lips.[13] Hegel, who was an avid reader of Herodotus, also would have known his description of the Egyptians as having "black skins and wooly hair."[14] Hegel cited in his *Lectures on the Philosophy of History* a story from James Bruce's *Travels to Discover the Source of the Nile,* and even if he had not read the book carefully, he must have noticed Bruce's conviction that Egypt had been populated from Ethiopia (VG, 230; LPW, 187).[15] There is no doubt therefore that Hegel was aware that the dominant view was that the ancient Egyptians had been black.

Hegel also would have been aware that in the late eighteenth century there had been a few countervoices to this idea. He would have known that Herder thought that the ancient Egyptians were from Southern Asia,[16] but he might not have been familiar with Christoph Meiners's argument that the Egyptians were closer in bodily formation to Indians than to Ethiopians and that the political institutions of India also bore resemblance to that of the Egyptians.[17] Hegel also knew the third edition of Johann Blumenbach's *De generis humani varietate nativa,* where a distinction was drawn between three different facial forms found in Egyptian art: the Ethiopian (Blumenbach's name for blacks), the Indian, and a third degenerate form specific to Egypt's climate.[18] However, Hegel perhaps was not aware that Blumenbach had placed the ancient Egyptians somewhere between the Caucasian and Ethiopian races.[19] At the turn of the century, some argued that ancient Egypt had been peopled from Arabia, but there were few prominent exponents of this view.[20] Among more recent works Hegel knew Baron Cuvier's monumental study *The Animal Kingdom,* which followed Blumenbach's division of the human species into three main races—the Caucasians, the Mongolian, and the Ethiopian—and located the Egyptians "very probably" among the Armenian or Syrian branch of the Caucasian stock. Cuvier explained: "It is from this branch, always inclined to mysticism, that have sprung the most widely extended forms of religion. Science and literature have sometimes flourished among its nations but always in a strange disguise and figurative style."[21] However, Hegel had almost certainly not read Cuvier's 1817 essay, in which he went farther and challenged the idea that Egyptian civilization was created by a "race of blacks," asserting instead that it was by men of "the same race as ourselves" who had "an equally large cranium and brain." He declared that there was a "cruel law which seems to have condemned to an external inferiority the races of depressed and compressed skulls."[22] However, although the anti-black prejudice that Cuvier expressed was widespread, his attack on the thesis that the ancient Egyptians were black seems to have had only a minor impact at the time.

Finally, we know that Hegel was aware of Giovanni Belzoni's exhibition of Egyptian antiquities in Picadilly in London in 1821, which made an important contribution to the growing enthusiasm for Egypt, and he had read Belzoni's travel journal, from the years 1815 to 1819, which was published in 1820 (V12, 290, 300; also VPW, 480, 492). One observation in particular contributed to the debate over the racial constitution of the Egyptians. He commented that most often Egyptian painters used a red color to portray skin color, "as if they were unacquainted with any colour to imitate the naked parts," but he judged that this was not because they could not paint it more realistically: "Yet it cannot be supposed that they did not know how to reduce their red paints to a flesh colour, for on some occasions, where the red flesh is supposed to be seen through a thin veil, the tints are nearly of the natural colour, if we suppose the Egyptians to have been of the same hue as their successors, the present Copts, some of whom are nearly as fair as the Europeans."[23] Although the remark explicitly assumes and does not prove that the ancient Egyptians were white, and although the evidence cited shows only that they did not paint their flesh as white, it was latched onto by subsequent commentators, such as Heeren in the 1826 edition of his *Ideen über die Politik, den Verkehr und den Handel*, as a direct refutation of Volney.[24] We know that Hegel read Heeren on Persia (VPW, 422). However, the basic framework of Hegel's treatment of the role of Africa in his treatment of Egypt was already set in 1822, and so it is clear that Heeren's 1826 text was not decisive for him on this point, if he read it at all. In the 1804 and 1815 editions, Heeren cited Herodotus's statement about the Egyptians being a black race with wooly hair as decisive proof that Egypt had many blacks, if it did not consist completely of blacks.

This sentence was omitted in 1826, as was the earlier conclusion that it was more than probable that the population of Egypt hailed from Ethiopia or Southern Africa (IP, 1804, 545, IP, 1815, 519, IP, 1826, 83). Heeren's 1826 edition thus marks a significant date in the debate about the racial identity of ancient Egyptian civilization, but it is noteworthy that even he was more intent on challenging Volney's arguments for a black civilization than on establishing a portrait of a white Egypt.

In sum, the consensus about the African nature of the ancient Egyptians, in whole or in part, was still largely intact at the beginning of the 1820s, and indeed, with a few exceptions, it was to last another twenty years. It would have been impossible in this context for Hegel to think of the ancient Egyptians as Caucasian and not mention it. However, if the Egyptians were black—whether or not they were Negroes, an important distinction too often ignored in the secondary literature but recognized by Heeren (see IP, 1804, 337, IP, 1815, 311, IP, 1826, 504–505)—then how did they find their place after the point at which Hegel had turned to the Caucasians? Hegel's answer seems relatively clear, but it remains problematic. He considered Egypt a province of the great Persian Empire (V12, 311). Hegel's immediate justification for considering Egypt in the context of Persia was based not on race but on the idea that historically the transition between Egypt and Greece came when Egypt was part of the Persian Empire (V12, 311; W2, 270; PH, 221). However, Hegel still had to explain why he located there the transition from nature to spirit that provided for liberation in the form of universal inwardness (V12, 268, 309), and, as I shall argue, the racial question resurfaces at that point.

When in the Introduction to the *Lectures on World History* Hegel announced that he would leave Africa behind, never to mention it again, he acknowledged that Egypt would be considered a stage in the movement of human spirit from east to west that does not belong to the spirit of Africa (VG, 234; LPW, 190). That is, it played no part in what he called "Africa proper." Because Hegel divided Africa into three parts in his account of the geographical basis of history, nobody seems particularly surprised to find a discussion of Egypt later in the book. There is sub-Saharan Africa, which Hegel also called "Africa proper," and which he said was "almost entirely unknown to us," before going on to a detailed and calumnious characterization of it. The centerpiece of that discussion was an account of how cannibalism was entirely compatible with the African principle (VG, 225; LPW, 183), a point he graphically illustrated in his discussion of the Ashanti: "A human being is torn to pieces, his flesh is cast to the multitude and greedily eaten by all who can lay hands on it (VG, 271; LPW, 220). As I have argued elsewhere, there is no known basis for this lurid story.[25] In addition to sub-Saharan Africa is European Africa, the coastland north of the desert. Finally, there is the river region of the Nile, which he placed in connection to Asia: "One might almost say that Africa consists of three continents which are entirely separate from one another" (VG, 213; LPW, 173; see also V12, 39–40). Hegel's division between the three parts of Africa means that his characterization of the inhabitants of the North Africa of his time as not Negroes or true Africans but akin to Europeans[26] tells us no more about his view of the racial identity of the ancient Egyptians than the fact that he listed Europeans, West Asians, Persians, and North Africans under the heading "Caucasians."[27]

This division of Africa has often been challenged by African writers, most notably Cheikh Anta Diop,[28] but it is noteworthy that it was already put in question at the time by an Englishman, Thomas Bowdich, who, in 1821, argued that an emigration from Egypt found its way, via Ethiopia, to the land of the Ashantis.[29] However, there is no evidence that Hegel was aware of Bowdich's treatise linking Egypt to West Africa, even though he had been Hegel's main source on the Ashantis.[30] My point here is simply that Hegel found that this division of Africa into three separate parts could not keep Egypt out of Africa, and thus Africa out of world history. For Hegel, Egypt may not have belonged to the spirit of so-called Africa proper, but sub-Saharan Africa returns with Egypt, his attempt to suppress it notwithstanding.

Hegel did not introduce his detailed treatment of sub-Saharan Africa into his lectures on history until 1824, but the only integral lecture course we have of the lectures is from 1822–1823 (V12). To see how Hegel's division of Africa collapsed in the section on Egypt, we must go to the composite texts in the complete works. Gans's 1837 edition of the lectures, drawn largely from the 1830–1831 lecture course on world history, provides only one direct reference to the relation of Egypt to Africa, but it is a dramatic one. Precisely at the moment of transition to Greece, Hegel drew a contrast within Egypt: on the one hand, the struggle of spirit for its liberation, and, on the other hand, a "naturalness, barbarous sensuality with African hardness, animal worship, the pleasure of living."[31] He illustrated the African side by referring to a woman who committed sodomy with a goat in a public marketplace. He also claimed that in Egypt human flesh was eaten and that human blood was drunk out of revenge. The reference is to Juvenal's *Satire* 14, a text that began by denouncing Egyptian animal worship and went on to claim that while it is forbidden there to eat sheep or goats, one may eat human flesh (xv. 13). Juvenal told the story of how, when in A.D. 127 two towns of upper Egypt were fighting, one fleeing man was captured and torn limb from limb and eaten raw on the spot (xv. 72–83). Juvenal, who had visited Egypt (xv. 45) dismissed it as a savage country (xv. 115). Hegel's point in recalling the story seems to have been to emphasize the connection with the yet more lurid details of his account of cannibalism south of the Sahara (VG, 224–33; LPW, 182–90). He could not have found a more dramatic way to establish in the minds of his audience that in his terms Egypt did belong to Africa.

Already in the 1822–1823 course Hegel introduced Egypt as "a difficult problem" (V12, 275). At the end of his discussion of Egypt, he returned to this characterization: "Here is the land of struggle, of dialectic, the land of problem." However, he added reassuringly: "If the problem is discovered, is determined, the solution is thereby given at the same time" (V12, 309). It is my argument here that the problem Hegel discovered was that of Egypt's relation to Africa, and he was therefore going to have to find a solution. Initially he characterized Egypt's relations with southern Africa as temporary or passing, falling into an older time. This enabled him to dismiss these relations as largely insignificant (V12, 274).[32] However, after quoting Herodotus's judgment at the beginning of the second book, that the Egyptians were the most rational people (*logiotatoi*) of all the peoples he had visited (II, 4 ff.), Hegel announced his astonishment that their reflective understanding or spirit, the intelligible organization, the fine institutions, and the admirable works of fine art, especially architecture, should be accompanied by another side that he called "African stupidity" (V12, 275). A little later Hegel again expressed surprise that the completely ordered political condition of a virtual police state is paired not with a calm religion, as one might expect, but with an African people that burns inwardly in its reserve, remains closed in on itself, and has nothing to do with the outside (V12, 279).[33] How could the Egyptians have been so rational and yet so stupid? Here Hegel's racial views impinge on the very movement of the dialectic.

To pursue this question further, it is necessary to examine briefly Hegel's conception of race.[34] Hegel's role in the history of race thinking has been largely underestimated and, to the extent that it has been addressed, largely misconceived. Scholars today often think anachronistically, focusing on a strictly biological conception of race or, more precisely, because biology was not yet an identifiable science as such, protobiological theories of race.[35] Furthermore, Hegel rejected the debate between monogenesis and polygenesis as being of no philosophical interest, speculating that it had been sparked by the idea that polygenesis would allow for a natural hierarchization of the races (PSS, II, 44–45).[36] In contrast to Kant, for whom that had been a question, Hegel focused on the study of recorded history and derived his understanding of race from it.

> The races are connected with and dependent upon localities, so that no conclusion can be reached with regard to there being an original difference between them. The question of racial variety bears upon the rights one ought to accord to people; when there are various races, one will be nobler and the other has to serve it. (PSS, II, 46–47)

Although this passage leaves room for more than one interpretation, I am inclined to understand it as Hegel's displacement of the question of the origins of racial variety from the status of an abstract question, which not only can never be answered with certainty but also lacks philosophical interest, to a question within the philosophy of world history (PSS, II, 44–45, 64–67). That is, the question of racial differences is addressed in an account of the objective working out of racial differences in history, as would be the case later with Robert Knox, Gobineau, and their successors, for whom climate, conquest, disease, and the impact of race mixing were the crucial factors. The history of Egypt offers a prime example of the history of racial contact in this sense, particularly if one sees it, as Blumenbach had done in his account of Egyptian art, as the copresence of three different types: the Ethiopian, the Indian, and a third degenerate form specific to Egypt's climate. Hegel understood Egypt as a meeting point of the races. In a passage added by Karl Hegel in his edition, we read, "We have here the African element [i.e., stirring and urgent impulses] in combination with Oriental massiveness, transplanted to the Mediterranean Sea, that grand locale of the display of nationalities" (W2, 253, 255–56; PH, 207). The first connection Hegel emphasized was that with Ethiopia: Egypt received its culture *(Bildung)* from Ethiopia (W2, 245; PH, 201). This was the standard conception of the time and confirms that Hegel had not opted for the less common view that Egyptian culture had its sole source in the East.[37] However, the fact that Hegel did not consider Egypt foreign to Ethiopia is confirmed by the fact that he located Egypt's decline from its contact with other peoples (W2, 247; PH, 202).

Hegel stressed that the two opposing principles that correspond to the African and the Oriental are not and cannot be fused. This is most apparent in the 1840 edition, as if Karl Hegel had made it a specific point of emphasis when reediting the text. Nature and Spirit remain only an abstract heterogeneous unity woven together into one knot (W2, 255; PH, 209), and yet still in the form of an antithesis: neither the immediate unity of less advanced nations, nor the concrete unity of the more advanced (W2, 267; PH, 218). That is why the sphinx, half human and half animal, is the perfect figure of Egypt as far as Hegel is concerned (W2, 243; PH, 199). The animal is the African: "barbarous sensuality with African hardness, Zoolatry" (W2, 267; PH, 218), whereas the human is already found in the Oriental's "struggle of spirit for liberation" (W2, 267; PH, 219). If Egypt is, on the one hand, superstition, and, on the other hand, forms of organization, the police, the mechanisms of the state, an agricultural economy, and so on (W2, 267; PH, 219), then it is because the Egyptians are Ethiopians, Indians, and, perhaps, if we follow Blumenbach, but it is not necessary, a third degenerate form specific to the climate. Although Hegel wrote in 1822 that Egypt is the land of struggle, of dialectic, and of the problem, and then told us that there is no problem in which the solution is not given at the same time (V12, 309), it seems that it is only in Karl Hegel's edition that the solution emerged with any clarity, although this should not surprise us, as the purpose of that edition, published only three years after Gans's edition, was intended not merely to include more from the early versions of the lectures but also to resolve certain problems in the exposition, of which the account of Egypt would be a prime example. If the Egyptian spirit cannot be content with the massive substantiality of spirit immersed in nature of the Orient, then it is, the 1840 edition explained, because it is African: "The coarse African nature disintegrated that unity and found the problem whose solution is free spirit" (W2, 269; PH, 220, trans. modified). It is thus specifically as African that the transition to Greece takes place, because the African serves here as a principle of negativity.[38]

More controversial is Hegel's claim that the downfall of Egypt comes with the arrival of the Caucasians on the scene in the form of the Persians. It is significant that Hegel does not explicitly highlight race mixing as the cause of their decline. Notwithstanding some comments on the subject in his discussion of America (VG, 201; LPW, 163–64), Hegel seems, unlike a number of his predecessors and contemporaries, to have not been as obsessed with race mixing as some of his contemporaries. By mid-century, race mixing was considered the decisive principle of the philosophy of history by such figures as Robert Knox and Gobineau. Nevertheless, Hegel does seem to have enthusiastically adopted the widespread conviction that weak races cannot survive the arrival of the Caucasians. In the case of the Native Americans, of course, Hegel's account was particularly graphic: They were gradually destroyed by the breath of European activity (VG, 200; LPW, 163). However, this genocidal destruction allowed him to formulate a more general law: "Culturally inferior nations such as these are gradually eroded through contact with more advanced nations which have gone through a more intensive cultural development" (VG, 201; LPW, 163). Something like this seems to be what Hegel had in mind as an explanation of Egypt's decline. Egypt was culturally inferior, precisely because it was this combination of two different principles, the African and the Oriental, that had never really formed a true union. For example, Egyptian religion was described as joining the African element with Oriental massiveness; it is African compactness (*Gedrungenheit*), together with the infinite impulse of spirit to realize itself objectively (W2, 253; PH, 207). However, another of Hegel's prejudices comes to the fore when he described this combination as closed off until it comes into contact with the Persians or, as he also suggests at one point, when the Greeks, specifically the Ionians and Carians, arrive on the scene and by their presence prepared Egypt for its decline (W2, 247; PH, 202). My thesis is that for Hegel, Egypt's African element was fundamental to Egypt's role as the point of transition to the Greek world. To understand that, one needs to understand the Oriental principle, for it is its copresence in Egypt with the African that made Hegel call Egypt the "land of problem."

This uncertainty about whether it was the Persians or Greeks that brought about Egypt's decline hints at an indeterminacy that also could be expressed in terms of the fact that Persia is still part of the Oriental world but racially is Caucasian. Hegel attempted to negotiate this disconnect between race and geographical division when he contrasted the inward transition from Egypt to Greece, the transition according to the concept, with the historical or outward transition from the Persian empire to Greece (W2, 270; PH, 221). In terms of the historical transition, the political unifying point of the Persian Empire was in the force of the Persian stock (*Stamm*) (V12, 311), albeit in comparison to Greece, it had weaknesses (W2, 271; PH, 222). Egypt provides the conceptual transition because it was in terms of its incomplete union of elements that he could present a "contradiction of principles which it is the mission of the West to resolve" (VG, 247; LPW, 201). More precisely, Nature and Spirit were combined here as contradictory with Egypt as their middle (*die Mitte*) (W2, 267; PH, 218). It is precisely because the African is a component of Egypt, a component that is unassimilable, forever doomed to remain outside of history, incapable of development and culture (VG, 234; LPW, 190), that Egypt supplies the negativity essential to the transition to Greece. To be sure, there is some ambiguity on Hegel's part on whether the African is or is not capable of culture, as indicated in the suggestion that Ethiopia passed its culture to Egypt, but it seems that he was most inclined to attribute a capacity for culture to Africans when he was contrasting them to Native Americans, to make the point that they are even less assimilable (VG, 202; LPW, 165). In any event, Hegel was saying that if one was simply telling the external story, one could pass directly from Persia to Greece: One would have no need for Egypt, which would be a mere diversion. In contrast, the logic of world history renders Egypt necessary, precisely because it is a contradiction that tries to combine what cannot be united except as heterogeneous: the African and "the massive substantiality of spirit immersed in nature," which is the Oriental spirit (W2, 269; PH, 220).

Hegel repeatedly acknowledged a historical transmission between Egypt and Greece, so it is surprising that when he drew the distinction between a historical transition to Greece and a conceptual transition, Egypt was identified not as the starting point of the historical transition but as the conceptual transition. However, this becomes intelligible when one observes that Hegel confined the historical transition to the Caucasian race, which is why history proper is said to begin in Persia. Race plays an even more decisive role in the way Egypt serves as the point of a conceptual transition to Greece. This is because it is only through the negativity that is introduced into world history by its passage through the African element of Egypt that the dialectical movement to Greece is possible. Indeed, it is likely that it was in the course of giving his account of Egypt in the period 1822–1823 that Hegel recognized the necessity of including a detailed account of the African as that which cannot be included, which is precisely why in May 1824 he set out in the Introduction to do precisely that. Hegel's notorious claim, that he left Africa to one side in the Introduction to the lectures on the philosophy of world history, cannot be taken at face value, but that does not mean that his treatment of Africa is any less sinister when linked to his discussion of ancient Egypt. This is because

Egypt, to many of Hegel's contemporaries, served as a counterexample to the most extreme racisms, whereas to Hegel it was an occasion for developing his ugly stereotypes of Africans.[39]

Notes

1. G. W. F. Hegel, *Die Vernunft in der Geschichte*, ed. J. Hoffmeister (Hamburg: Felix Meiner, 1980), 234; trans. H. B. Nisbet, *Lectures on the Philosophy of World History* (Cambridge: Cambridge University Press, 1975), 190. (Henceforth, VG and LPW, respectively.) I outline what I consider scandalous about this discussion in "Hegel at the Court of the Ashanti," in *Hegel after Derrida*, ed. Stuart Barnett (London: Routledge, 1998), 41–63.

2. G. W. F. Hegel, *Vorlesungen über die Philosophie der Weltgeschichte*, ed. Karl Heinz Ilting, Karl Brehmer, and Hoo Nam Seelmann, Vorlesungen 12 (Hamburg: Felix Meiner, 1996), 233. (Henceforth V12.)

3. G. W. F. Hegel, *Vorlesungen über die Philosophie der Geschichte*, 2d ed., ed. Karl Hegel, *Werke*, vol. 9 (Berlin: Dunker und Humblot, 1840), 211; trans. J. Sibree, *The Philosophy of History* (New York: Dover, 1956), 173. (Henceforth, W2 and PH, respectively.) See Robert Bernasconi, "With What Must the Philosophy of World History Begin?," *Nineteenth-Century Contexts* 22:2 (2000): 171–201.

4. See Robert Bernasconi, "Black Skin, White Skulls: The Nineteenth-Century Debate over the Racial Identity of the Ancient Egyptians," *Parallax* 43, April 2007, forthcoming. Clearly this topic recalls Martin Bernal's *Black Athena* and the controversy it provoked. I do not explore this debate here both because I have addressed it elsewhere and because neither side throws much light on the issues raised in this chapter. Martin Bernal, *Black Athena*, vol. 1 (New Brunswick, NJ: Rutgers University Press, 1987). (Henceforth, BA.) See also Mary Lefkowitz, *Not Out of Africa* (New York: Basic Books, 1996); ed. Mary Lefkowitz and Guy Maclean Rogers, *Black Athena Revisited* (Chapel Hill: University of North Carolina Press, 1996); Martin Bernal, *Black Athena Writes Back* (Durham, NC: Duke University Press, 2001).

5. C. F. Volney, *Voyage en Égypte et en Syrie,* in *Oeuvres complètes* (Paris: Firmin Didot, 1838), 131–32; trans. as *Travels through Egypt and Syria* (New York: David Longworth, 1798) 53–54.

6. C. F. Volney, *Les ruines, ou meditation sur les revolutions des empires* (Paris: Desenne, 1792), 22; trans. as *The Ruins of Empires* (Baltimore, MD: Black Classic Press, n.d.), 17, emphasis in the original.

7. Philosophers are, of course, familiar with Hume's famous claim of 1753–1754, that "there never was a civilized nation of any other complexion than white," but that was written before the revival of interest in Egypt that came at the end of the eighteenth century. Volney can thus be read as an answer to Hume.

8. C. F. Volney, *Voyage en Égypte et en Syrie*, 133; trans. as *Travels through Egypt and Syria*, vol. 1, 55.

9. Henri Grégoire, *De la literature des nègres* (Paris: Maradan, 1808), 1-34; trans. David Bailie Warden, *An Enquiry Concerning the Intellectual and Moral Faculties, and Literature of Negroes* (Armonk, NY: M. E. Sharpe, 1997), 1–14.

10. G. W. F. Hegel, *Vorlesungen über die Philosophie der Weltgeschichte*, ed. Georg Lasson (Hamburg: Felix Meiner, 1988), 461. (Henceforth, VPW.) See also W2, 242; PH, 198. On Hegel's copy of Volney, see Otto Pöggeler, "Einleitung," in *Vorlesungen über Naturrecht und Staatswissenschaft* (Hamburg: Felix Meiner, 1983), xvi.

11. See G. W. F. Hegel, *Vorlesungen über die Ästhetik*, *Theorie Werkausgabe* 14 (Frankfurt: Suhrkamp, 1970), 300; trans. T. M. Knox, *Hegel's Aesthetics* (Oxford: Oxford University Press, 1975), vol. 2, 658. The evidence is that Hegel must have read Denon at least by 1823. Although his lectures on the philosophy of art in that year do not name Denon, the description of Egyptian architecture recalls that which is attributed to him in the posthumous version: *Vorlesungen über die Philosophie der Kunst*, ed. Annemarie Gethmann-Siefert, Vorlesungen 2 (Hamburg: Felix Meiner, 1998), 220.

12. Vivant Denon, *Voyage dans la basse et la haute Égypte* (London: Samuel Bugster, 1807), vol. 1, 98; trans. E. A. Kendal, *Travels in Upper and Lower Egypt* (London: DARF, 1986), reprint of 1802, 101.

13. Denon, *Voyage*, vol. 1, 73; trans. as *Travels*, vol. 1, 67.

14. The passage, which describes Sesostris's army, includes the phrase, "they have black skins and wooly hair" (book 2, 103–104). The significance of the passage has since been challenged. For a discussion, see Frank M. Snowden, *Blacks in Antiquity* (Cambridge, MA: Harvard University Press, 1970).

15. James Bruce, *Travels to Discover the Source of the Nile* (Edinburgh: Archibald Constable, 1805), vol. 2, 308–35. If Hegel had read this the second edition, he would have had even more evidence, from the appendices by Alexander Murray, that the ancient Egyptians were black.

16. J. G. Herder, *Ideen zur Philosophie der Geschichte der Menschheit*, ed. M. Bollacher (Frankfurt: Deutscher Klassiker, 1989), 501; trans. T. Churchill, *Outlines of a Philosophy of the History of Man* (New York: Bergman, n.d., reprint of London, 1800), 343.

17. Christoph Meiners, "Commentatio de veterum Aegyptiorum Origine," in *Comment. hist. et phil. Goetting*, vol. 10, 57–79. I am grateful to Eun-Jueng Lee for supplying me with a copy of this text.

18. Johann Friedrich Blumenbach, *De generis humani varietate nativa* (Göttingen: Vandenhoek and Ruprecht, 1795), 187–88; trans. Thomas Bendyshe, *On the Natural Varieties of Mankind* (London: Longman, Green, Longman, Roberts, and Green, 1865), 231. The evidence that Hegel knew this text is set out by Michael Hoffheimer in "Hegel, Race, Genocide," *The Southern Journal of Philosophy* 39 (2001): 61, n. 91.

19. John Frederick Blumenbach, "Observations on Some Egyptian Mummies opened in London," *Philosophical Transactions* 84 (1794): 193.

20. This view is dismissed by Alexander Murray in one of his appendices to Bruce's *Travels to Discover the Source of the Nile*, vol. 2, 489. However, Murray failed to provide a source. He perhaps had William G. Browne in mind. See *Travels in Africa, Egypt, and Syria from the Year 1792 to 1798* (London: T. Cadell Jun. and W. Davies), vol. 1, 159–66.

21. M. le. Chevalier Cuvier, *Le règne animal distribué d'après son organisation* (Paris: Deterville, 1817), vol. 1, 95; trans. as *The Animal Kingdom Arranged after Its Organization* (London: Henry G. Bohn, 1863), 38.

22. Georges Cuvier, "Extrait d'observations faites sur le cadavre d'une femme connue à Paris et à Londres sous le nom de Vénus Hottentote," in *Discourse sur les revolutions du globe*, ed. G. Cuvier, P.-Ch. Joubet, and L. Passard (Paris: Passard, 1817), 221–22. I am grateful to T. Denean Sharpley-Whiting for supplying me with a copy of this text.

23. Giovanni Belzoni, *Narrative of the Operations and Recent Discoveries within the Pyramids, Temples, Tombs, and Excavations in Egypt and Nubia* (London: John Murray, 1820), 239.

24. A. H. L. Heeren, *Ideen über die Politik, den Verkehr und den Handel der vornehmsten Völker der alten Welt*, part 2, division 2 (Göttingen: Vandenhoek und Ruprecht, 1826), 84. I have also consulted the editions with the same publisher from 1804 and 1815. (Henceforth designated as IP, followed by the date of the edition.)

25. Bernasconi, "Hegel at the Court of the Ashanti," 46.

26. M. J. Petry, *Hegel's Philosophy of Subjective Spirit*, (Dordrecht, Holland: D. Reidel, 1978), vol. 1, 49. (Henceforth, PSS, followed by the volume number.)

27. F. N. Colin and H. Schneider, "Hegels Vorlesungen notizen zum subjektiven Geist," *Hegel-Studien* 10 (1975): 22.

28. Cheikh Anta Diop, *Antériorité des civilizations nègres* (Paris: Présence Africaine, 1967); trans. Merer Cook, *The African Origin of Civilization* (Chicago: Lawrence Hill, 1974). See also Théophile Obenga, *Cheikh Anta Diop, Volney et le Sphinx* (Paris: Présence Africaine, 1996), 22.

29. T. Edward Bowdich, *An Essay on the Superstitions, Customs, and Arts Common to the Ancient Egyptians, Abyssinians, and Ashanties* (Paris: J. Smith, 1821), 5.

30. T. E. Bowdich, *Mission from Cape Coast Castle to Ashantee* (London: John Murray, 1819). See Bernasconi, "Hegel at the Court of the Ashanti," 45–51.

31. G. W. F. Hegel, *Vorlesungen über die Philosophie der Geschichte*, ed. Eduard Gans, *Werke* 9 (Berlin: Dunker und Humblot, 1837), 227–28.

32. Hegel said the same of the Hyksos, or shepherd kings, whom he understood as coming from Southern Africa, although they are now usually understood to have came from the North. While their rule may have only been about a century (1680–1580 B.C.), Josephus claimed that their rule was over 500 years. See W. W. How and J. Wells, *A Commentary on Herodotus* (Oxford: Oxford University Press, 1961),

vol. 1, 418. I am uncertain of Hegel's source; Herodotus does not mention them by name.

33. Hotho's manuscript read "African people," whereas Griesheim's read "African element."

34. In addition to the essay by Michael Hoffheimer, cited later, see also on this topic his "Race and Law in Hegel's Philosophy of Religion," in *Race and Racism in Modern Philosophy*, ed. Andrew Valls (Ithaca: Cornell University Press, 2005), 194–216..

35. For examples of this tendency, see Joseph McCarney, *Hegel on History* (London: Routledge, 2000), 143–44; Bernard Bourgeois, *Etudes Hégeliennes* (Paris: Presses Universitaires de France, 1992), 264.

36. On Hegel's approach to the question of hierarchy and much else, see Michael Hoffheimer, "Hegel, Race, Genocide," *Southern Journal of Philosophy* 39 (2001): 35–62.

37. According to Josiah Nott, writing in 1854, the idea that the Egyptians were specifically Negroes (as opposed to being more generally black) was already being challenged by Champollion and Rosselini, while the idea that Egypt's civilization came from Ethiopia was not under attack until George Gliddon's *Chapters in Egypt* in 1843 and Samuel George Morton's *Crania Aegyptica* in 1844. See J. C. Nott and George Gliddon, *Types of Mankind* (Philadelphia, PA: Lippincott, Grambo, 1854), 212–13.

38. One should be clear that Hegel did not think of the Egyptians as Negroes, but that does not mean that they were not black. On the distinction between Egyptian fetishism and that of the Negroes, see G. W. F. Hegel, *Vorlesungen über die Philosophie der Religion. Teil 2: Die bestimmte Religion*, Vorlesungen 4, ed. Walter Jaeschke (Hamburg: Felix Meiner, 1985), 195; trans. Peter Hodgson, *Lectures on the Philosophy of Religion*, vol. 2: *Determinate Religion* (Berkeley: University of California Press, 1987), 291.

39. I would like to thank Amit Sen and Michael Hoffheimer for their suggestions on how to improve an earlier draft of this chapter.

Part 4

Identity and Difference in the *Philosophy of Right*

Chapter 10

Identity and Difference in Hegel's Model of Ethical Normativity

Erin E. Flynn

> . . . [The laws and powers of the ethical substance] are not something *alien* to the subject. On the contrary, the subject bears *spiritual witness* to them as to *its own essence*, in which it has its *self-awareness* [*Selbstgefühl*] and lives as in its element which is not distinct from itself—a relationship which is immediate and closer to identity than even [a relationship of] *faith* or *trust*.[1]

I

It is a powerful vision. The individuals in such a community do not simply trust in their laws and institutions, they have something more than even faith in these powers. In fact, they identify themselves, their innermost essence, with these governing norms. They are somehow even self-aware through them. The vision is all the more powerful when we consider that for Hegel the inhabitants of such a community must be *subjects*. That is, to put it very roughly, they must be capable of differentiating themselves, individuating themselves, and holding at a critical distance the world in which they find themselves. The subject that identifies with these laws and institutions is, in Hegel's terms, a *moral* subject. Indeed, this relationship is for Hegel the origin and endgame of the historical emergence of moral subjectivity.

Hegel's vision therefore preserves, or purports to preserve, the basic concept of the modern autonomous individual, and yet it also is supposed to position that modern individual within a structure of law and institution with which the individual identifies as the source and aim of her own liberty, and not merely as an external check upon the liberty of others and hence protection of her liberty. The fact that the individual who identifies herself with ethical institutions in this way is supposed to be a moral subject with personal rights, distinct even in the context of such identification, has led a number of recent interpreters to regard Hegel's concept as a plausible, normative ideal.[2] The idea, very generally, is that Hegel's formula for the unity of identity and difference allows for a normative model that can account for the substantive authority of objective norms while at the same time admitting that their normative appeal must be grounded by the subject's ability to identify with them. I intend to ask whether or not this ideal of a differentiated subject identifying with the laws and institutions of her society is plausible from *within* the structure that Hegel articulates in his *Philosophy of Right*. And I intend to ask this question with a particular ethical institution in mind: legal punishment.

II

Before turning to the question of punishment, however, I want to characterize logically the relation of identity between differentiated moral subjects and objective ethical institutions. This characterization will depend largely on identifying the principal deficiencies of abstract right and morality, the first two practical standpoints of the *Philosophy of Right*, which Hegel claims necessitate the standpoint of ethical life. I have two objectives in so doing. First, I intend to show how ethical life is plausibly to be considered a unity of identity and difference. Second, I want to suggest at least a minimal condition for what this unity might mean in the context of a practical philosophy.

Hegel defines the personal will of abstract right as a will that is an abstract self-identity, hence, only implicitly free. He says, for instance, that "[p]ersonality begins only at that point where the subject has . . . a consciousness of itself as a completely abstract 'I' in which all concrete limitation and validity are negated and invalidated" (PR, §35R). The will of the person comes to be in his consciousness of being able to refuse to identify with any content. As far as the personal will is concerned, it is immediately its essence, immediately free. Or, as Hegel says, "The person is the individuality of freedom in pure being-for-itself" (PR, §35A). In this relationship of immediacy, Hegel says that "there is knowledge of the *self* as an *object* [*Gegenstand*], but as an object raised by thought to simple infinity and hence purely identical with itself" (PR, §35R). And finally, at this stage of abstraction, Hegel claims that "[i]f I say that I am free, 'I' is still this being-within-itself [*Insichsein*] without any opposition" (PR, §34A).

This definition of the abstract personal will echoes Hegel's depiction in the *Logic* of the relationship of *identity*. Just as the abstract 'I' of the person is without opposition, "[f]ormal identity . . . abstracts from distinction."[3] And just as personality is distinguished by its self-consciousness as an abstract 'I', Hegel uses the figure of self-consciousness to exemplify the relation of self-identity. "It is his identity as consciousness of himself that distinguishes man from nature in general, and particularly from animals, which do not achieve a grasp of themselves as 'I', i.e. as their pure self-unity" (EL, §115A).

The relationship of identity is for Hegel a relationship of essence, so inasmuch as the will's essence is its freedom, it makes sense to say that the personal will of abstract right is taken to be a simple self-identity with its freedom. But what does this mean in the practical context? There are two implications that I would like to emphasize. First, it means that the personal will is indifferent to its particular content. As I mentioned earlier, the freedom of the personal will is largely a matter of being able to refuse to identify with any particular content at all. The will is just free, no matter the content in which it happens to invest. So Hegel claims, "[S]ince particularity, in the person, is not yet present as freedom, everything that depends on particularity is here a *matter of indifference*" (PR, §37A). This leads to a second implication, that the will's particular content is already determined without any reference to the will's freedom. That is, the formal fact that the content is willed, and nothing distinct about the *source* of the content or the *manner* of the willing, is all that matters to the person's freedom.[4] So "although it [the personal will's particular content] is present—as desire, need, drives, contingent preference, etc.—it is still different from personality, from the determination of freedom" (PR, §37). For the personal will, then, its motivation is not a problem for its self-determination. Unless externally constrained, whatever motivates it shall result in a free action.

III

Of course, this indifference to content is unstable precisely when we have motivations that run counter to our own freedom. The *moral* will reflects upon such a possibility and is therefore aware of its content, its motivation, as different from and in opposition to its freedom, or essence. As a result, Hegel claims, morality is "the point of view of *consciousness* (see §8)—in general the point of view of the difference, *finitude*, and *appearance* of the will" (PR, §108). The moral will acknowledges the particular content of the will as an *appearance* of essence, not to be immediately identified with freedom.

Again, we may ask what this means in a practical context. In contrast to the personal will, Hegel had claimed that in morality "there is already an opposition; for in this sphere I am present as an individual will, whereas the good is universal, even though it is within me" (PR, §34A). Hence, the will of the moral subject, while knowing itself to be free, *requires* freedom of itself. It must *posit* itself as free (see PR §106R). And so the "question of the self-determination and motive [*Triebfeder*] of the will and of its purpose now arises in connection with morality" (PR, §106A). So one practical implication is that the moral will cannot remain indifferent to its content. As moral agents, we must concern ourselves with our motivations. But the moral subject is principally aware of its motivations as different from or as the mere appearance of its freedom. It is, after all, possible that its motivations run counter to its own freedom. This difference encourages Hegel to say that "the moral point of view is consequently the point of view of *relationship, obligation*, or *requirement*" (PR, §108). The particular moral will is drawn to its essence, its own freedom, as to what it ought to be, as to its duty. And so a second practical implication is that with morality the notion of an ideal, a norm, or a commandment truly emerges.[5]

And yet the moral will is, according to Hegel, merely formal. Normative obligation emerges but famously lacks motivational content. We are therefore left with two necessary, but as yet disparate (hence, insufficient), conditions for the will's freedom: motivational content and normative standing. Furthermore, Hegel has identified them with the logical standpoints of identity and difference, respectively. Their union would therefore appear to promise motivational content that has normative standing—a union of identity and difference. This is precisely what we find in Hegel's concept of ethical life.

IV

Ethical life therefore appears to promise to be the will's motivating ground, or sufficient reason, for acting. Since, for Hegel, this motivating ground cannot be identified with just *any* inclination of the will, he identifies it as a *totality*, the reason for the particular inclination, raised to the level of an objective, real feature of the world.

In the *Logic*, it is precisely as ground, or sufficient reason, that identity and difference are unified (see EL, §121). And this, Hegel claims, is "*essence* posited as *totality*" (EL, §121). In the ethical sphere this means that we identify the freedom of the will with (at least) that which gives it sufficient reason to act. And what does this, according to Hegel, is the totality of social relations that will provide it with its norms. This totality makes the free will what it is—it is the will's own motivating ground, that in terms of which the will determines itself. And this helps explain the relation of substantiality that Hegel continuously emphasizes in ethical life. But in order to be a genuine ground, ethical life must in fact provide sufficient reasons to motivate the will. The norms into which the ethical agent is educated must be available to her practical reason as genuine reasons for acting. If they are, then it makes sense to say that the ground of ethical life unifies the will's identity with and difference from its freedom, for a motivating reason or ground is what we take as our own when we act. And our freedom is indeed constituted by acting on or from our own grounds. A reason or ground, however, cannot be a ground unless distinct—unless it calls to us, pulls or urges us. What is required, therefore, if ethical life is to be such a unity, is that it provide real norms that are both distinct from us and yet our own. That is the sense in which ethical life is a unity of our identity with and difference from our own essence. The question is whether or not Hegel's concept of ethical life makes good on this promise of being such a motivating ground.[6]

V

As I mentioned earlier, I want to test this notion in the context of legal punishment. Hegel must be able to represent punitive norms as such motivating grounds. Now I am not concerned with what is ordinarily presented as Hegel's justification of legal punishment. I want instead to draw our attention to two facts about his presentation of the administration of legal punishment that should lead us to doubt that it *could* serve as such a motivating ground.

The first fact has to do with punishment's place in the sphere of ethical life. As an aspect of the administration of justice, it belongs in civil society. In civil society, the individual interacts with others as a private person. It is the emergence of this sphere that for Hegel shows that modern ethical life provides for the development of the private interests of individuals. And for this reason the state can in turn be a unity justified to and motivating these subjects, as opposed to a force that motivates by submerging or repressing subjectivity and privacy, as in feudalism. As many commentators have noted, the sphere of civil society is therefore the sphere in which the modern moral individual achieves actuality. It is therefore also the essential achievement of the distinct rationality of modern ethical life.

So far it would seem that punishment's place as an institution of civil society would position it well to satisfy the subjective requirements of ethical life. Since civil society is that sphere in which the individual is most free to pursue private ends, should not its institutions be least alien to her? But this is not the case, according to Hegel. For while Hegel insists that civil society is necessary for the development of the subject's individuality, he also insists that its institutions lack sufficient normative authority. The "interdependence" of private individuals in civil society is at best an "external state" or a "state of necessity" (PR, §183). In fact, civil society remains a sphere of "difference" (PR, §182) and "appearance" (PR, §184) in which individuals pursue private interests and satisfy their needs using others principally as a means to achieve those private ends. If there are institutions necessary to such mutual satisfaction, then they are at best coincidentally related to the individual's private ends, at least insofar as he is a *Bürger*.

The problem with civil society, in light of Hegel's model of ethical rationality, therefore looks something like this. To actualize my freedom requires that reason, which obtains objectivity in social norms, determine my action. But in civil society these norms are *not* action's determining ground. They are rather external constraints on action. Hence, civil society is an "external state" along similar lines to those described by Kant for the *Rechtstaat*. Therefore, it seems as though there are no grounds on which this bourgeois individual might regard the norms of civil society as his own essence, as even part of *his* end. There is, rather, an accidental, or an external, coordination between the subjective grounds for action and these objective norms. Hence, acting within this totality does not actualize the agent's freedom. On the contrary, Hegel is both extreme and prescient when it comes to seeing that the principles organizing civil society lead to "a spectacle of extravagance and misery as well as . . . physical and ethical corruption" (PR, §185). In civil society the right of the "subject's particularity to find satisfaction" (PR, §124R), which for Hegel distinguishes modern ethical rationality, is an agent of boundless extravagance and dissolution.

Hegel *does* identify as a universality the *interdependence* required for the mutual pursuit of our own self-interest. Into this interdependence our particular interest "passes over" in civil society. But it explicitly is *not* for Hegel the "unity . . . of ethical identity" (PR, §186). As he puts it, the two spheres of particularity and universality remain in civil society self-sufficient principles. "Individuals," he says, "as citizens [*Burger*] of this state, are *private persons* who have their own interest as their end" (PR, §187). This end is sufficient to motivate them as bourgeoisie. At the same time, however, the structures of interdependence necessary for the pursuit of that end—structures of the market, the administration of justice, and the police—are therefore also necessary for the constitution of this sphere. The problem is that in civil society the necessary condition for the pursuit of private interest is not itself taken as an end of that interest. It is rather used only as a means to it. Hence, the interest of this common or universal continuum (*Zusammenhang*) "is not present in the consciousness of these members of civil society" (PR, §187). This is why Hegel says that the unity of particularity and universality in civil society is "present not as *freedom*, but as . . . *necessity*" (PR, §186). The norms governing this *Notstaat* are not the agent's own. And for Hegel this means that the bourgeoisie do not have the actualization of their own freedom as their end. For what we as private persons lack is precisely a non-arbitrary structure for endorsing our ends. Our private self-determination is for Hegel an inward arbitrariness, which cannot have "an existence [*Dasein*] in the external" (PR, §187R). On the contrary, the norms of civil society are only external constraints on this private self-determination. As such, in this sphere spirit cannot be "*at home* and *with itself* in this *externality* as such" (PR, §187R).

Now we may not accept Hegel's depiction of civil society. And we may also reject Hegel's implication that external laws and institutions can constitute reasons for acting, to say nothing of the apparent claim that without them we can have no nonarbitrary endorsement of ends, hence, no self-determination. Yet if these are in fact Hegel's claims, then we must accept that for Hegel my aims as *bourgeois* lack the universality required for me to be genuinely free. If that is so, then how are the civil institutions that integrate these private aims supposed to have the kind of strong normative claim that Hegel asserts for them? If civil society is supposed to produce this "spectacle of extravagance and misery . . . physical and ethical corruption," then how is education into its institutions supposed to yield an agent who regards the norms of these institutions as her own motivating grounds for action? How indeed when education into such institutions seems to require the acknowledgment that within them only our private ends constitute motivating grounds? It hardly seems plausible in such a context that the practical reason of the convict, pursuer of private ends, would come to regard, beyond even faith and trust, the judgment of the court as his very essence, especially since that judgment mandates the severest truncation of precisely his pursuits as a bourgeois individual.

VI

Legal punishment's status as an institution of civil society therefore raises serious questions about the extent of its normative authority. Furthermore (and this is the second dubious fact, to which I alluded earlier, about Hegel's presentation), what Hegel has to tell us about the convict deepens my doubts about just how the convict is supposed to bear spiritual witness to the imposition of civil society's punitive norms. Two elements stand out. One has to do with the extravagant claims Hegel makes on behalf of the convict's reconciliation to his punishment. The other has to do with the contingency of the convict's identification with the jury, upon which that reconciliation is based. My claim is that in the context of civil society Hegel simply cannot make good the strong, normative claims made on behalf of the institutions of administrative justice. He cannot, in other words, show that the rational will of the convict must regard the institution as his own ethical substance and freedom.

As to the claims he makes on behalf of the criminal, Hegel says that punishment

> subjectively . . . applies to the criminal in that *his law, which is known by him* and is *valid* for him and *for his protection*, is enforced upon him in such a way that he himself finds in it the satisfaction of justice and merely the enactment of *what is proper to him* [*das Seinigen*]. (PR, §220)

Here we have a striking example of the kind of strong claim of identification that Hegel makes between the individual and the laws and institutions of her ethical life. Hegel insists that the rational validity of ethical laws extends all the way down even to those who suffer from their implementation. This is an extremely high, and in some sense admirable, standard against which to hold actual institutions. But on what basis can Hegel make such a claim?

Hegel asserts that two subjective conditions are necessary to meet this standard of ethical rationality. First, the law broken must be (1) known by the criminal and (2) valid for her and for her protection. Second, in the punishment's administration and enforcement, the criminal must find (1) the satisfaction of justice and (2) what is proper to her. I will assume that the first condition is met. The law in question is publicly known, enacted according to legitimate political procedures, and for the protection of the citizenry. But how are we to understand the satisfaction of the second condition? How are we guaranteed in knowing that the criminal grasps her punishment as what she deserves? This question involves the finest grain of identification between the individual and the institution. It involves the most subjective of the subject's identification, hence, the point at which identity and difference would be most radically unified in ethical life (the point at which these objective standards and the subjective conditions of their enactment unite).

Hegel emphasizes a number of points about the administration of justice meant to show that our "*duty to submit to the court's authority*" (PR, §221), which corresponds to our "*right to stand in a court of law*" (PR, §221), meets this most subjective requirement. Failing this, of course, the duty would be empty. He claims, for instance, that "the rights of the subjective consciousness include not only that of making the laws publicly known . . . but also the possibility of knowing [*zu kennen*] how the law is *actualized* in particular cases" (PR, §224). The reason for this publicity, as Hegel notes, is that "a primary characteristic of a right is that the citizens should have confidence in it" (PR, §224A). They should be "convinced that justice [*Recht*] is actually being done" (PR, §224A). To convince them of this, two aspects of the dispensation of justice in the court of law must be manifest: determinations of fact and determinations of law (see PR, §225, 227). I will focus on the former, since determinations of fact in a court of law lead, I claim, to an unstable core of contingency that threatens to undermine the most basic claims Hegel has made on behalf of the identification between the individual and the institution of justice's administration.

Determinations of fact, to which Hegel refers as the "*knowledge* [*Erkenntnis*] of the case in its *immediate* individuality [*Einzelheit*]" (PR, §227), do not require legal expertise. Instead, this is "knowledge to which *every educated person* may aspire" (PR, §227). That fact takes crucial determinations in the trial out of the hands of legal experts and places them into the hands of *any* educated person, supposedly allowing the convict to grasp them. Furthermore, the "essential factor" in making determinations of fact regarding the actions of the accused lies in determining the "insight and intention" (PR, §227) of the accused. Failure to properly perceive insight and intention, to determine the state of mind of the accused, would necessarily result in the convict's alienation from the verdict, hence, an explicit violation of Hegel's formula of ethical rationality. But what is particularly telling is Hegel's admission that the knowledge in question concerns only "subjective certainty," and no "absolutely objective determination" (PR, §227), nor "truth in the higher sense" (PR, §227A). "For these reasons," Hegel says, "the ultimate factors in such a decision are *subjective conviction* and conscience" (PR, §227). This seems dangerously contingent ground upon which to base the strong claims of identity and rationality that Hegel makes for ethical institutions. In fact, Hegel admits that short of confession the judgment of the court will retain something alien to the convict (see PR, §227A). Since forced confession is impermissible, we seem to be left with only *subjective conviction* to assure us that the convict finds the verdict just and proper. Is this not to make the vaunted union of identity and difference the flimsiest of accidents in our administration of justice?

VII

What overcomes this contingency, Hegel claims, is the jury trial. In it the right of the accused is satisfied "by the *confidence* which can be placed in the subjectivity of those who arrive at the verdict" (PR, §228). But how does the jury trial guarantee such confidence? That "confidence," Hegel says, "is based primarily on [the jury's] equality with the concerned party in respect to their particularity—their social status [*Stand*] and the like" (PR, §228). What allows for subjective identification with the verdict is therefore the *equality* of the accused with the jury. "Equality" here translates *Gleichheit*, and it is telling that Hegel uses it in this context. In the *Logic* he explains: "Equality [sameness or likeness, we might instead say] is only an identity of [terms] that are *not the same*, not identical with one another" (EL, §118). It would make sense that in civil society, the concrete sphere of difference, of *Recht* differentiated in and coordinating the mutually indifferent wills of bourgeois individuals, the extent of identity should be mere likeness. And *Gleichheit*, in the *Logic*, emerges only subsequently to the appearance of *Untershied.* (Its explication belongs in fact to a section under the heading *Unterschied.*) The best we could hope for in terms of identification in the court of law is therefore identity subordinated to difference, rather than united with it.

This logical point also is reflected in the composition of the jury, making the problem all the more trenchant, for Hegel's gloss on *Gleichheit* is that it concerns the "social status [*Stand*] and the like" of the accused and the jury. In the context, therefore, of the pursuit of private interests governed by personal rights, Hegel reduces the requirement of subjective identification to a matter of likeness within classes.[7] This is, in effect, to preserve premodern modes of social identification, via class likeness, in the modern social structure. Hegel's prescient grasp of the divisions of modern civil society encourages this obvious violation of his own formula for modern ethical rationality. Because civil society is a sphere of private, often class-based competition, any claim for universal subjective identification in its courts must be illusory. For even if sufficient likeness to overcome the threat of contingency could be established *within* classes, interclass violations would remain impossible to adjudicate. The historical fact that interclass violations very often are difficult to adjudicate may indicate that Hegel recognizes something important about historical conditions of justice, but it certainly does not help to show that an adequate system of justice could be established in the civil society he describes.[8]

Hegel attempts to soften the blow of these conflicts by appealing to the notion of *Bildung*. *Bildung* is especially important in the context of civil society, for by means of *Bildung* individuals are awakened to valid ethical norms as objective features of their social reality. *Bildung* therefore operates as a kind of buffer against the privacy of interests, which characterizes civil relations. This is manifest in the jury trial in that we require not merely a jury of peers but of *educated* peers. For any educated person can competently make determinations of fact in the court of law (see PR §227). But the concept of *Bildung* only echoes the problems of class already established. *Bildung* is not sufficient to establish the likeness required to ensure the general administration of justice across a civil society, for *Bildung* must be particular to class if indeed class interests are diverse. Those norms central to the coordination of interests within one class may be irrelevant to the coordination of interests within another. What is more, *Bildung* raises explicitly the specter of uneducated classes. The severely impoverished could not hope for *any* satisfactory administration of justice under these conditions. Again, that this fact fairly accurately represents the actual condition of justice in the world, not to mention the fact that Hegel is well aware that severe poverty compromises justice generally, does not speak in favor of Hegel being able to announce that the necessary conditions of justice have been met in bourgeois society. In fact, it does not even speak in favor of Hegel having shown that these conditions of justice *could* be established by the conceptual development of civil society, since its institutions seem to include contingencies as part of their necessary conditions.[9]

In any event, it seems clear that Hegel has not established that punitive norms constitute motivating grounds for the bourgeois person's practical reason. Hence, the "*duty to submit to the court's authority*" has not been established, and the institution is not properly regarded as the person's substance. At best Hegel has established that the satisfaction of the necessary conditions of ethical rationality is in part contingent. But that will not do for Hegel's basic claim about *Sittlichkeit*, which is supposed to show that the actualization of *Recht* is necessary.

Notes

1. G.W. F. Hegel, *Elements of the Philosophy of Right*, ed. Allen Wood, trans. H. B. Nisbet (Cambridge: Cambridge University Press, 1991), §147. (Hereafter cited internally as PR.) References to Hegel's remarks on sections will be followed by R, while references to additions to sections will be followed by A.

2. For recent readings emphasizing aspects of the "right of subjectivity," see "Hegel's Ethical Rationalism," in Robert B. Pippin, *Idealism as Modernism* (Cambridge: Cambridge University Press, 1997), 417–50; Allen W. Wood, *Hegel's Ethical Thought* (Cambridge: Cambridge University Press, 1990); Michael Hardimon, *Hegel's Social Philosophy: The Project of Reconciliation* (Cambridge: Cambridge University Press, 1994); Frederick Neuhouser, *Foundations of Hegel's Social Theory: Actualizing Freedom* (Cambridge, MA: Harvard University Press, 2000); Robert R. Williams, *Hegel's Ethics of Recognition* (Berkeley: University of California Press, 1997).

While each of these readers casts Hegel's ethical thought in importantly distinct ways, each is also at pains to emphasize a genuine subjectivity in the context of modern ethical life. Whether it is Pippin's emphasis on subjective motivations, Wood's on ethical subjectivity, Neuhouser's on subjective freedom, Hardimon's on reconciliation between subjects and modern institutions, or Williams's on the role of mutual recognition among subjects, each resists the view that the Hegelian picture subsumes the individual beneath a totalitarian state or community.

3. G.W .F. Hegel, *The Encyclopedia Logic*, trans. T. F. Geraets, W. A. Suchting, and H. S. Harris, (Indianapolis, IN: Hackett, 1991), §115R. (Hereafter cited internally as EL, with references to remarks and additions following the convention explained in note 1.)

4. Hegel seems quite clearly to have in mind here the kind of traditional compatibilist accounts of freedom central to the natural right theories of Hobbes and Locke.

5. Indeed, the very commandment of abstract right (be a person and respect others as persons ([see PR, §36]) cannot be heeded except by moral subjects.

6. It also should be noted that ethical life is more than mere ground for Hegel. It is an actuality and a substance. It is not quite true that it determines its content out of itself, for it is not pure Concept. And yet it is clear that its purposes are more substantial than mere grounds, which can be put to any end (see EL, §122R). In this respect, the doctrine of essence maps onto the *Philosophy of Right* not merely in terms of identity, difference, and ground but also in terms of its larger sections: essence (abstract right), appearance (morality), and actuality (ethical life). The latter takes up and unites the essence and the appearance as the actual ground of the determinateness of the will. Ground is still an appropriate concept with which to describe the actual, since it is ground that reveals that essence has its essence in appearance—in what emerges from the ground. When actuality unites essence and appearance, then it does so as the actual ground, the substance, uniting the two elements. In fact, one might say that appearance itself is the manifestation of the second moment of essence: difference.

7. I realize that my use of "class" to translate "*Stand*" is contentious, but "estate" is archaic, and "status" misses the point. I hope it suffices to say that "class" here refers simply to quasinatural social divisions identified according to the particular social and economic interests of, for instance, a union of skilled laborers or agricultural landowners. When I claim that Hegel in effect preserves premodern modes of social identification, then I mean that my political identity, when I stand before a court of law, is defined according to these particular "class" interests. The conflict to which Hegel seems necessarily led, then, is that his inclusion of the particularity of the accused brings with it the disintegration of the sphere of conflicting civil interests.

8. The problems that class conflicts pose for a retributive theory of punishment are well known, and Hegel is not oblivious to them. For a general take on the issue, see Jeffrey Murphie, "Marxism and Retribution," in *Punishment*, ed. A. J. Simmons et al. (Princeton, NJ: Princeton University Press, 1995). For an extended discussion of Hegel's sensitivity to the problem, see Mark Tunick, *Hegel's Political Philosophy: Interpreting the Practice of Legal Punishment* (Princeton, NJ: Princeton University Press, 1992), 113–20.

9. One might argue that Hegel's conditions necessitate some kind of classless society. Perhaps even the notion of general education, or *Bildung*, suggests that.

However true this may be, it is not Hegel's model of civil society as it is supposed to actually exist. Nor is it even consistent with Hegel's presentation of the conditions of just punishment, since there he makes explicit reference to class *distinction* in outlining those necessary conditions.

Chapter 11

Political Identity and the Dynamics of Accountability in Hegel's *Philosophy of Right*: Patriotism and Trust in the Modern State

Jason J. Howard

My goal in this chapter is to examine one of the more controversial aspects of Hegel's *Philosophy of Right*, which is the status of conscience for legitimating the political identity of the state. Much quality scholarship has gone into this issue over the last two decades in showing the pivotal place of conscience for understanding modern ethical life.[1] My concern here is not the moral import of conscience per se but how Hegel conceives of the constitutive interrelationship between the identity of the political and personal accountability. In specifying this interconnection Hegel shows us how the legitimacy of the political itself, as the objective expression of a just society, is related to how we measure the terms of our own accountability. To tackle this issue, in which the warrant of the political issues from the dynamics of personal culpability, is to understand how the indelible reality of human choice, what Hegel refers to as the "formal conscience," is concretized in more and more substantial forms of personal responsibility. Hegel's characterization for these genuine forms of personal responsibility is the "true conscience" (*Das wahrhafte Gewissen*) (*PR*, §137).[2]

As Hegel sees it, the truth of the political, its authority as a genuine expression of a common cultural undertaking, rests on how people become conscious of this larger identity through coming to terms with the facticity of their own accountability, along with the freedom of choice that such accountability presupposes. This chapter argues that in specifying how this connection unfolds in all its complexity, Hegel provides us with a compelling account of why the truth of political identity, if it is to be the expression of a free and just solidarity, is dependent on the extent to which individuals can recognize aspects of their own accountability within the larger dynamic of political governance. It is my contention that the dynamism of accountability itself is what propels human agents beyond their own self-interest and immediacy, which issues in the constant negotiation of our "second nature" as trusting and trustworthy social agents whose rightful *topos* is the creation of a free and just society.[3] My account of this interrelationship between the development of accountability and the achievement of a legitimate political identity proceeds as follows. The first part of this chapter gives a brief overview of modern ethical life, specifying the significance of the modern state in providing citizens with the opportunity of discovering the abstract character of formal conscience for themselves, which enables agents to overcome the restless indeterminacy of a life beset by endless choices. The second part examines the status of the "true conscience" and the role it plays in showing the connection between autonomy and personal responsibility, specifying how this notion is active at the level of personal disposition (*Gesinnung*) in the various levels of ethical life. The third part demonstrates how the true conscience reaches its final form of concreteness as "patriotism" in clarifying how citizens discover why it is that the truth of their own interiority gains its objective confirmation in forging a viable political identity, the truth of which ensues in the mediation of genuine differences. The chapter concludes by indicating how the negotiation of a political identity is also an ethical achievement in that it shows the actuality of the free will to emerge in the reality of a social commons that solidifies our second nature in the creation of a trusting and just society.

The State and Modern Ethical Life

In a very general sense we can say that the *Philosophy of Right* seeks to indicate under what conditions modern individuals can be assured that freedom is not a fiction but the truth of their experience as cultural subjects. In order to prove this, Hegel must specify how the modern state "*should be recognized*" if its relationship to freedom is to be coherently discerned (*PR*, Preface, emphasis).[4] With this goal in mind, my reading of the *Philosophy of Right* is oriented toward indicating how the abstract (formal) character of conscience is overcome in modern ethical life insofar as it supplies a determinate context from which the internal certitude of conscience can find a fuller register for its choices than just immediate particularity.[5] This process reaches its apex in the realization that political identity is founded on a constant negotiation that revolves around the attempt to explicate the underlying concern of all self-conscious agency, namely, that of giving the free will determinate actuality in the forging of a recognizable spiritual identity.

As Hegel clarifies, the term *right* designates the free will in its concrete existence (*PR*, §29).[6] It is through right that we become conscious of what it means to be free. The task Hegel sets himself is to delineate the manifold gradations in which the right of the free will is effective. Thus as Hegel stipulates, the right of the free will becomes "formalized," as well as the accompanying duties associated with this right, as stages in the concretization of freedom (*PR*, §30).[7] The status of conscience for assessing the rationality of modern political identity is a pivotal concern in this regard, because if it turns out that the "true conscience" is simply subjectivity purified of its inwardness and innermost convictions, then the state cannot be said to properly respect the "sanctuary" (*Heiligtum*) of personal conviction, leaving the subject no choice but to appropriate the interests of the state as his or her own (*PR*, §137, Remark).[8]

Hegel makes it quite clear that what distinguishes modern ethical life is the degree to which it has managed to organize the fundamental distinctions and differentiations inherent to self-conscious communities in accordance with the truth of self-determination, which is most evident in the ability of such communities to mediate singular self-insistence with the universality of common purposes and goals. Thus as Hegel specifies, to say modern ethical life makes freedom concrete is to say that particular individuals have both developed themselves to their full potential and recognize this potential for themselves, as well as acknowledge how their own sense of individuality gains its most concrete form in the task of mutual determination, appropriating the larger initiatives of the community as the register of their own personal accountability (*PR*, §260).[9]

The very credibility of the modern state, then, is based on its ability to allow subjects to discover their own inwardness and independence, differentiating themselves from the encompassing totality in which they find themselves in order to discern to what extent they are legitimately bound to the common projects that underscore the world in which they live. Indeed, the stronger the state, the stronger its ability to let individuals assert their own independence against the norms of the community. The central insight here is that self-conscious existence is always embedded in horizons whose legitimacy appears to stand outside the subjects whose lives it circumscribes. In this sense, to be self-conscious means to be born to alienation, set in contradiction against the immediacy that initially conditions us. The intuitive awareness of who I am as a particular individual is constantly being undone insofar as the actual experience of being independent is mediated by sources seemingly beyond my own factical immediacy. In other words, I live in a world that has already established what it means to be a "particular individual," and thus I am implicated in a set of conceptual distinctions operating well before I become conscious of them. The crowning achievement of modern ethical life lies in both its implicit recognition of this situation as well as its capacity to acknowledge what consequences this has for the civil, moral, religious, and lastly political framework of human societies.

Seen along these lines, the possibility of appropriating the underlying norms of the modern state does not depend on some timeless act of critical reflection that is posited between the subject and the government but on the capacity of the state to acknowledge the multiple ways in which subjects appropriate the fact of their own individuality, creating the space necessary for the differentiation of their so-called natural immediacy and conscious mediation to gradually unfold. Although everyone is self-conscious, not everyone is reflective to the same degree or extent. Indeed, this is one of the cardinal problems in organizing modern society, especially if this society claims to endorse the right to self-definition as its governing political agenda.[10]

Given the aforementioned qualifications, modern ethical life can be broadly defined as the arena in which individuals learn how to navigate the differences that condition them. In this sense the overall integrity of ethical life depends on the ability to educate conscious subjects into their fuller possibilities as *self-conscious* agents. What makes this process an experience of inward liberation and not simply one of internal subjugation, although moments of this dynamic are not without elements of subjugation, is that modern ethical life rests on the necessity of appropriation as a process of development. As a consequence, the various communities that make up ethical life, that of the family, civil society, and the state, recognize that what functions as "reasons" for participating in its manifold relationships are multifarious in both their extent and degree of evidential force. A case in point is the status of legal rights. The modern ethical state grants all subjects the same legal rights, regardless of one's color, religion, class, or sex, thereby ensuring that this process of appropriation unfolds itself as universally as possible, offsetting the contingencies that afflict us as particular individuals. Many of these rights are effective before we consciously reflect on them, which is to say they serve as objective conditions that provide us with the possibility of discovering our own individuality. Without these laws there would be no way to effectively ensure that individuals have the opportunity of articulating the measure and sense of their own particularity, because there would be no way to guarantee the social space necessary for such articulation to ensue.

The granting of legal rights, however, is not some trade-off or contract between state and citizen in which we are obliged to repay our debt to society later in life, although this is one of the ways we initially come to understand the duty of citizenship but the recognition that self-consciousness is necessarily irreducible to its natural instance as biological individual. It is this deeper insight that anchors the potentiality of ethical life as a whole. That is why ethical life can truly be described as a "*second nature*" (*PR*, §§4, 151, emphasis added).[11] To be sure, we come into the world bearing distinctions that already differentiate us from the natural world, which is evident in the fact that even children have certain inalienable rights accredited to them (*PR*, §174).[12]

As should be readily apparent, conscience is pivotal in bringing this second nature to fruition insofar as conscience, as inner conviction, is what ultimately secures our "ethical" possibilities at the level of personal recognition. As Hegel specifies, once self-consciousness realizes its power of internal justification and differentiation, its formal freedom as conscience, "everything depends on the kind of content which it gives itself" (*PR*, §138, Remark).[13] Indeed, the very stability of modern ethical life rests, to a large extent, on overcoming this formal freedom of differentiation by properly appropriating it. The only way it is properly appropriated, or checked, is by having one's freedom firmly grounded in substantial projects that fulfill one's indwelling desire for independence in a way that authentically completes one's inherent pursuit of such independence. It is precisely because of this drive toward independence that political identity plays such a crucial role in founding the rationality of modern ethical life, for without a substantial sense of political identity the larger import or point of our own independence remains in confusion. To be sure, what differentiates modern ethical life from that of earlier epochs, for example, that of the Greek *polis*, is that the concretization of our "second nature" as rational agents allows itself to be more fully discerned in its ramifications so that we do not remain outstanding witnesses to our own experience of being individuated. In such cases, we remain implicitly alienated from the encompassing relationships that draw our world into focus, and we do not recognize ourselves as being integrally involved in working out the *meaning* of human nature.[14]

To have one's freedom genuinely fulfilled is not to nullify this formal right of choice, which would be impossible in principle, but to have one's own innermost projects and interests also confirmed at the concrete level of social participation—the intensity of inwardness becomes coupled with substantial content.[15] As long as self-conscious agents refuse to give an account of their interests within the domain of concrete human interaction, the freedom that defines self-conscious agency can never become objective. What I want to emphasize here is that such formal freedom—the infinite determinability of the will—is never fully overcome, because to overcome the propensity for such abstraction would be to reify the dynamism of self-consciousness itself. Seen as such, the rationality of ethical life is based on the ability of its multiple communities to demonstrate *in practical ways* how such instances of abstraction are either illegitimate, or at the least, inadequate, responses to the multiple demands of social existence. If the modern state were to truly overcome such formal freedom, then it would inadvertently deprive particular subjects of the opportunity of discerning the rationality of their own experience, for the abstract character of formal freedom would no longer be something we discern for ourselves but dictated from without.

We overcome the formality of conscience through recognizing how we are responsible for sustaining the social commons. Although this responsibility can be understood in a variety of ways, I want to focus on the awareness of political identity as the recognition of our own capacity to be accountable, and what this implies for the governance of a just society. As a citizen of a given state, certain rights define the extent and limitations of my freedom, what can and cannot be done to me, along with what I can and cannot do to others. Because these rights are ascribed to me immediately, they do not initially seem to have much in common with personal culpability but with "external necessity," appearing as an indifferent force of legislation to the subjects whose lives it governs. It is this indifference itself that is broken down in seeing the living universality that underscores the practical reality of the world of rights. As long as the true connection between rights and personal responsibility remains unclear, the truth of political identity lacks a substantial foundation, for we misunderstand how it is that a just and rational society expresses an *ethical achievement* and is not just a way of organizing citizens.

The Place of the "True Conscience"

The various phases of ethical life—the family, civil society, and the state—demarcate the stages in which the particular individual comes to concrete selfhood by specifying the diverse ways in which *being an individual* gains confirmation in the universal substantiality of modern ethical life. As Hegel affirms, it is here within the dynamism of ethical life that ". . . the self-will of the individual and his conscience (*die Eigenwilligkeit und das eigene Gewissen des Einzeln*), in its attempt to exist for itself and in opposition to the ethical substantiality, have disappeared" (*verschwunden [ist]*) (*PR*, §152).[16] What I want to argue here, following the general interpretive framework of many recent interpretations of the *Philosophy of Right*, is that this supposed disappearance of personal conviction needs to be understood against the conceptual backdrop of Hegel's overall methodology and the larger aims of his social and political philosophy.[17] Hegel develops his position cognizant of the "resistance" inherent to the natural will, in which subjects mistake the hyperbole of choice for true liberation, and he understands that this immediacy must be willingly mediated in a way that makes the import of our decisions more transparent so as to make accountability an imperative and not just an option. What makes up the rationality of the modern state, then, is not due to some unseen system of self-perpetuation that utilizes particularity as "it" sees fit in order to fulfill the epistemological priority of immanent knowing but rather, because the genuine concerns of real subjects always persist beyond the moment of singular appropriation and fulfillment. Moral authority, just as much as political authority, should never be based on warrants whose sole proof resides in the primacy of individual reflection, otherwise subjects remain locked in a state of perpetual alienation from each other's *true motives* in which social consensus is constantly at risk of devolving into factions of conspiracy theories.[18] Such attitudes must be shown to be abstractions, which is impossible outside a viable notion of political identity, for it is only at the level of state initiatives that trust can be revealed in its fuller register as the truth of the free will made into practical policy. To be sure, without the universality that trust provides, our "second nature" would remain confined to the level of possibility for we could never provide enough compelling evidence from which to undertake the mediation of substantial differences to any genuine degree. In accordance with this insight, the rational state develops ". . . *those relations* (*der Verhältnisse*) which are necessitated by the Idea of Freedom" (*PR*, §148, Remark), thereby enabling the given solidarity that unites us to be confirmed not only inwardly but outwardly as well.[19]

Taking the aforementioned considerations into account, I now want to specify in some detail how Hegel construes the place of the "true conscience" and its significance in providing the practical anchor, as it were, for construing the sense of our own accountability. Hegel's description of the true conscience runs as follows: "True conscience is the disposition (*Gesinnung*) to will what is good *in and for itself*; it therefore has fixed principles, and these have for it the character of determinacy and duties which are objective for themselves" (*PR*, §137, emphasis).[20] Unlike the formal conscience, whose motives and legitimacy remain indeterminate because they lack any objective ground, the true conscience is a "communal conscience" in which agents recognize themselves as members of a given ethical community.[21] Saying that this form of ethical agency is a disposition does not entail the assimilation of all action to mere habit but emphasizes that this mode of agency is born of our experience as members of a community in which we learn to see the value that certain relationships have played in shaping our own sense of what is implied in being an individual. What makes these relationships valuable in the first place is not based on something I simply determine on my own but the experience of empowerment and responsibility they engender within me; it is this that ought to impel me to take up these relationships as my own proper duty. What is more, it is precisely through these relationships that the vernacular of personal responsibility gains a substantial sense and content.

The pull of conscience as "the *formal aspect* of the activity of the will . . . " (*PR*, §137, emphasis added) is abated or overcome in the concreteness of ethical life to the extent that we realize, in a very practical way, *the impossibility of differentiating ourselves from the world without disowning our own freedom as determining agents at the same time*.[22] That is not to say that we cannot differentiate ourselves from the demands the world places upon us, which remains a real possibility, but that the elements of this withdrawal will depend on more than what I can or cannot obtain for myself as an individual; in short, that if there are genuine disagreements, which Hegel does not deny, then these disagreements must themselves bear evidence of a universal freedom in jeopardy of being misconstrued, misunderstood, or otherwise violated.[23] It is my contention that the most obvious proof for this violation will manifest itself at the level of political identity in the organization and implementation of state priorities. Consequently, claims of individual misrecognition do not automatically entail that a given relationship is problematic or suspect, which would then give rise to the immediate reformulation of this relationship and its legitimacy. In this regard people's private interests remain just that, their private interests, yet in pursuing these interests people inevitably encroach upon other public goods at which point the question of how one prioritizes issues of responsibility comes into relief—how these priorities are assessed depends on what relationships can be adjusted and to what degree.[24]

Agents who endorse the abstract immediacy of formal conviction live in a world underwritten by suspicion where anything that does not meet the approval of their individual standpoint is seen as a threat, and where every sacrifice is compensated with the promise of some personal reward. Agents who act on behalf of genuine conviction, in contrast, live in a world underwritten by trust in which they recognize the relationships that engage them as the determination of freedom in movement, the institutions that organize their interests as the deposit of freedom in action. The habitual activity that Hegel takes as one of the hallmarks of genuine conviction is not a submission to the status quo but the result of the sedimentation of trust that is shaped over time, which implicitly rests on the collective resolve of a mutual history forged in the common goal of bringing the ideal of freedom to fruition. The moment our resolve loses interest in the common project of recognizing freedom in actuality, which depends on negotiating differences rather than denying them, this resolve loses its rational legitimacy. As a consequence, to assume the true conscience could be just as active in a totalitarian regime as in a rational state is to overlook the substantial connection between genuine conviction and justice, a point we will return to shortly. What makes a political system totalitarian is precisely that it refuses to grant the infinite right of the individual the space to confirm his or her freedom in practical ways, for to do so would be to concede the illegitimacy of its own political hegemony.

We experience our freedom most concretely in the projects we undertake to redefine the meaning of the contingency that engulfs us as particular individuals. In negotiating our differences, the true conscience comes to prominence as that mode of acting that recognizes one's own integrity to be tied up with upholding those forms of determinate universality that subsist through empowering the infinite actuality of the free will. To choose not to uphold or respect these forms as they subsist within a given content is to neglect those very avenues that grant us the opportunity of reconciling ourselves with our deepest sources of alienation, especially the experience of individuation. Moreover, the transition beyond the abstraction of the formal conscience to the genuine or true conscience ensues through the practical recognition of freedom in the concrete norms and institutions that govern the actual commerce of self-conscious existence—that in genuinely upholding such norms and institutions one is actively taking part in the fulfillment of freedom as the rightful determination of spiritual existence. It is because of this that one recognizes the forging of a transparent political identity as the practical bastion of the free will, for it is through this political identity that the trust we have in each other finds its most dramatic enactment.

The upshot of this is that any society that is concerned with freedom cannot seek to eliminate the contingency and indeterminacy that condition us as particular individuated beings, because it is only through experiencing this contingency firsthand that we come to realize that our existence is always more than our immediate facticity is capable of explaining. It is natural to mistake the immediacy of reflection, the formality of conscience, for the truth of self-consciousness and "resist" having to mediate the manifold demands that confront us, denying the complexity of the relationships shaping our experience at the same time. This is part and parcel of our immediacy as knowing agents, insofar as whatever *appears* true must initially issue in self-certainty. Each phase of ethical life, that of the family, civil society, and state, is a means of demonstrating how the certainty of self-reflection, or the givenness of who we consider ourselves to be, is in a continual process of being redefined and thus is always more than simply immediate. As the individual learns to discern the relationships that embrace him or her, so he or she discovers the necessity of partaking in these relationships through participating in their constitutive actuality. Following Hegel's account, "piety" in the family, "rectitude" in civil society, and "patriotism" for the state are all instances of true conviction at work in uncovering the relationship between personal liberty and accountability.[25] I now want to examine the third form of true conscience, that of patriotism, in order to stipulate the relationship between personal accountability and political identity in more detail.

True Conscience and Political Identity

In working out the sense and limits of my own accountability I come to recognize in a practical way that my formal freedom of self-definition, which appears exemplified in the universality of personal choice indicative of civil society, remains indeterminate outside the substantial forms of articulation inherent to the common history that ethical life encapsulates.[26] In this sense, our "*highest duty* is to be members of the state" (*PR*, §258), since it is in contributing to the achievement of the state as the substantial locus of communal definition that one also ensures that the multiple forms of right that make up self-conscious existence are actualized to their fullest potential.[27] As Hegel explains, the spheres of the family and civil society provide us with an immediate sense of our existence as separate individuals, whereas we discover the larger history of our own individuality within the social institutions that sediment this history. Thus we discover our identity as not only "private" but also "substantial" persons through actively participating in the projects, goals, and ends of the state (*PR*, §264).[28] It is only in this recognition of the state as the locus of self-definition that the *achievement* of freedom as a process of mutual interaction and recognition becomes intuitively objective. It is institutions that transcribe the constitution of a specific nation as the history of a common people into actuality and that provide, as Hegel explicitly specifies, the objective foundation of trust that will come to inform our ethical disposition (*des Zutrauens und der Gesinnung der Individuen*) (*PR*, §265).[29]

The particular forms and instances of personal freedom evident in both the family as well as civil society, along with those rights and duties applicable to each sphere, are testament to transforming categories of thought, and not just the desires or choices of individual subjects, that, in short, it is in our capacity to organize our desires and choices that make them substantial, thus capable of being both recognized and fulfilled, and not just the fact that we have desires and can make choices. What I want to emphasize here is that this becomes most explicit at the level of political identity in the form of state institutions that secure the common work of self-organization as the communal project of freedom. In the dictates of its constitution, judicial organization, larger administration, and foreign policy, the state reveals itself to be an ethical entity that encapsulates the concerns of its citizens by making them explicit. The immediate authority of the family, just as much as the opposing interests and welfare of distinct individuals in competition against each other within civil society, occurs within a wider context of a common language and history. This common history animates the entire organization of ethical life and is most objective in those institutions that maintain the priorities of this culture as a whole, which are the manifold estates and institutions of the state.

As Hegel explains, the state is the will of the people made objective at the level of social customs and concrete projects. Hence, as Hegel indicates, the state is "the actualization of the ethical Idea" (*PR*, §257). Yet the actuality of this idea remains incumbent on the extent people recognize themselves in its common reality, finding their own intentions (*Gesinnung*) fulfilled in concrete forms of free existence.[30] Otherwise put, the state secures the reality of free recognition in demonstrating the actuality of freedom to exist at the level of concrete existence and not just subjective intention. In recognizing how our underlying concerns extend themselves beyond the immediacy of our own given particularity, the meaning of freedom is changed at the same time. Hegel sees this realization concretized in that form of conscientious agency he calls the "political disposition" or "patriotism," which is also the most substantial form of the "true conscience" (*PR*, §268).[31] What grounds the political disposition in discussion here is precisely that of "trust" (*Zutrauen*), whose degree of evidential concreteness varies depending on the agent in question, and which centers on "the consciousness that my substantial and particular interest is preserved and contained in the interest and end of an other (in this case, the state), and in the latter's relation to me as an individual (*als Einzelnem*)" (*PR*, §268).[32] That Hegel qualifies this disposition with the term *trust* I think is highly significant, for it underscores the fact that those who act with a true conscience are aware that their actions are centered on maintaining a relationship of recognition that by its very nature is thoroughly dynamic in character. To say one acts from a disposition informed by trust is to say that one acknowledges a certain degree of evidential concreteness in making one's choices, and that this evidence, namely, that the fundamental aims of the state are experienced as trustworthy, takes precedence in making one's choices.

Hegel makes it quite clear that in discussing the issue of patriotism he does not mean simply a "willingness" to give up one's life for the sake of the state, which is a rather simplistic grasp of genuine patriotism, but a general disposition shaped by the practical insight that one's experience is essentially tied to those communities that determinately empower one's possibilities as a particular individual (*PR*, §268, Remark).[33] What patriotism verifies is the reality of subjective intention in making the *knowledge* of the state concrete. As Hegel emphasizes, one only undertakes the burden of making "*extraordinary* sacrifices" on account of having had practical experiences that confirm one's particular individuality to be embedded in the common experiences we share as individuals. If there is nothing of these common experiences that can lend itself to articulation, and thus verification, then there is nothing with which to legitimately motivate people to make sacrifices in the first place.[34] What qualifies patriotism as the most substantial form of the true conscience is that it illustrates the intention of particular subjects who realize that their own individual fulfillment is tied to the endeavors they undertake to forge an institutional world of common intersubjective experience. Consequently, what is true about their experience is not confined to themselves alone but the common truth that underscores their own independence, that of freedom. In other words, subjects of true conscience appreciate why their own particular concerns need not be defined in antithesis to a larger political identity in order to remain "their own," for they recognize that the warrants that ground this identity look to the freedom we all presuppose as thinking agents, in which the indelible reality of choice is given a coherent sense and viable goal. Indeed, it is the presence of a larger political identity and its explicit concern for self-definition that reveals how my own interests as a subject are extended beyond the site of my own particularity, which is also why the true source of any genuine political identity must be how responsibility is earned, shared, and implemented, and not simply the brokering of individual power.

Conclusion: The Dynamics of Accountability and the Truth of Political Identity

As social agents we experience cultural existence most viscerally in light of how we formulate the terms of our own accountability. It is precisely because of this that the legitimacy of any political identity depends not only on how the right to self-definition is articulated through political practices but, more importantly, on how the authority that supports these practices is discovered and experienced by the agents whose lives such policies attest to governing. The discovery of our accountability to each other in the spheres of the family, civil society, and the state is a testament to how we circumscribe our common accountability as a community in terms of the reality of mutual determination, which requires substantial acts of trust if such accountability is to issue in anything beyond that of mundane agreement. Seen as such, those institutions that solidify our political identity, such as the practical administration of the principles of a given state's constitution, also serve to render an objective account of our own priorities. If these priorities continually change or are irresponsibly enacted, then so too the political identity they seek to engender will remain caught up in the contingency of personal initiative, and the achievement of the political as the objective expression of our own autonomy becomes indecipherable from the politics of opportunism. It is in this slip, so to speak, that genuine political identity initiates its disintegration into nationalist ideology.

Hegel's analysis of the true conscience and its ties to the legitimacy of political identity looks to how we articulate what is involved in being accountable, giving an analysis of how we identify our own individuality with the political dynamic of state governance. In pursuing this very theme, Hegel offers a practical demonstration of how the reality of our own resolve comes to prominence in shaping both who we are and who we want to be. If we are to appreciate Hegel's project in its full political relevancy then the place of conviction is crucial, because it is the *tension* of conscience that fosters the possibility of genuine responsibility and retains my particularity at the same time, which is the minimal condition for a free and just society.[35]

Indeed, Hegel's description of the true conscience is crucial to understanding his conception of political identity, for people have to recognize themselves as being recognized in a way that respects and accommodates what matters most to them as *particular individuals*. How we conceive our own individual identity inevitably conditions the ways in which we recognize other individuals and how they recognize us. It is precisely because of this dynamism that the identity of politics is reflected in how we construe the measure of our own accountability.

Since being self-conscious is all about how we become conscious of what is implied in being a self, the more abstract the connection between political identity and personal accountability, the more prone we are to restrict the truth of freedom to individual prerogative and caprice. It is precisely because of this interconnection or reciprocity that a good government is a just government, because if the state is rational then the edifice of its principles is rooted in the knowledge that denying the accountability of the political is to dissolve the substantiality of freedom in restricting its providence to the realm of the "mere" ideal. Understood along these lines, it should be clear why Hegel's account of the true conscience is so indispensable in appreciating his conception of political identity. To be sure, if Hegel cannot stipulate the connection between individual conviction and the objective imperative of political responsibility, then he cannot indicate how the truth of self-consciousness issues in its ability to make itself actual, since the true value of one's personal freedom must remain indeterminate.[36] In showing how accountability unfolds as a process of actualization, Hegel demonstrates why the truth of recognition is not inherent to any one object or experience but the way in which we organize the fundamental categories of our lives. The point of political identity is not to deny this ongoing endeavor but to affirm it as the practical guarantor of our own rationality.

The recognition of the political as the objective expression of the terms in which we construe the sense of our own responsibility is what institutes the connection between the political and the intimacy of personal accountability. The upshot of this is that the ethical currency of freedom is not simply limited to subjective insight but embedded in actual forms of community that harness, foster, and make objectively concrete the ways in which we are accountable to each other, and why. The concern here is *not* sociology but the makings of a just society, or how we recognize what holds a just society together, which is not just acknowledging the fact that people are separate individuals but realizing that no one is reducible to being only a simple individual. This means that we how interact with others shapes the lexicon through which the connection between self-interest and accountability can become explicit. If we cannot discern the ways in which politics genuinely accommodates our own concerns and *obligations*, then the political identity of the state must appear outside these concerns as something contingent, after the fact, or, at worst, imposed.

To close, human communities are continually forged through the ability of their members to differentiate themselves from their common identity, coming to terms with the meaning of such differentiation as the community matures. Realizing that we ought to have a say in how differences determine the community is the political moment just as much as it is the ethical moment, because how we come to terms with this responsibility determines the fate of the community as a whole. Hegel's account of conscience shows the *tension* inherent in negotiating this wider responsibility, which risks reading the imperative toward liberty solely through the lens of personal prerogative rather than seeing it as an indication of the patience required in forging any free society. Our sense of political identity is concretized in the pathos of these extremes, in which we come to discern that the final truth of the political is that it shows us how we mediate the alienation inherent in being an individual. Indeed, the truth of being human is inseparable from this process of self-discovery, where the reality of choice and the weight of self-determination arise *together* in propelling us outside our own immediacy to the actuality of the political community. It is here that the history of our accountability to each other has its fullest register in the trust we have in one another to forge a free and just society.

Notes

1. Comprehending the positive place of conscience entails getting a clear grasp of what Hegel understands by the term *genuine* or *true conscience*. The problem, however, is that Hegel spends very little time explicitly developing *genuine* forms of conscience, as the proliferation of different interpretations surrounding this issue attests. With reference to the *Philosophy of Right* see the following: Michael Mitias, *Moral Foundations of the State in Hegel's* Philosophy of Right: *Anatomy of an Argument* (Amsterdam: Editions Rodopi B.V., 1984); Thomas Mertens, "*Recht und Unrecht des Gewissens in Hegels Rechtsphilosophie*," *Archiv für Rechts-und Sozialphilosophie* 74 (1988): 477–90; Daniel O. Dahlstrom, "The Dialectic and the Necessity of Morality in Hegel's *Philosophy of Right*," *The Owl of Minerva* 24 (1993): 181–89, also "*Die Zweideutigkeit des* Gewissens," *Hegel-Jahrbuch* (1993–1994): 430–38; Gabriel Amengual, "*Das Gewissen Als Höchste Recht Des Subjekts*," *Hegel-Jahrbuch* (1993–1994): 430–38.

2. G. W. F Hegel, *Grundlinien der Philosophie des Rechts*, ed. E. Moldenhauer and K. M. Michel, *Werke in zwanzig Bänden*, vol. 7 (Frankfurt am Main: Suhrkamp Taschenbuch Wissenschaft, 2000), 254; G. W .F Hegel, *Elements of the Philosophy of Right*, ed. Allen Wood, trans. H. B. Nisbet (Cambridge: Cambridge University Press, 1996), 164. (Hereafter cited as *PR* [*Werke* 7], trans. Nisbet.)

3. As many critics have noted, Hegel's account of political identity looks to Rousseau quite closely for its general outline, agreeing with Rousseau that political society does not arise out of an explicit contract but the way in which our interests are thematized. For an exceptionally concise account of the importance of Rousseau for Hegel, see Frederick Neuhouser, *Foundations of Hegel's Social Theory: Actualizing Freedom* (Cambridge, MA: Harvard University Press, 2000), esp. 55–82. A point that Neuhouser overlooks, however, as does most secondary literature, is the pivotal role of conscience for Rousseau in recognizing how the general will completes our original moral instinct toward the good, and consequently the importance this insight plays for Hegel. See especially Rousseau's *Emile*, book IV, "The Confession of Faith of the Savoyard Vicar," Rousseau, *Emile or on Education*, trans. Alan Bloom (London: Penguin Books, 1991), 266–94, and the *Social Contract*, book II, ch. XII; book III, ch. XIV, in Rousseau, *The Social Contract*, trans. Christopher Betts (New York: Oxford University Press, 1994), 89–90, 125.

4. *PR*, preface, *Werke* 7, 26, Nisbet, 21. The account of conscience provided here is different from the *Phenomenology* insofar as the earlier text can be seen as providing a speculative account of the history of consciousness that encapsulated

the ways in which the experience of moral imputation itself comes to concreteness in the growing awareness of self-conscious agents. This movement reached its apex when self-consciousness realized that its concrete singularity is what establishes the legitimate criteria of meaningful action, and not abstract ideals or laws, which signal the dawning of conscience proper (ch. VI of Spirit, section C, subsection C, "Conscience. The 'beautiful soul,' evil and its forgiveness"). See G. W. F Hegel, *Phänomenologie des Geistes,* ed. Hans Friedrich and Heinrich Clairmont (Hamburg: Felix Meiner, 1988), 415–42; G. W. F Hegel, *Phenomenology of Spirit,* trans. A.V. Miller (New York: Oxford University Press, 1977), 383–409. (Hereafter cited as *Phän.*) In breaking through this final immediacy, self-consciousness discovers the substantiality of its own existence in the all-encompassing reality of knowing, which ties its sense of singular existence to the depth of its mutual recognition. Viewed from this standpoint, the predominant place of conscience appears to shift in the *Philosophy of Right,* offsetting the epistemological and metaphysical centrality of conscience in the *Phenomenology* to a seemingly less centralized if nevertheless significant moment. It is easy to infer from this that conscience plays a much more marginal role in Hegel's later thought, which I think is unjustified once the pivotal place of conscience is seen in its fuller light. In this regard I strongly agree with such thinkers as Karol Bal and Jay Bernstein, who see conscience as crucial both thematically and methodologically to Hegel's project as a whole. See Karol Bal, "*Der Begriff Gewissen als zentrale Kategorie der Hegelschen Ethik,*" *Hegel-Jahrbuch* (1987): 226–34; Jay Bernstein, "Conscience and Transgression: The Persistence of Misrecognition," *Bulletin of the Hegel Society of Great Britain* 29 (1994): 55–70.

5. As Gabriel Amengual points out, for many critics Hegel's idea of conscience presents the perfect entrance point from which to expose his insensitivity to morality, and individual subjectivity in particular. See Amengual, "*Das Gewissen Als Höchste Recht Des Subjekts,*" 430. This chapter seeks to reveal how these criticisms, both from the general standpoint of libertarian criticisms of Hegel's formulation of freedom and that of internal criticisms related to the place of conscience within his wider system, largely misunderstand the relationship between individual conviction (*Gesinnung*) and political identity. For an example of these criticisms, see J. Findlay, *Hegel: A Re-examination* (London: Allen and Unwin, 1958), M. Theunissen, "*Die verdrängte Intersubjektivität in Hegel's Philosophie des Rechts,*" in *Hegel's Philosophie des Rechts,* ed. D. Henrich and H. P. Horstmann (Stuttgart: Klett-Cotta, 1982), 317–81.

6. *PR,* §29, *Werke* 7, 80, trans. Nisbet, 58.

7. *PR,* §30, *Werke* 7, 83, trans. Nisbet, 59.

8. *PR,* §137, Remark, *Werke* 7, 254, trans. Nisbet, 164. This charge of emptiness is perhaps best formulated by Ernst Tugendhat when he claims that "conscience in Hegel is no more simply conceptual, but moral perversion." See *Selbstbewußtsein und Selbstbestimmung* (Frankfurt am Main: Suhrkamp, 1979), 349.

9. *PR*, §260, *Werke* 7, 406–407, trans. Nisbet, 282.

10. Hegel's problem in the *Philosophy of Right*, then, is not so much that he "assumes a principal distance between actor and act . . . doer and deed," which becomes the condition of recognition for the sovereignty of spirit, which is the claim put forth by Ferdinand Maier. See "*Kontingenz und Identität. Handlungstheoretische Erwägungen zur Dialektik der Moralität*," *Hegel-Jahrbuch*, (1987): 128–38, 130. Rather, the issue is that this "principal distance" is itself operative in varying degrees, which is sometimes explicit while other times not. Thus it is not that all agents recognize themselves as operating under the same "global direction of the will," but that such transparent purposefulness is never entirely possible. The "civilizing instinct of ethical life," as Maier refers to it (133), is the possibility of overcoming the alienation of being individuated, and not just reconciliation with objective cultural norms. Maier discounts the possibility of individually negotiating this participation in an ethically significant way, because he does not take seriously Hegel's attempt to integrate the formal conscience within a fuller paradigm of moral participation. Ludwig Siep makes a similar criticism in his seminal book *Anerkennung als Prinzip der praktischen Philosophie—Untersuchungen zu Hegels Jenaer Philosophie des Geistes* (München: Karl Alber Freiburg, 1979), esp. 280–90.

11. *PR*, §4, *Werke* 7, 46, trans. Nisbet, 35; *PR*, §151, *Werke* 7, 301, trans. Nisbet, 195.

12. *PR*, §174, *Werke* 7, 327, trans. Nisbet, 211.

13. *PR*, §138, *Werke* 7, 264, trans. Nisbet, 166.

14. A. S. Walton puts the point quite succinctly in stating that the difference between modern ethical life, as opposed to Greek, is that the modern form provides not only the "criteria" but also the "institutional expression" of its own capacity for "self-assessment." See "Hegel: Individual Agency and Social Context" in *Hegel's Philosophy of Action*, ed. Lawrence Stepelevich and David Lamb (Atlantic Highlands, NJ: Humanities Press, 1981), 75–93, 89.

15. See Hegel's discussion of formal freedom in *PR*, §15, *Werke* 7, 65–68, trans. Nisbet, 48–49.

16. *PR*, §152, *Werke* 7, 303, trans. Nisbet, 195–96.

17. See Paul Franco, *Hegel's Philosophy of Freedom* (New Haven, CT: Yale University Press, 1999); Adriaan Peperzak, *Modern Freedom: Hegel's Legal, Moral, and Political Philosophy* (Dordrecht, Holland: Kluwer, 2001). My interpretation differs from the aforementioned accounts in focusing specifically on the role of conscience in legitimizing modern political identity.

18. The accounts of culture in the *Phenomenology* (ch. VI of Spirit, section B) as well as that of morality (ch. VI of Spirit, section C) are case studies in just this point (*Phän*, 323–94, 395–415; Miller, 296–363, 365–83.) Yet what is not so clear in the *Phenomenology* is how these two spheres interrelate within a single world of spiritual consciousness, which is the concern of the *Philosophy of Right*.

19. *PR*, §148, *Werke* 7, 297, trans. Nisbet, 192.

20. *PR*, §137, *Werke* 7, 254, trans. Nisbet, 164.

21. Karol Bal emphasizes this point in the article, "*Der Begriff Gewissen als zentrale Kategorie der Hegelschen Ethik*," 230.

22. *PR*, §137, *Werke* 7, 254, trans. Nisbet, 164.

23. As Hegel explains: "But such *collisions* (*Kollisionen*) must be genuine ones, for moral reflection can invent collisions for itself wherever it likes and so give itself a consciousness that something *special* is involved and that *sacrifices* have been made" (*PR*, §150, *Werke* 7, 299, trans. Nisbet, 193). This does not mean that everything I do must have the sanction of the state body, but that when conflicts do arise I cannot immediately assume that I am in the right simply because my own individual principles do not garner the respect I deem they deserve.

24. For a further discussion of this point, see Walton, "Hegel: Individual Agency and Social Context," 88; Michael O. Hardiman, "The Project of Reconciliation: Hegel's Social Philosophy," *Philosophy and Public Affairs* 21 (1992): 165–95, 182.

25. The family is that place in which the natural undergoes its most immediate transformation in the creation of a free unity between biologically distinct individuals (man and woman) (*PR*, §170, *Werke* 7, 323, trans. Nisbet, 209). With this in mind, we can say that the major ethical task of the family is the education (*Bildung*) of children into free persons as well as the preservation of the integrity of the free union of marriage in the public forum of mutual recognition. Hegel characterizes the ethical obligation commensurate with such activity as "piety." In contrast to the family, civil society speaks to that transition in which my own particularity becomes increasingly evident as I come to terms with the newfound sense of my own independence. With this transition the compact organization of the family loses its primacy as the "obligating factor," and ethical life "appears to be lost" (*PR*, §181, *Zus*.; *Werke* 7, 338, trans. Nisbet, 219). It is normal that in facing the vast expanse of civil society in all its multiplicity we react to this "difference" with a sense of reserve and even skepticism. It is this latent sense of antagonism and competition that draws the reality of formal freedom into explicit relief as we stake a path for ourselves as particular individuals. Hegel indicates "rectitude" as that disposition that is operative in civil society, in which one gains a sense of commitment toward others beyond one's immediate family (*PR*, §207, *Werke* 7, 359, trans. Nisbet, 238). It is this expanding network of social relations that solidifies our common concern for security and independence, that is, for self-determination, in practical and self-evident ways.

26. If we closely follow Hegel's account of civil society it becomes apparent that conscience is not "an ethical standard operating on the fringe of society," which is how Allen Wood interprets the place of conscience in his influential book *Hegel's Ethical Thought* (New York: Cambridge University Press, 1990), 188. The formality of individual conviction is integral to the existence of self-consciousness and the relation of self-consciousness to life itself in the form of desire. Every stage

of ethical life can be seen as an attempt to mediate the formality of the subjective will, which places conscience at the heart of Hegel's entire moral, social, and political endeavor.

27. *PR*, §258, *Werke* 7, 399, trans. Nisbet, 275.

28. *PR*, §264, *Werke* 7, 411, trans. Nisbet, 287.

29. *PR*, §265, *Werke* 7, 412, trans. Nisbet, 287.

30. *PR*, §257, *Werke* 7, 398, trans. Nisbet, 275.

31. *PR*, §268, *Werke* 7, 413, trans. Nisbet, 288. Daniel Dahlstrom provides an informative account of the various criticisms directed toward Hegel's formulation of the true conscience in the article "*Die Zweideutigkeit Des Gewissens,*" *Hegel-Jahrbuch* (1993–1994): 439–44.

32. *PR*, §268, *Werke* 7, 413, trans. Nisbet, 288.

33. *PR*, §268, *Werke* 7, 413, trans. Nisbet, 289. It is this very idea of direct sacrifice for political gains that is the rationale of the French revolution and the politics of suspicion that it perpetuates. See the *Phenomenology*, chapter VI on Spirit, section B, subsection III, "Absolute Freedom and Terror" (*Phän*: 385–94; Miller, 355–63.)

34. J. O'Malley gives a good account of how political disposition serves as the counterpole in guaranteeing the "actuality of freedom" against the potential "mechanism of the state." See J. O'Malley, "*Die Wurzeln der Freiheit als politische Gesinnung im subjektiven Geist,*" in *Psychologie und Anthropologie oder Philosophie des Geistes*, ed. Franz Hespe and Burkhard Tuschling (Stuttgart: Frommann-Holzboog, 1991), 422–36, 424.

35. The idea of the true conscience that Hegel puts forth in the *Philosophy of Right* follows through on Rousseau's insight, that conscience is in many ways the fulcrum of the particular and general will. As Stefan Hübsch succinctly points out: "It is not against conscience but with and through it that Hegel has given a means both complex and simple for the solution of Rousseau's most penetrating of problems: how is the unity of universal and subjective will to be thought, which must underlie every organized human community if it should be more than a contingent or violent association of individual people." See Stefan Hübsch, *Philosophie und Gewissen: Beiträge zur Rehabilitierung des philosophischen Gewissensbegriffs* (Göttingen: Vandenhoeck & Ruprecht, 1995), 117–18 (my translation).

36. Thus as Gabriel Amengual clarifies: "As the sensuous outcome (result) of reason, intention (*Gesinnung*) is equally the unity of subjective particularity and objective (institutional) and communal universality." See Amengual, "*Das Gewissen Als Das Höchste Recht Des Subjekts,*" 432 (my translation).

Chapter 12

Substantial Freedom as Identity of Rights and Duties

Maria G. Kowalski

In *Philosophy of Right,* Hegel boldly asserts that each individual has a right to freedom, but he also argues that an individual finds his substantial freedom in duties. Enveloped in these two claims is an apparent contradiction. The main objective of this chapter is to assess how Hegel's conception of substantial freedom (*substantielle Freiheit* [PR, §149, §257])[1] as being an *identity of rights and duties* resolves this contradiction and to show how this conception reflects a distinctively modern conception of freedom. Substantial freedom is the union of subjective and objective freedom and entails both that an individual choose the proper object of will and that the proper object be the realization of his essentially free nature. The identity of right and duty, according to Hegel, is a "factor [*Bestimmung*] of the greatest importance, and the inner strength of states is embodied in it." Earlier in this passage he asserts that "there is a single principle for both duty and right, namely the personal freedom of human beings" (PR, §261R). Given the nature of these claims, Hegel's theory must prove that duties and freedom are indeed compatible.[2] In spite of the importance that Hegel attaches to the role of rights and duties in his social and political philosophy, the notion of duty has not received much consideration. This chapter will show why the concept of duty is indispensable to understanding the distinctively modern nature of Hegel's conception of freedom. The central element of Hegel's political theory is the individual's essential nature as a free will willing its own freedom; my argument is that *the will's fundamental right and duty is freedom*, expressed in terms of self-determination and self-realization. The argument presented here entails a set of claims. First, rights and duties are grounded on the notion of free will; the most important right and duty is the right and duty the self has to itself to realize its essential freedom. Second, the respect and dignity of each individual is expressed and vindicated in the inviolability of the fundamental right and duty to realize[3] freedom. And third, freedom must be properly understood as the identity of rights and duties, an identity that is realized only in the rational and ethical state. Since Hegel predicates his conception of *Sittlichkeit* on the self-determining powers of the self, all rights and duties that an individual acquires in the state must be in accordance with the concept of the fundamental right to freedom as inviolable.

Freedom is something the free will must will, that is, has a duty to will. Hegel's objective in the *Philosophy of Right* is to present the institutions that are required by the content and structure of freedom; the concept of freedom from which the ethical institutions are immanently derived is a concept of freedom as an inviolable right. It is this inviolability of the right to freedom that grounds the obligations that a member of a community has. The right to freedom means that the duties to which a person as a free will submits must be derived from the free will itself. The emphasis on the importance of freedom in Hegel's political philosophy is not new. In fact, many interpreters have made this claim.[4] However, there is very little consistency in the interpretation of the meaning of Hegel's conception of freedom. I attribute this lack of consistency to the fact that the relationship between rights and duties and freedom has up to now been consistently neglected. Freedom is indeed the central theme of Hegel's *Philosophy of Right*, but his conception of freedom cannot be properly understood and validated without understanding that it is the right and duty of our essential nature as free wills that makes freedom the inviolable right that it is. What is missing from the literature on Hegel's political and social philosophy is an understanding of Hegel's ethical and political system as being built upon the essential right to freedom that all individuals have by virtue of possessing free will.

Hegel's argument is that rational social and political institutions are necessary in order for an individual to realize freedom. The rationality of the state derives from its ability to make it possible for members to actualize individual freedom and to fulfill the duty each individual has to realize his essential nature as free. The duty to belong to a social and political community is not in Hegel's philosophy justified by the claim that a state is rational (though it must be rational for substantial freedom to be realized) but from the duty to self that each individual has to actualize concrete freedom. One of the advantages of Hegel's conception of freedom as identity of rights and duties is that it can justify citizens' support for the state and its policies, even when those policies demand that an individual sacrifice his or her particular interests for the sake of the whole. The reason individuals can support and accept the ends of the rational state is because in the state, individuals, as citizens, have a common objective, a universal objective of realizing freedom. In realizing substantial freedom, individuals achieve their highest right. Political and social institutions embody substantial freedom only if they provide the conditions such that rights and duties have a relationship of identity.

If individuals are to fully embrace the duties they have as social members, then doing one's duty, according to Hegel, must not be just a demand that is imposed or that is coercive; rather, fulfilling one's duties as a social member must be the means of realizing one's own interests as a particular being. This argument is in clear contradiction to the communitarian arguments that claim that an individual's identity is exhausted by his or her social roles, by the duties he or she is committed to by virtue of his or her social membership.[5] In Hegel's view, the duties an individual has as a social member must reflect and address particular interests and objectives, because the source of these duties is the duty to self that a being has to realize his or her own essential nature as free will. While it is true that Hegel insists that a political association should be viewed as a community, the kind of community he envisions is a modern one and not the traditional type, for only the modern community is capable of achieving substantial freedom, and only the modern community accords full recognition and articulation of individual rights. The kind of ethical community that Hegel constructs is one in which the individual autonomy and rights of each individual to self-determination are the defining elements of both the structure and the objective of the rational state. In other words, his conception of the ethical community is a particularly modern one.

Ground of Rights and Duties

At the core of Hegel's grounding and defense of individual rights is the idea—to use Rawls's terminology—of "personal inviolability,"[6] an inviolability of the free will which, because it expresses the idea of respect for individual freedom, can never be sacrificed for the sake of satisfying other objectives or interests. The moral significance of abstract right is that its priority delineates the grounding of right on a consideration other than need and necessity; rather, following Kant, Hegel bases the notion of right on the autonomy of free will, which constitutes personality.[7] Its abstract nature clearly indicates that it is not a fully conceived notion of right; Hegel's main point in this section is primarily to find the origin and justification of rights and duties. This points to the requirement of having a personality and of presenting individuals as having the capacity for rights and duties. And because abstract right grounds the notion of right, it establishes the importance of the priority of right itself. Rights do not follow from an individual's role or position in the society.

At the stage of abstract right, Hegel is concerned with establishing the normative grounds for the minimal claims about rights and duties, but he also establishes the normative grounds upon which a more complete conception and development of rights and duties will be realized. For Hegel, abstract right and duties are based on a certain conception of "free will," which is the defining characteristic of "personality." The conception of a person as a free will, for Hegel, is the ground of rights. The general commandment of right, "*be a person and respect others as persons*" (PR, §36), expresses the self-consciousness that has itself for its object. The duty to treat others never merely as means but always also as ends is grounded on this conception of the self as a self-conciousness that has itself for its object.

In order to identify, realize, and protect the abstract freedom of a person, Hegel, in his formulation of abstract right, defines right by abstracting from all considerations of particular interests, desires, and utility. All contingent matters are stripped away until only the free will remains as the essential end in itself. Abstract right is thus based upon a notion of a moral personality that is free and equal. Hegel's derivation of rights from the abstract notion of the will bears some affinity for Rawls's insistence that mutual recognition of one another's rights can be realized only through a process of abstracting individuality from all of its contingencies, from particularity, until all differences are removed, until something resembling the pure will remains.[8] For Kant the fundamental principle of moral duty is "(a)ct so that you treat humanity, whether in your person or in that of another, always as end and never as a means only."[9] The ground of any duty, following this categorical imperative, is the inherent value of the free will or practical rationality of the individual to whom the duty is owed. In abstract right, Hegel conceives of duties in essentially the same way: Hegel agrees with Kant, that inherent to all human beings is a concept of rational will, and that only rational wills are ends in themselves.

Hegel's philosophy of right posits the duty to self as being fundamental to our inherent nature as free, and because this duty to realize freedom is essential to our human nature, one cannot release oneself from it. One's consciousness of one's essential right to freedom engenders the duty to self to seek and actualize concrete freedom in the world. "Personality," Hegel claims, "is that which acts to overcome [*aufzuheben*] this limitation and to give itself reality—or, what amounts to the same thing, to posit that existence [*Dasein*] as its own" (PR, §39). The limitation that Hegel is referring to is the limitation of "being merely subjective" (PR, §39). The duty to self to actualize one's freedom entails that one's will find expression for itself in the external world. The individual of abstract right, then, has a duty to himself or herself because he or she ought to affirm his or her own moral status and the particular rights and duties that follow from the fundamental right and duty to realize freedom; the individual also has duties to others not to violate their rights.

"A person," Hegel claims, "is therefore a subject which is aware of this subjectivity, for as a person, I am completely for myself: the person is the individuality of freedom in pure being-for-itself" (PR, §35A). To be aware of one's subjectivity is to have the consciousness of oneself as having the capacity for rational agency and the capacity to realize one's essential nature as free. As a free will, a "being-for-itself," a person has the consciousness of being something determined, insofar as one is a "free will," and as something indeterminate, insofar as "free will" is an abstraction, a universal. It is by virtue of being a "free will" that a being who is "for itself" gains consciousness of its duty to self to endow its "free will" with external concrete determination such that it can realize individual freedom.

The will has a duty to will its determination but it cannot achieve freedom unless it wills rationally. The opposite of the rational will that is "free and for itself" is the will that is arbitrarily determined by "natural drives" (PR, §15). A will is genuinely free when it rationally reflects and evaluates the possible choices available and undertakes those projects that will serve to actualize its essential nature. "This self-consciousness which comprehends itself as essence through thought and thereby divests itself of the contingent and the untrue constitutes the principle of right, of morality, and of all ethics" (PR, §21R). What this remark emphasizes is that for Hegel the will is genuinely free when it rationally deliberates, and its choices reflect the will's consciousness of itself as a free will.

It is Hegel's argument that as a free will a person has a duty to self to bring about a more concrete realization of freedom; this realization entails a movement from being purely "for itself" to finding more concrete expression in the world external to the will. Concrete freedom and individuality can be achieved only when the will becomes determinate not merely in the universal sense as a free will but as particular being with particular interests, goals, and so on. Hegel claims that "the Idea of the will is in general the *free will which wills the free will*" (PR, §27). This, I think, rather succinctly defines what the duty to self entails. The duty of the person as a "free will" entails the development and the preservation of its essential capacity to "will the free will." In other words, the duty to self is a duty to acquire consciousness and understanding of one's own nature by confronting and being engaged in the world that is external to the self and that provides the means through which the self can have consciousness of itself as a self with the capacity to will. The self's relationship with the "other" becomes more complex with the development of Hegel's political and social philosophy, but the basis for that development is set forth in abstract right where the self comes to have consciousness of itself, the other, and its duty to overcome the separateness that exists between itself and the other.

One's awareness of one's selfhood, of being a free will, thus entails a duty to self to realize one's freedom by developing and enabling the will to will freely. Hegel defines a person as a self-consciousness, a self-determining will that is aware of its right and duty to realize its freedom. Ultimately, the objective is for one to become a completely realized individual, and this is achieved when the universal and the particular elements of one's personhood are united within the context of a certain kind of political state. The imperative to "be a person" means nothing less than that every person has a duty to self to actualize his or her capacity for rights by appropriating things that lack free will. The second part of this imperative is that one ought to respect others as persons (PR, §36). The duties that the imperative to respect others as persons invokes are negative insofar as this imperative stipulates that a person ought not to violate or infringe the rights of the other, that is, "not to *violate* personality and what ensues from personality" (PR, §38). These duties are not positive in the sense that they specify particular actions a person would be obligated to take in one's relation to others. Abstract right abstracts from all particular interests and desires as well as any kind of general conceptions of well-being; therefore, it entails only a prohibition against interference with the rights of others—the right of another to be a person and to give himself or herself existence.

It is by virtue of being a rational agent, a "person," that one has a duty to self to realize one's essential nature as free. Since both the right and duty to realize freedom are not derived from some contingent sources, such as desire or virtue, but from the individual's being inherently rational, the rational agent cannot give up this right and thereby be released from the duty he or she has to himself or herself. It is important to understand that insofar as the rational agent recognizes that the duty to self to realize freedom is for his or her own benefit, he or she does not regard it as a burden but as a rational self-regarding requirement. An individual has a duty to himself or herself because he or she is conscious of being a "person" with a right to freedom; a person has a duty to others by virtue of his or her consciousness of them as being persons with rights.

One difficulty that may arise at this point is that the "self-regarding" nature of the fundamental right and duty of all individuals to realize their inherent nature as free may seem to yield an egoistic conception of the self. This interpretation would be unacceptable, as Hegel clearly rejected all ethical theories based on an egoistic conception of self. Rights for Hegel entail claims to the fulfillment of an individual's essential nature as free; the fundamental right and duty to freedom that each individual has requires the individual to act with respect to other persons and their rights. Thus as a rational agent, every person has a right to freedom against all other persons, and all other persons have the same right against him or her such that he or she has correlative duties toward them. At the level of abstract right, these duties are negative: each person must refrain from activities that would interfere with the right of others. The concept of personality does not lead to unfettered individualism, because substantive freedom can be realized only in a pluralistic ethical context in which each person's right to freedom is granted full recognition. It is important, I think, to recognize that although Hegel reveals the inadequacy of any theory that limits itself to the formal or abstract conception of the rights of the person, constituting the first stage of the development of right, such prioritization is not a denial of the essential importance of the inherent right to individual freedom.

Moralität

Like "abstract right," *Moralität* is an abstraction that is fully realized only in the ethical realm of *Sittlichkeit*. Whereas in abstract right one was shown to have a duty to self to realize oneself as a *person*, the duty associated with *Moralität* is the duty one has to give oneself the determination of a *subject*, and as a subject one has a duty to will the "good." The consciousness of oneself as a "subject" is a definitive aspect of modernity and crucial to one's identity. The definitive aspect of *Moralität* is the "reflection of the will into itself and its identity for itself" (PR, §105); this means that one has a consciousness of oneself as a particular, rational, moral, and free being—a "subject." The subjective will has a right and a duty to express and realize its subjective end concretely. The source of this inviolable right to subjectivity and subjective freedom is the essential nature of the will as free and self-determining. Thus the moral will comprehends that it has a duty to will its own determination, for in this process it expresses its capacity for freedom. The moral point of view is an element of the right of the subjective will, because in "accordance with this right, the will can *recognize* something or *be* something only in so far as that thing is *its own*, and in so far as the will is present to itself in it as subjectivity" (PR, §107).

In the realm of *Moralität*, the will is not only in itself but also for itself; the "reflection of the will into itself and its identity for itself, as opposed to its being-in-itself and immediacy and the determinacies which develop within the latter, determine the *person* as a *subject*" (PR, §105). The moral point of view is thus concerned with the subject, the individual's inward conscience. At the stage of abstract right, the will expresses itself externally. In morality the will's objective is its own subjectivity, its own inward state. Morality embodies the "development of the *right* of the subjective will" (PR, §107R). The individual recognizes and knows himself or herself as being absolute and self-determining, hence, the will in this realm follows only the dictates of its own reason.

The external embodiment of the will in "things," such as property, represents an expression of the will—albeit a very limited one. "In [abstract] right, the will has existence in something external, but the next stage is for the will to have existence in itself, in something internal. It must have being for itself, as subjectivity, and be confronted with itself. This relation to itself is that of *affirmation*, but it can attain this only by superseding its immediacy" (PR, §104A). For "affirmation" to be achieved, *Moralität* entails the will willing itself by self-consciously determining and willing its own moral ends. Whereas in abstract right, the notion of right was associated with prohibitions, in morality the "determination of my will with reference to the will of others is positive—that is, the will which has being in itself is inwardly present in what the subjective will realizes" (PR, §112A). The concept of morality, claims Hegel, "is the will's inner attitude (*Verhalten*) towards itself" (PR, §112A). To be a subject means that one has consciousness of oneself as a particular individual, and it is this consciousness of oneself as a particular individual that makes morality less abstract than the notion of "personality" in abstract right. The distinguishing characteristic of morality is the notion of subjectivity, which for Hegel means that each individual has a consciousness of himself or herself as a subject, a rational and moral agent.

Whereas in abstract right the will is infinite in itself, in morality the will is "*infinite* not only *in itself* but also *for itself*" (PR, §105). The transition to morality is marked by the will's identity "for itself"; it is not being merely reflected "in itself." "The worth of a human being," writes Hegel, "is measured by his inward actions, and hence the point of view of morality is that of freedom which has being for itself" (PR, §106A). Whereas abstract right imposes the command to be a "person" and respect others as persons, the command of morality is to be a "subject" and respect others as subjects. In other words, one has both a right and a duty to realize oneself as a subject and to respect others as subjects. The moral point of view involves the development of the will that is still an abstraction, but it is an abstraction that involves self-consciousness, which was lacking in the more formal abstraction at the level of abstract right. "Person" as an abstraction involved only the recognition of formal freedom; "subjectivity" emerges with the advent of self-consciousness, of being able to recognize oneself as a contingent individual.

By claiming that the subjective will has a right, Hegel is making the point that the will has the right to determine the content of its "subjectivity," to recognize and become only that which it recognizes as holding its content, to identify the core of its consciousness as a self. The subject's particularity has a right to find its satisfaction—Hegel refers to this as the right of "subjective freedom" (PR, §124R). Hegel's claim is that *Moralität* is a higher development of freedom, because the will in this sphere cultivates its individual subjectivity. The "moral point of view," according to Hegel's argument, "is the development of the *right* of the subjective will—or its mode of existence—

whereby this subjective will further determines what it recognizes as its own object [*Gegenstand*] so that this becomes the will's true concept—i.e. becomes objective in the sense of the will's own universality" (PR, §107R). The right and the duty of the moral subject is thus to consciously determine himself or herself.

The first criterion that a moral act must satisfy is the demand that it ensue from a responsible will. A moral agent cannot be held accountable for an act unless he or she consciously willed it, unless the act is an objectification of his or her subjective consciousness and an expression of his or her self-determined purpose. What characterizes an action as moral is that it corresponds to the will's purpose. This condition is demanded by the right of the moral will to recognize "only what was inwardly present as purpose" (PR, §114A). The second aspect, on the other hand, is concerned with the "intention behind the action—that is, of the relative value of the action in relation [*Beziehung*] to me" (PR, §114A). The last aspect relates not just to "the relative value of the action, but its universal value, the *good*" (PR, §114A). The "good is the intention, raised to the concept of the will" (PR, §114A).

An action is moral for Hegel when it fulfills the following requirements: (1) "it must be known by me in its externality as mine"; (2) "its essential relation [*Beziehung*] to the concept is one of obligation"; and (3) "it has an essential relation [*Beziehung*] to the will of others" (PR, §113). The first requirement refers to the subject's recognizing the consequences of his or her actions in externality and recognizing that the external determination follows from his or her intentions. Moral action must correspond to the subject's purpose and intent. The obligation that arises from the expression of the will as moral is due to the will's intention also having a universal content, hence, the subjective will's relation to universality is one of obligation. Given the universal content in the relationship between subjective will and universal will, the existence of subjective will is not limited to an immediate thing or property; its existence is itself immediate. The commandment of abstract right, "Be a person and respect others as persons," contained neither an "*explicit* reference to the concept, which is not yet opposed to or distinguished from the subjective will, nor does it have a *positive* reference to the will of others" (PR, §113R). In fact, the fundamental imperative of abstract right is prohibitive, and the essential relation of the subjective will to the will of others is negative. Morality, however, involves positive relations to others insofar as it demands that the subjective will be in conformity with the universal will.

We have seen that insofar as the commandment of abstract right is essentially prohibitive, the relation of a person's will in relation to another is negative. The duty that is involved in this kind of relation is not positive but negative—it only stipulates that one ought not act in such a fashion that the act would violate the respect that one ought to have for others. In reference to abstract right, the negative duty one has to others is expressed in terms of prohibitions; in morality, the will seeks its determination in reference to the will of others. The welfare of others comes to play a part in the will's determination. The will having a positive reference to the will of others seems to suggest that the needs and interests of others ought to be considered in the process of willing. Yet Hegel does not provide an argument that defines the duty a will has to others in the realm of morality. Allen Wood is on solid ground when he asserts that "Hegel's argument provides for a universality of concern only in the minimal sense that it removes the presumption that subjectivity concerns solely the subject's own well-being."[10]

In Hegel's theory the "expression of the will as *subjective* or *moral* is action" (PR, §113); therefore, the first duty that the will has in the sphere of *Moralität* is to will, to exercise the "*abstract* or *formal* right of action, according to which the content of my action, as accomplished in *immediate* existence [*Dasein*], is entirely *mine*, so that the action is the *purpose* of the subjective will" (PR, §114). The second duty of morality is not only to realize the "relative value" of the action in relation to me but also to realize its "universal value, the *good*" (PR, §114A). The universal value that Hegel invokes in this particular passage refers to the "ought" imperative of Kantian philosophy. That the intention should also be universal, as opposed to being purely particular, follows from the objectification of the will. The subjective will must become the universal will, but before the will reaches its universal being, it must go through this determinacy of subjectivity, for "[o]nly in the will as subjective will can freedom, or the will which has being *in itself*, be actual" (PR, §106).

One has a duty to realize one's essential free will, but why must this duty be fulfilled through one's self-realization as a "subject"? In abstract right, Hegel's argument is that the free will gives itself an existence through primarily things (*Sache*), external objects (*Dinge*), but "this mere immediacy of existence is not in keeping with freedom, and the negation of this determination is the sphere of *morality*. I am then free no longer merely in this immediate thing (*Sache*), but also in a superseded immediacy—that is, I am free in myself, in the subjective realm" (PR, §33A). In the realm of *Moralität*, "everything depends on my insight, my intention, and the end I pursue" (PR, §33A). The kind of freedom the will strives to achieve in the sphere of *Moralität* is in reference not to some external "other" but in relation to itself as subjectivity. In the sphere of *Moralität* one has a duty to own one's actions by having a greater consciousness of the subjective aspect of willing by choosing the content of one's will. "The moral will," Peperzak claims, "is a reflexive will, a will that is its own object or a will that owns, knows and wills itself."[11] One who consciously chooses the content of one's willing views oneself as being responsible and accountable for one's actions and embraces one's moral actions with intention and purpose.

Substantial Freedom

Substantial freedom, which can be realized only in *Sittlichkeit*, is the unity of objective freedom and subjective freedom, where the former refers to the laws and institutions of the rational social order, and the latter refers to the capacities and attitudes associated with the individual.[12] The inherent rationality of the political and social institutions for Hegel means that these institutions provide the circumstances in which the individuals can attain objective freedom *and* subjective freedom. Subjective freedom for Hegel denotes the nature of the relationship that a citizen has to the state. One forms an identity with the political and social institutions when one considers these institutions as embodying one's essence, end, and the product of one's activity (PR, §257). Hegel's claim that a citizen has such a strong identity with the social and political institutions can at first glance strike one as being too strong and even contrary to the idea of being an autonomous rational agent. A closer examination, however, yields an argument that I believe does not contradict Hegel's emphasis on rational autonomy but instead gives full support to it and also supports Hegel's claim that duties realize freedom. The main idea behind Hegel's argument is that a member of the ethical state who, without any reflection, complies with the requirements of the legal and political institutions does not necessarily achieve freedom. Subjective freedom can be achieved only when the citizen's following of the rules and laws of the social order is *consciously willed.*

When one views the rational political and social institutions as representing one's own rational essence, then the state ceases to be an "other," something alien and external to one's identity. This conscious identification with the rational political and social structures to which Hegel refers is fundamental to one's realization of freedom, because what motivates and enables this kind of identity is one's expression of one's rational autonomous nature and duty to realize one's own essence. To view the state as being the product of one's own activity, one must first come to understand one's role as an agent who collectively makes the political and social institutions possible and through whose support the institutions will continue to exist and function properly. The fact that Hegel claims that the identity between the member and the state is one of "essence" and not purely instrumental does not undermine one's right to pursue one's own particular interests. In fact, Hegel insists that one cannot achieve freedom if particular interests are neglected.

Hegel speaks of the unity between social members and the political and social institutions as being one of "essence." This claim needs further clarification in order to show that the claim of identity does not undermine Hegel's notion of autonomy and does not lead to the mistaken interpretation that a social member must sacrifice his or her own particular interest in order to achieve this identity of "essence." This clarification also will allow us to see why Hegel makes the claim that duties and rights have a relationship of identity in *Sittlichkeit.* It is important to recognize that Hegel's claim, that the universal and particular wills are united in the ethical state, does not mean that the individual is no longer a separate entity from the state and no longer has particular interests. A proper understanding of the relation between the social member and the state thus hinges upon proper understanding of what Hegel means by "essence."

Hegel's claim that citizens ought to regard the political and social institutions of *Sittlichkeit* as their own "essence" must not be interpreted to mean that individuals are who they are by virtue of their membership alone. In fact, Hegel associates this kind of unreflective "immediate" unity with ancient Greece and rejects it because it offers no possibility for autonomy and subjective freedom. The ancients lacked self-conscious understanding of themselves as being particular individuals, and therefore, they lacked the capacity for autonomy and self-determination. What is distinctive of and essential to self-conscious identity is reflection, the ability to abstract from anything externally given, an "other," and to make it one's own—to embrace the "otherness" by overcoming it.

To understand Hegel's claim that with respect to their "essence" social members have a relationship of identity with their political and social institutions, it is necessary to understand how his notion of reflection brings about such a unity of identity. Our identities are formed within and shaped by the particular world in which we live. This in itself, according to Hegel, does not provide a full account of the notion of identity that he has in mind, but it is essential in understanding how one comes to have the particular self-identity one has. Being a member of a particular state and having particular roles to fulfill provide one with a framework within which one can define oneself. Through forming social attachments and by becoming an active member of a society, one gains recognition and acquires social roles that are self-affirming.[13]

It is in the context of this knowledge of how individuals come to attain subjective freedom in the state that Hegel's bold assertion, that the individual's "*highest duty*" (PR, §258) is to be a member of the state, is to be understood. The obligatory aspect of this duty follows from the centrality of social engagement in the formation of self-identity and the recognition of one's particularity. Hegel argues that the "individual attains actuality only by entering into *existence* [*Dasein*] in general, and hence into *determinate particularity*" (PR, §207). Being "someone," becoming a "determinate particularity," and finding in one's social commitments and duties the source of one's essential self is what the "highest duty" entails. Through social engagement individuals gain consciousness of themselves and recognition by others as being of value. Hegel views social participation as self-positing and self-affirming in the sense that the individual has the means and the opportunity to give external expression to his or her subjectivity. Because of this the individual comes to regard social membership as being his or her "highest duty" and as being valuable in itself.

The notion of social participation that Hegel articulates is not one that is passive in nature, such that one fulfills one's duty to the state without comprehending or acknowledging that those duties express one's own essential self. Such passive fulfillment of duties does not lead to the realization of subjective freedom. It is only when one consciously undertakes and fulfills one's social roles that one actively posits one's particular identity. "The *right of individuals* to their *subjective determination to freedom*," according to Hegel's argument, "is fulfilled in so far as they belong to ethical actuality; for their *certainty* of their own freedom has its truth in such objectivity, and it is in the ethical realm that they *actually* possess *their own* essence and their *inner* universality" (PR, §153).

While the ethical state is undeniably prior to and independent of any particular social member, the political and social institutions themselves cannot maintain their viability without the support of the citizens. The fact that the members of *Sittlichkeit* recognize that they can find their subjective freedom only by being in a state does not for Hegel automatically mean that they will see the "essence" of the state as encompassing their own essence. Thus we are back to the issue of what exactly is the "essence" that Hegel posits as being the grounding substance of the members' identity with the state. The "essence" of this identity, the essence of the state that individuals recognize as being the substantive source of their identity, I argue, is rationality.[14] The unity of "essence" to which Hegel refers in his political philosophy involves political and social institutions fulfilling the requirement of being rational and universal, in the sense that their objective and justification are the realization of freedom. When the institutions meet this criterion of rationality, then the member of the state comes to understand his or her duties to the state as flowing from the duties he or she has to his or her own self. The duty to realize this freedom thus becomes the duty to produce and maintain the means to realizing that freedom.

I have argued that Hegel asserts that the identity the social member has with the political and social institutions is an identity of "essence" and that the "essence," he refers to is rationality. The second task will be to explore how the rationality of the state relates to the duties that members have in the state. This account of the rationality of the state is crucial insofar as the duties one has in the state must be compatible with one's realization of one's objective freedom. One can achieve objective freedom if one can give a rational justification for fulfilling one's duties and supporting the political and social institutions that give rise to these duties.

The concept of objective freedom is critical to Hegel's argument, because it provides a justification of why one acts rationally when conforming to the requirements of the political and social institutions of *Sittlichkeit*. Objective freedom addresses the issue of what the context of the political and social institutions must be in order for those institutions to be considered inherently rational by the citizens. When members of the ethical state successfully achieve objective freedom, that means they view the institutions as having a universal validity.[15] Objective freedom means that the institutions embody in their content and structure a realization of freedom that can be universally recognized and validated.

The state is essentially rational in the sense that it is a self-determining entity consistent with the ideal of a self-determined will that can exist independently or *für sich.* "The principle of modern states," Hegel claims, "has enormous strength and depth because it allows the principle of subjectivity to attain fulfillment in the *self-sufficient extreme* of personal particularity, while at the same time *bringing it back to substantial unity* and so preserving this unity in the principle of subjectivity itself" (PR, §260). If individuals are to realize freedom through social membership, then the political and social institutions must be set up and must function in such a way that members' particularity is secured. Freedom for Hegel entails the unity of the will, in the will's ability to determine itself as something particular and at the same time to view itself as being universal. "Only by making resolutions can the human being enter actuality" (PR, §13A); by "resolving, the will posits itself as the will of a specific individual" (PR, §13). The will, therefore, must limit itself, must "resolve" on a particular thing or action, in order to be actual. The process whereby the will chooses an objective for its willing must be one that is reflective and not blind or arbitrary.

Ethical duties, Hegel claims, liberate members of the ethical community because in fulfilling duties they engage in a process that enables them to actualize themselves. Self-actualization and self-determination are by nature contextual. Perhaps this point is all too obvious, but it is important for showing that the relationship between the individual and society is codependent in nature. Hegel's discussion of subjective and objective freedom shows the indispensability of a context for self-realization and freedom, and that the identity of right and duty is an indispensable element of this context. At the center of Hegel's understanding of what freedom is is the idea that "[f]reedom is to will something determinate, yet to be with oneself [*bei sich*] in this determinacy" (PR, §7A). While a particular determination is not a sufficient condition of freedom, determination itself is a necessary element in self-realization, and one must be *bei sich selbst* in the object of the determination that one's will wills. The expression *bei sich selbst,* for Hegel, means being with oneself, self-sufficient or at home.[16]

The critical element in Hegel's discussion of freedom consists in his insistence that duties can liberate an individual in the sense of enabling each individual to actualize himself or herself only if the freedom is one in which the will is "completely *with itself* [*bei sich*], because it has reference to nothing but itself, so that every relationship of *dependence* on something *other* than itself is thereby eliminated. It is *true*, or rather it is *truth* itself, because its determination consists in being in its *existence* [*Dasein*]" (PR, §23). Two important points must be made based on the text just quoted. One is concerned with the relational aspect of freedom, and the second is concerned with how the antithetical relationship between the self and other is "eliminated"—though "eliminating" here means overcoming the other and not suppressing and destroying the other. Duties allow and enable the individual will to find and define its truth in existence. To say that the will must have "reference to nothing but itself" does not mean that it should will without any reference to that which exists outside of itself; rather, what Hegel is saying is that the will must will with reference to some context in order to find its own truth, its own self, and only then can the relationship of dependence on the "other" as a self-defining mechanism be transformed into a relationship where the opposition between the self and the other is overcome. It must be stressed here that the process of self-determination is not static but dynamic, meaning that the self continuously engages in positing the "other" and overcoming this "otherness."

Remaining with oneself, *bei sich*, for Hegel means being with oneself in the objects of one's willing, one's self-determination, and positing oneself as "determinate." Self-determination can only be realized through self-activity that aims to define itself for itself and through itself. The content of one's determinations cannot be the product of the abstract "I" itself. Duty expresses self-determination in that duty is "the *self-determination* of the 'I,' in that it posits itself as the negative of itself, that is, as *determinate* and *limited*, and at the same time remains with itself [*bei sich*], that is, in its *identity with itself* and universality" (PR, §7). Inherent in this proposition is a paradox, a paradox that seems to claim two self-contradictory things at the same time: duty is an "other" and is at the same time a self-determined identity. Duty is an "other" in the sense that it is initially something that seems to impinge on our negative freedom, something that appears contradictory to freedom.

Duty for Hegel represents an "other," an object whose "otherness" must be overcome through self-positing activity. It is a medium that allows the self to form its self-identity and achieve freedom through interaction with the empirical realm in that the very nature of duty calls for recognition of the contextual aspect of self-determination. The rational self must be dialectically engaged with the empirical context. Hegel asserts that the "essential element of the will for me is duty . . . it is in the true sense my own objectivity that I bring to fulfillment in doing so. In doing my duty, I am with myself [*bei mir selbst*] and free" (PR, §133A). Hegel thus identifies substantial freedom with *Beisichselbstsein*; in other words, to be free in this absolute sense is to be *bei sich selbst*, or with oneself.

A "self being with itself" is a complicated phrase that draws on the individual's potential for and full articulation of self-consciousness, the realization of the other, and the achievement of self-realization and self-mastery through the overcoming of the other, of anything that is external to itself. The free self finds itself via a self-positing activity that is not purely an activity of reason but has an empirical element to it as well. It is in this empirical element that the difference between Hegel's view and Kant's and Fichte's lies. Wood succeeds in capturing this point particularly well when he says: "Kant and Fichte don't tell us not to care about what is other than the self, but they do draw a sharp distinction between the rational self and everything empirical, and they regard the freedom of the self as compromised by any motive reflecting the self's relation to empirical otherness."[17] The self engages in self-positing activity always in relation to an other; it becomes "with itself" when it achieves independence from the other by overcoming its otherness. It needs the other for achieving self-awareness and for molding its own self-identity, but it must overcome the "otherness" of the identity and dependence on the other in order to achieve self-sufficiency and identity with itself. "*Beisichselbstsein in einen Andern*, being with oneself in an other," is a necessary step to being "with oneself."

The concept of duties as an absolute abstraction or universality contains "the element of *pure indeterminacy* or of the 'I''s pure reflection into itself, in which every limitation, every content, whether present immediately through nature, through needs, desires, and drives, or given and determined in some other way, is dissolved" (PR, §5). As an abstraction, duty is an "other," an external element that stands in opposition to self. Self-determination for Hegel means not only that the self moves from the abstraction of the self to recognizing that its true self-determination must acknowledge desires, drives, and so on, but it means as well that the "other" is also recognized as possessing a content and is not limited to its universal or abstract nature. At the abstract level, duties will appear as something the individual must fulfill, as in Kant's ethical system, but they will not be recognized by a self as being self-positing, for it is in the recognition of the content of duties that the self can recognize its own determination.

Unlike Kant, Hegel does not see an insurmountable conflict between doing one's duty and having and fulfilling one's desires. One reason for this is that the realization of freedom is not only essential to one's being but is so critical in the realization of one's essential nature that at the highest level duty and desire coincide. The second reason duty and desire coincide is a social one: To realize our freedom, we must be in a society with others, and the duties that we come to have to others or to society itself make social being possible. Even if we are naturally inclined to give preference to our interests rather than to the interests of others, we fulfill duties that we owe to others because they serve our own interests. Hegel's justification of the duties we owe to others is not purely instrumental insofar as he views the duties that we acquire in society to be an expression of our fully realized rationality.

Hegel contends that a will is free when it is "completely *with itself* [*bei sich*], because it has reference to nothing but itself, so that every relationship of *dependence* on something *other* than itself is thereby eliminated" (PR, §23). I think it is important to understand here what Hegel does and does not mean by nondependence on other. Hegel is not satisfied to say that mutual dependence of each individual on every other is a sufficient condition for freedom. The only type of dependence that Hegel admits as being compatible with freedom is self-dependence. Thus in order for duties to be compatible with freedom, they must capture the idea of self-dependence. How exactly does one achieve self-dependence? One becomes self-dependent when one's will makes the universal its content.

Two elements enable the will to make the universal its content: thought and self-consciousness. The process through which Hegel claims the "particular is superseded and raised to the universal is what is called the activity of *thought.* The self-consciousness which purifies and raises its object, content, and end to this universality does so as *thought asserting itself* in the will. Here is the *point at which it becomes clear* that it is only as *thinking* intelligence that the will is truly itself and free" (PR, §21R). A little later in the same passage, Hegel writes that "self-consciousness which comprehends itself as essence through thought and thereby divests itself of the contingent and untrue constitutes the principle of right, of morality, and of all ethics" (PR, §21R). Self-consciousness comes to understand its essence, which is the free will, through thought whose activity also enables the will to abstract itself from the contingent and untrue, by which Hegel means something other than its essence, and to find its true determination. He says, "It is *true*, or rather it is *truth* itself, because its determination consists in being in its *existence* [*Dasein*]—i.e. as something opposed to itself—what it is in its concept; that is, the pure concept has the intuition of itself as its end and reality" (PR, § 23). Self-dependence is in Hegel's moral and political philosophy understood to be the same as self-determination: The free will is self-referential and self-determining.

It may seem at first glance that Hegel's conception of freedom as embracing self-determination and self-sufficiency contradicts his claim that each individual has a duty to be a member of a state. The contradiction is inherent in his argument that an individual can attain his or her determinations by being a member of a state; that is, he or she gains self-sufficiency by entering a relationship of dependence on something external to his or her own self. How does Hegel reconcile duty to belong to a community and his notion of freedom as self-determination, self-sufficiency, and independence from being determined by another? Hegel could have argued that all individuals are equally dependent on each other in a community, or that their dependence is not upon other individuals but rather upon the state itself; but in either case, the individual is free, because he or she is not dependent on other individuals. Hegel, however, does not make this argument, because neither case would bring about true reconciliation for him. The fact that each individual is equally dependent on other members or the whole state itself does not mean that freedom has been achieved. The "otherness" inherent in this dependence—even if the dependence is the same among all individuals—is not overcome.

While the notion of individual rights and their exercise has been taken to be rational, fulfilling one's obligations has not often been deemed to be the expression or the realization of one's freedom. Hegel wants to show that the performance of one's duties, whether they be duties to self or others, is not only rational but also essential in the pursuit and realization of one's freedom. The notion of duty for Hegel is not reducible to the principle of duty for duty's sake; nor is it to be equated to duty for the sake of social ends. One who fulfills the obligations expected of one purely because that is what is expected from one as a citizen, or because one fears sanctions resulting from nonperformance, is not free and does not contribute to the realization of freedom in the social and political community. Fulfillment of obligations for Hegel must be based on self-conscious and free activity.

The principle of duty is one of freedom only when the condition that the duties of an individual be fulfilled of his or her own free will is met. To carry out the imperatives dictated by a particular duty does not in itself mean that one is unfree or that one's freedom is constrained. Indeed, Hegel would go so far as to state that the fulfillment of an obligation can be a more substantive expression of one's freedom. It is a more substantive and complete expression of freedom because it is an act of self-conscious free will. Since in duties we find and express our individualism, duties are moral imperatives as well as rational activity. They are also of practical necessity in that a social order cannot maintain its viability in the absence of civic order.

In stating that the "state is the actuality of concrete freedom" Hegel is arguing that the duties a citizen has in a society enable and facilitate the realization of the citizen's freedom. Contrary to the contractarian view that sees the entrance into a state as necessitating each individual to give up some of his or her own freedom so that he or she and everyone else can exercise their rights to certain kinds of freedoms in the state,[18] Hegel does not see the state as having this purely instrumental function. If the citizen is to realize his or her freedom in the state, then his or her identity with the state, according to Hegel, is dependent on the ability of the institutional structures to facilitate the development of subjective freedom. Being a member of a particular state is central to the formation of self-identity.

Hegel maintains that people must be able to actualize themselves as individuals, both in the sense that they actualize their own individuality and their social identity. What this means for Hegel is that the social and political constructs must be such that they enable and encourage this kind of actualization. But even more important, each individual has a duty to seek this actualization, precisely because each individual has a right to his or her "particularity." The notion of the state that Hegel presents has as its foci the rights of individuals. In exercising one's rights, one actualizes oneself, but this actualization can take place only within a realm of a rational and an ethical community where each individual's rights are recognized.

Self-determination and self-development for Hegel always imply a social context within which one comes to recognize both the rights and duties one has due to possessing a free will. To realize oneself as an individual means to recognize and understand that each person has an aspect of his or her personhood that is social. Ethical life, including family, civil society, and the state, with its social customs and practices, provides a framework that allows each individual to recognize his or her capacity for self-realization and freedom. What the argument has shown is that the role of duties in Hegel's political philosophy is to facilitate the realization of freedom. Duties must be understood as being compatible with freedom. Indeed, they are its substantive actualization. The right to freedom is not violated but is indeed respected when the rational self is aware of the need for fulfilling duties as serving the objective of creating a social context that allows the potential for self-realization.

Notes

1. References that include PR are to *Grundlinien der Philosophie des Rechts*, translated as *Elements of the Philosophy of Right*, trans. H. B. Nisbet, ed. Allen W. Wood (Cambridge: Cambridge University Press, 1991). Citation is by paragraph number and, when relevant, R for Remarks and A for Additions. I would like to express my gratitude to Frederick Neuhouser for his detailed criticism of this work.

2. On the most superficial level, there is a striking similarity in Hegel's and Rousseau's reflections that freedom and constraint are compatible, but a closer look reveals how different they are. Rousseau's political theory, from the Hegelian perspective, relies on a notion of the will that is arbitrary, and his theory never moves beyond this arbitrariness. For a more comprehensive discussion of Rousseau and Hegel, see Paul Franco, *Hegel's Philosophy of Freedom* (New Haven, CT: Yale University Press, 1999), 174; Frederick Neuhouser, *Foundations of Hegel's Social Theory: Actualizing Freedom* (Cambridge, MA: Harvard University Press, 2000), 60–62, 78–81.

3. I use the terms *actualization* and *realization* interchangeably. For a full discussion of "actual," see Allen W. Wood, *Hegel's Ethical Thought* (Cambridge: Cambridge University Press, 1990), 10.

4. For examples of recent literature on Hegel's conception of freedom, see Franco, *Hegel's Philosophy of Freedom*; Neuhouser, *Foundations of Hegel's Social Theory;* Adriaan T. Peperzak, *Modern Freedom: Hegel's Legal, Moral, and Political Philosophy* (Dordrecht, Holland: Kluwer, 2001).

5. Well-known communitarian theories have been presented by the following: Alasdair MacIntyre, *After Virtue: A Study in Moral Theory* (Notre Dame, IN: University of Notre Dame Press, 1984); Michael Sandel, *Liberalism and the Limits of Justice, Liberalism and Its Critics* (New York: New York University Press, 1984); Charles Taylor, "Atomism," in *Philosophy and the Human Sciences: Philosophical Papers* (Cambridge: Cambridge University Press, 1985), 187–210.

6. J. Rawls, *A Theory of Justice* (Cambridge, MA: Harvard University Press, 1971), 3. But as Stephen Houlgate points out, "although basic rights and liberties are inalienable within a Rawlsian well-ordered constitutional democracy, they do not have an absolute priority in such a state." See Stephen Houlgate, "Hegel, Rawls, and the Rational State" in *Beyond Liberalism and Communitarianism: Studies in Hegel's Philosophy of Right* , ed. Robert R. Williams (Albany: State University of New York Press, 2001), 270, n. 50.

7. Unlike Kant, however, Hegel does not invoke a contractual basis for grounding property rights.

8. Rawls, *A Theory of Justice*, 3.

9. Immanuel Kant, *Foundations of Morals*, in *Critique of Practical Reason and Other Writing in Moral Philosophy*, ed. Lewis White Beck (Chicago: University of Chicago Press, 1949), 87.

10. Allen Wood, *Hegel's Ethical Thought* (Cambridge: Cambridge University Press, 1990), 136.

11. Peperzak, *Modern Freedom*, 327–28.

12. For my understanding of subjective freedom and objective freedom I am indebted to Neuhouser's excellent discussion in chapters 3 and 4 of *Foundations of Hegel's Social Theory*.

13. For a fuller discussion of recognition, see Wood, *Hegel's Ethical Thought*, chapter 4; R. Pippin, *Hegel's Idealism* (Cambridge: Cambridge University Press, 1989), chapter 7; Robert R. Williams, *Recognition: Fichte and Hegel on the Other* (Albany: State University of New York Press, 1992), chapter 8; Ludwig Siep, *Anerkennung als Prinzip der Praktischen Philosophie* (Munich: Alber, 1979).

14. Wood expresses a similar thought when he claims that "Hegel's theory is still universalistic because it appeals to principles that claim universal validity for all thinkers . . . the ethical is a universal, objective standard for the rational assessment of social institutions. A relationship is 'ethical' only if it is capable of derivation from the universal concept of free will." See Wood, *Hegel's Ethical Thought*, 212.

15. The universalistic interpretation of Hegel's ethics is made by Allen Wood in *Hegel's Ethical Thought*, 212.

16. For a more complete discussion of the meaning of *bei sich selbst*, see Wood, *Hegel's Ethical Thought*, 45–46.

17. Wood, *Hegel's Ethical Thought*, 45.

18. For an informative discussion on Hegel and contract theory, see J. W. Gough, *The Social Contract* (Oxford: Oxford University Press, 1957), chapter XI; Patrick Riley, *Will and Political Legitimacy* (Cambridge, MA: Harvard University Press, 1982), chapter 6; Seyla Benhabib, "Obligation, Contract, and Exchange: On the Significance of Hegel's Abstract Right," in *State and Civil Society: Studies in Hegel's Political Philosophy*, ed. Z. Pelczynski (Cambridge: Cambridge University Press, 1984), 159–77.

CONTRIBUTORS

Robert Bernasconi is Moss Professor of Philosophy at the University of Memphis. He is the author of two books on Heidegger and numerous articles on Hegel and twentieth-century continental philosophy. He also has edited a number of books on race, including *The Idea of Race,* with Tommy Lott and four series of reprints with Thoemmes Press, the most recent of which is *Race, Hybridity, and Miscegenation.*

Andrew Buchwalter is associate professor of philosophy and department chairperson at the University of North Florida. He is the author of *Culture and Democracy: Social and Ethical Issues in Public Support for the Arts and Humanities.* He is completing two books, a monograph on the contemporary significance of Hegel's political thought and a collection of essays comparing and contrasting Hegel with seminal thinkers on a diverse range of issues. His current research focuses on globalization theory and the relationship of religion and politics.

Martin J. De Nys is associate professor of philosophy at George Mason University. His principal research interests are in nineteenth-century philosophy, especially Hegel, Marx, and Kierkegaard, transcendental phenomenology, the philosophy of religion, metaphysics, and radical social theory. He is the author of a number of articles dealing especially with issues in the philosophy of Hegel and the philosophy of religion.

Erin E. Flynn is assistant professor of philosophy at Ohio Wesleyan University. Since completing his dissertation, *Conflict and Attunement: The Limits of Punishment in Hegel's* Philosophy of Right, he has been researching and publishing primarily in philosophy of action, philosophy of law, and post-Kantian German philosophy. He also is writing a novel about Hegel's *Phenomenology of Spirit.*

Philip T. Grier is the Thomas Bowman Professor of Philosophy and Religion at Dickinson College. He has published a book on Marxist ethical theory, edited the volume *Dialectic and Contemporary Science*, and published articles on Hegel's Logic, the philosophy of history, and Russian Hegelianism. He was vice president of the Hegel Society from 2002 to 2004.

Jason J. Howard is a recent graduate from the Katholieke Universiteit, Leuven, and he is currently an assistant professor of philosophy at Viterbo University. He has published articles either on or related to Kant, Hegel, and the philosophy of William Desmond. His specialty is the development of moral conscience in German idealism, and his present research involves the articulation of a substantial Hegelian ethic.

Maria G. Kowalski is a recent graduate of the doctoral program at Columbia University, Department of Political Science. She is currently adjunct assistant professor at New York University and Columbia University, and she is completing a book on Hegel's political philosophy.

William Maker is professor of philosophy and chair of the Philosophy and Religion Department at Clemson University. He is the editor of *Hegel on Economics and Freedom* and *Hegel and Aesthetics*, and he is the author of *Philosophy without Foundations: Rethinking Hegel.* He has also published numerous articles on Hegel and contemporary philosophy. He was vice president of the Hegel Society of America from 1994 to 1996.

Angelica Nuzzo is professor of philosophy at Brooklyn College and Graduate Center, City University of New York, and she was a Fellow at the Radcliffe Institute for Advanced Studies at Harvard (2000–2001) and a recipient of an Alexander von Humboldt Fellowship (2004–2005). She is the author of two books on Hegel, *Rappresentazione e concetto nella logica della Filosofia del diritto* and *Logica e sistema*, the monograph *System*, and *Kant and the Unity of Reason.* Her numerous essays on German idealism and modern philosophy appear in journals such as the *Journal of the History of Philosophy*, *Hegel-Studien*, and the *Owl of Minerva*.

Patricia Anne Simpson is associate professor of German at Montana State University. Her research interests include the philosophy, literature, and theory of German classicism and romanticism.

She has published widely on contemporary culture as well. Her book *The Erotics of War in German Romanticism* is forthcoming. Simpson also is coeditor of *The Enlightened Eye: Goethe and Visual Culture.*

Robert R. Williams is Professor of German and Religious Studies at the University of Illinois at Chicago, past president of the Hegel Society of America, author of *Hegel's Ethics of Recognition* and *Recognition: Fichte and Hegel on the Other*, editor of *Beyond Liberalism and Communitarianism: Studies in Hegel's Philosophy of Right*, and translator of Hegel's *Lectures on the Philosophy of Spirit 1827/29*, forthcoming, and several articles on Hegel and German idealism.

Richard Dien Winfield is Distinguished Research Professor of Philosophy at the University of Georgia and the author of the following: *Reason and Justice*, *The Just Economy*, *Overcoming Foundations: Studies in Systematic Philosophy*, *Freedom and Modernity*, *Law in Civil Society*, *Systematic Aesthetics*, *Stylistics: Rethinking the Artforms after Hegel*, *The Just Family*, *Autonomy and Normativity*, *The Just State: Rethinking Self-Government*, and *From Concept to Objectivity: Thinking through Hegel's Subjective Logic.*

Christopher Yeomans is assistant professor of philosophy at Kenyon College. He works on the history of modern philosophy (with particular interest in Kant and Hegel) and the philosophy of action. He is currently at work on a book on the logical structure of Hegel's philosophy of action and theory of the will.

INDEX

Q

R

S

W

Y

Z